THE GOLD STANDARD
DAT BIOLOGY
Book I of IV

Gold Standard Contributors
• 4-Book GS DAT Set •

Brett Ferdinand BSc MD-CM
Karen Barbia BS Arch
Brigitte Bigras BSc MSc DMD
Ibrahima Diouf BSc MSc PhD
Amir Durmic BSc Eng
Adam Segal BSc MSc
Da Xiao BSc DMD
Naomi Epstein BEng
Lisa Ferdinand BA MA
Jeanne Tan Te
Kristin Finkenzeller BSc MD
Heaven Hodges BSc
Sean Pierre BSc MD
James Simenc BS (Math), BA Eng
Jeffrey Cheng BSc
Timothy Ruger MSc PhD
Petra Vernich BA
Alvin Vicente BS Arch

DMD Candidates

E. Jordan Blanche BS
[Harvard School of Dental Medicine]
Stephan Suksong Yoon BA
[Harvard School of Dental Medicine]

Gold Standard Illustrators
• 4-Book GS DAT Set •

Daphne McCormack
Nanjing Design
· Ren Yi, Huang Bin
· Sun Chan, Li Xin
Fabiana Magnosi
Harvie Gallatiera
Rebbe Jurilla BSc MBA

RuveneCo

The Gold Standard DAT was built for the US DAT.

 The Gold Standard DAT is identical to Canadian DAT prep except QR and ORG. Also, you must practice soap carving for the complete Canadian DAT.

 The Gold Standard DAT is identical to OAT prep except PAT, which is replaced by OAT Physics; see our Gold Standard OAT book for Physics review and OAT practice test.

Be sure to register at www.DAT-prep.com by clicking on GS DAT Owners and following the directions for Gold Standard DAT Owners. Please Note: benefits are for 1 year from the date of online registration, for the original book owner only and are not transferable; unauthorized access and use outside the Terms of Use posted on DAT-prep.com may result in account deletion; if you are not the original owner, you can purchase your virtual access card separately at DAT-prep.com.

Visit The Gold Standard's Education Center at www.gold-standard.com.

ISBN 978-1-927338-09-4

Address all inquiries, comments, or suggestions to the publisher. For Terms of Use go to: www.DAT-prep.com

RuveneCo Inc
Gold Standard Multimedia Education
559-334 Cornelia St
Plattsburgh, NY 12901
E-mail: learn@gold-standard.com
Online at www.gold-standard.com

Table of Contents

EXAM SUMMARY

The Dental Admission Test (DAT) consists of 280 multiple-choice questions distributed across quite a diversity of question types in four tests. The DAT is a computer-based test (CBT). This exam requires approximately five hours to complete - including the optional tutorial, break, and post-test survey. The following are the four subtests of the Dental Admission Test:

1. Survey of the Natural Sciences (NS) – 100 questions; 90 min.
   - General Biology (BIO): 40 questions
   - General Chemistry (CHM): 30 questions
   - Organic Chemistry (ORG): 30 questions

2. Perceptual Ability Test (PAT) - 90 questions; 6 subsections; 60 min.
   - Apertures: 15 questions
   - Orthographic or View Recognition: 15 questions
   - Angle Discrimination: 15 questions
   - Paper Folding: 15 questions
   - Cube Counting: 15 questions
   - 3-D Form Development: 15 questions

3. Reading Comprehension (RC) – 50 questions; 3 reading passages; 60 min.

4. Quantitative Reasoning (QR) – 40 questions; 45 min.
   - Mathematics Problems: 30 questions
   - Applied Mathematics/Word Problems: 10 questions

You will get six scores from: (1) BIO (2) CHM (3) ORG (4) PAT (5) QR (6) RC.

You will get two additional scores which are summaries:
   (7) Academic Average (AA) = BIO + CHM + ORG + QR + RC
   (8) Total Science (TS) = BIO + CHM + ORG

Common Formula for Acceptance:

GPA + DAT score + Interview = Dental School Admissions*

*Note: In general, Dental School Admissions Committees will only examine the DAT score if the GPA is high enough; they will only admit or interview if the GPA + DAT score is high enough. Some programs also use autobiographical materials and/or references in the admissions process. Different dental schools may emphasize different aspects of your DAT score, for example: PAT, BIO, TS, AA. The average score for any section is approximately 17/30; the average AA for admissions is usually 18-20 depending on the dental school; the AA for admissions to Harvard is around 22-23; the 100th percentile is usually 25 meaning that virtually 100% of the approximately 13 000 students who take the DAT every year have an AA less than 25. Only a handful of students score 25/30. Our two student contributors scored 27/30 (AA).

The DAT is challenging, get organized.

dat-prep.com/dat-study-schedule

1. How to study:

1. Study the Gold Standard (GS) books and videos to learn
2. Do GS Chapter review practice questions
3. Consolidate: create and review your personal summaries (= Gold Notes) daily

2. Once you have completed your studies:

1. Full-length practice test
2. Review mistakes, all solutions
3. Consolidate: review all your Gold Notes and create more
4. Repeat until you get beyond the score you need for your targeted dental school

3. Full-length practice tests:

1. ADA practice exams
2. Gold Standard DAT exams
3. TopScore Pro exams
4. Other sources if needed

4. How much time do you need?

On average, 3-6 hours per day for 3-6 months

WARNING: Study more or study more efficiently. You choose. The Gold Standard has condensed the content that you require to excel at the DAT. We have had Ivy League dental students involved in the production of the Gold Standard series so that pre-dent students can feel that they have access to the content required to get a score satisfactory at any dental school in the country. To make the content easier to retain, you can also find aspects of the Gold Standard program in other formats such as:

Is there something in the Gold Standard that you did not understand? Don't get frustrated, get online.

dat-prep.com/forum   dat-prep.com/QRchanges-2015

Good luck with your studies!

Gold Standard Team

GOLD STANDARD
MULTIMEDIA EDUCATION

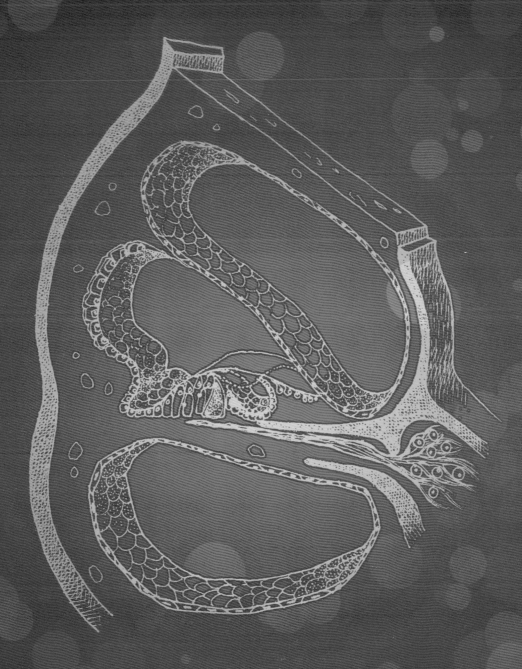

BIOLOGY

Memorize	Understand	Importance
tructure/function: cell/components omponents and function: cytoskeleton NA structure and function ransmission of genetic information litosis, events of the cell cycle ell junctions, microscopy	* Membrane transport * Hyper/hypotonic solutions * Saturation kinetics: graphs * Unique features of eukaryotes	2 to 5 out of the 40 Biology DAT questions are based on content in this chapter (in our estimation). * Note that between 25% and 50% of the questions in DAT Biology are from 5 chapters: 1, 2, 14, 15, and 16.

DAT-Prep.com

Introduction

Cells are the basic organizational unit of living organisms. They are contained by a plasma membrane and/or cell wall. Eukaryotic cells (*eu* = true; *karyote* refers to nucleus) are cells with a true nucleus found in all multicellular and nonbacterial unicellular organisms including animal, fungal and plant cells. The nucleus contains genetic information, DNA, which can divide into 2 cells by mitosis. Please note: we will begin to explore characteristics specific to plant cells in Chapter 17.

Additional Resources

Free Online Q&A + Forum

Video: Online or DVD

Flashcards

Special Guest

1.1 Plasma Membrane: Structure and Functions

The plasma membrane is a semipermeable barrier that defines the outer perimeter of the cell. It is composed of lipids (fats) and protein. The membrane is dynamic, selective, active, and fluid. It contains phospholipids which are <u>amphipathic</u> molecules. They are amphipathic because their tail end contains fatty acids which are insoluble in water (*hydrophobic*), the opposite end contains a charged phosphate head which is soluble in water (*hydrophilic*). The plasma membrane contains two layers or "leaflets" of phospholipids thus it is called a bilipid layer. Unlike eukaryotic membranes, prokaryotic membranes do not contain steroids such as cholesterol.

The <u>Fluid Mosaic Model</u> tells us that the hydrophilic heads project to the outside and the hydrophobic tails project towards the inside of the membrane. Further, these phospholipids are <u>fluid</u> - thus they move freely from place to place in the membrane. Fluidity of the membrane increases with increased temperature and with decreased saturation of fatty acyl tails. Fluidity of the membrane decreases with decreased temperature, increased saturation of fatty acyl tails and increase in the membrane's cholesterol content. The structures of these and other biological molecules are discussed in Chapter 20 of this book (= BIO 20).

Glycolipids are limited to the extracellular aspect of the membrane or outer leaflet. The carbohydrate portion of glycolipids extends from the outer leaflet into the extracellular space and forms part of the glycocalyx. "Glycocalyx" is the sugar coat on the outer surface of the outer leaflet of plasma membrane. It consists of oligosaccharide linked to

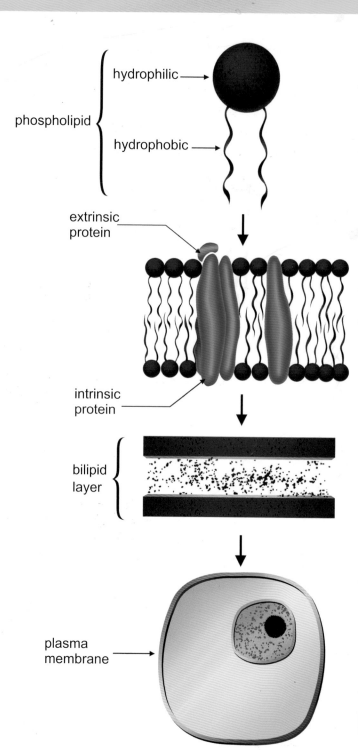

Figure IV.A.1.1: Structure of the plasma membrane. Note that: hydro = water, phobic = fearing, philic = loving

protein or lipids of the plasma membrane. The glycocalyx aids in attachment of some cells, facilitates cell recognition, helps bind antigen and antigen-presenting cells to the cell surface. Distributed throughout the membrane is a mosaic of proteins with limited mobility.

Proteins can be found associated with the outside of the membrane (extrinsic or peripheral) or may be found spanning the membrane (intrinsic or integral). Integral proteins are dissolved in the lipid bilayer. Transmembrane proteins contain hydrophilic and hydrophobic amino acids and cross the entire plasma membrane. Most transmembrane proteins are glycoproteins. They usually function as membrane receptors and transport proteins.

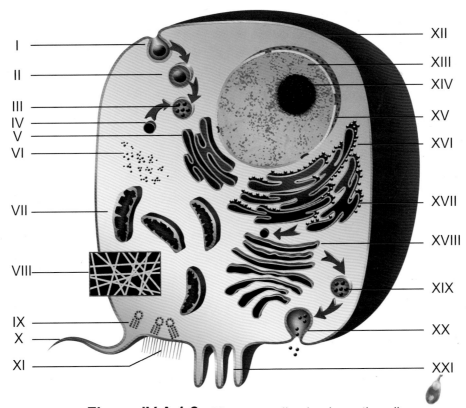

Figure IV.A.1.2: The generalized eukaryotic cell
To learn about the special characteristics of plant cells, see Chapter 17.

I	endocytosis	VIII	cytoskeleton (further magnified)	XV	nuclear envelope
II	endocytotic vesicle	IX	basal body (magnified)	XVI	cytosol
III	secondary lysosome	X	flagellum	XVII	rough endoplasmic reticulum
IV	primary lysosome	XI	cilia	XVIII	Golgi apparatus
V	smooth endoplasmic reticulum	XII	plasma membrane	XIX	exocytotic vesicle
VI	free ribosomes	XIII	nucleus	XX	exocytosis
VII	mitochondrion	XIV	nucleolus	XXI	microvillus

Peripheral proteins do not extend into the lipid bilayer but can temporarily adhere to either side of the plasma membrane. They bond to phospholipid groups or integral proteins of the membrane via noncovalent interactions. Common functions include regulatory protein subunits of ion channels or transmembrane receptors, associations with the cytoskeleton and extracellular matrix, and as part of the intracellular second messenger system.

The plasma membrane is semipermeable. In other words, it is permeable to small uncharged substances which can freely diffuse across the membrane (i.e. O_2, CO_2, urea). The eukaryotic plasma membrane does not have pores, as pores would destroy the barrier function. On the other hand, it is relatively impermeable to charged or large substances which may require transport proteins to cross the membrane (i.e. ions, amino acids, sugars) or cannot cross the membrane at all (i.e. protein hormones, intracellular enzymes). Substances which can cross the membrane may do so by simple diffusion, carrier-mediated transport, or by endo/exocytosis.

1.1.1 Simple Diffusion

Simple diffusion is the spontaneous spreading of a substance going from an area of higher concentration to an area of lower concentration (i.e. a concentration gradient exists). Gradients can be of a chemical or electrical nature. A chemical gradient arises as a result of an unequal distribution of molecules and is often called a concentration gradient. In a chemical (or concentration) gradient, there is a higher concentration of molecules in one area than there is in another area, and molecules tend to diffuse from areas of high concentration to areas of lower concentration.

An electrical gradient arises as a result of an unequal distribution of charge. In an electrical gradient, there is a higher concentration of charged molecules in one area than in another (this is independent of

Figure IV.A.1.2.1a: Isotonic Solution.
The fluid bathing the cell (i.e. red blood cell or RBC in this case; see BIO 7.5) contains the same concentration of solute as the cell's inside or cytoplasm. When a cell is placed in an isotonic solution, the water diffuses into and out of the cell at the same rate.

the concentration of all molecules in the area). Molecules tend to move from areas of higher concentration of charge to areas of lower concentration of charge.

Figure IV.A.1.2.1b: Hypertonic Solution.
Here the fluid bathing the RBC contains a high concentration of solute relative to the cell's cytoplasm. When a cell is placed in a hypertonic solution, the water diffuses out of the cell, causing the cell to shrivel (crenation).

Figure IV.A.1.2.1c: Hypotonic Solution.
Here the surrounding fluid has a low concentration of solute relative to the cell's cytoplasm. When a cell is placed in a hypotonic solution, the water diffuses into the cell, causing the cell to swell and possibly rupture (lyse).

Osmosis is the diffusion of water across a semipermeable membrane moving from an area of higher water concentration (i.e. lower solute concentration = hypotonic) to an area of lower water concentration (i.e. higher solute concentration = hypertonic). The hydrostatic pressure needed to oppose the movement of water is called the osmotic pressure. Thus, an isotonic solution (i.e. the concentration of solute on both sides of the membrane is equal), would have an osmotic pressure of zero.

{Memory guide: notice that the "O" in hyp-O-tonic looks like a swollen cell. The O is also a circle which makes you think of the word "around." So IF the environment is hypOtonic AROUND the cell, then fluid rushes in and the cell swells like the letter O}.

1.1.2 Carrier-mediated Transport

Amino acids, sugars and other solutes need to reversibly bind to proteins (carriers) in the membrane in order to get across. Because there are a limited amount of carriers, if the concentration of solute is too high, the carriers would be saturated, thus the rate of crossing the membrane would level off (= saturation kinetics).

The two carrier-mediated transport systems are:

(i) <u>facilitated transport</u> where the carrier helps a solute diffuse across a membrane it could not otherwise penetrate. Facilitated diffusion occurs via ion channels or carrier proteins and transport molecules down a concentration of electrochemical gradient. Ions and large molecules are therefore able to cross the membrane that would otherwise be impermeable to them.

ii) <u>active transport</u> where energy (i.e. ATP) is used to transport solutes <u>against</u> their

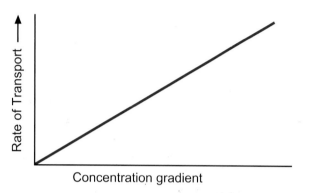

Simple Diffusion: the greater the concentration gradient, the greater the rate of transport across the plasma membrane.

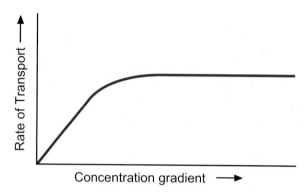

Carrier-mediated Transport: increasing the concentration gradient increases the rate of transport up to a maximum rate, at which point all membrane carriers are saturated.

Figure IV.A.1.3: Simple diffusion versus Carrier-mediated transport.

concentration gradients. The Na$^+$–K$^+$ exchange pump uses ATP to actively pump Na$^+$ to where its concentration is highest (outside the cell) and K$^+$ is brought within the cell where its concentration is highest (see Neural Cells and Tissues, BIO 5.1.1).

1.1.3 Endo/Exocytosis

Endocytosis is the process by which the cell membrane actually invaginates, pinches off and is released intracellularly (endocytotic vesicle). If a solid particle was ingested by the cell (i.e. a bacterium), it is called phagocytosis. If fluid was ingested, it is pinocytosis.

The receptor-mediated endocytosis of ligands (e.g. low density lipoprotein, transferrin, growth factors, antibodies, etc.) are mediated by clathrin-coated vesicles (CCVs). CCVs are found in virtually all cells and form areas in the plasma membrane termed clathrin-coated pits. Caveolae are the most common reported non-clathrin-coated plasma membrane buds, which exist on the surface

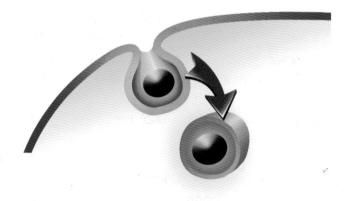

Figure IV.A.1.4: Endocytosis.

of many, but not all cell types. They consist of the cholesterol-binding protein caveolin with a bilayer enriched in cholesterol and glycolipids.

Exocytosis is, essentially, the reverse process. The cell directs an intracellular vesicle to fuse with the plasma membrane thus releasing its contents to the exterior (i.e. neurotransmitters, pancreatic enzymes, cell membrane proteins/lipids, etc.).

The transient vesicle fusion with the cell membrane forms a structure shaped like a pore (= *porosome*). Thus porosomes are cup-shaped structures where vesicles dock in the process of fusion and secretion. Porosomes contain many different types of protein including chloride and calcium channels, actin, and SNARE proteins that mediate the docking and fusion of vesicles with the cell membrane. The primary role of SNARE proteins is to mediate vesicle fusion through

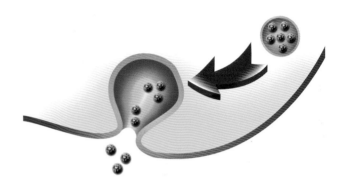

Figure IV.A.1.5: Exocytosis.

full fusion exocytosis or open and close exocytosis. The former is where the vesicle collapses fully into the plasma membrane; in the latter, the vesicle docks transiently with the membrane (= "kiss-and-run") and is recycled (i.e. in the synaptic terminal; BIO 1.5.1, 5.1).

1.2 The Interior of a Eukaryotic Cell

Cytoplasm is the interior of the cell. It refers to all cell components enclosed by the cell's membrane which includes the cytosol, the cytoskeleton, and the membrane bound organelles. Transport within the cytoplasm occurs by cyclosis (circular motion of cytoplasm around the cell).

Cytosol is the solution which bathes the organelles and contains numerous solutes like amino acids, sugars, proteins, etc.

Cytoskeleton extends throughout the entire cell and has particular importance in shape and intracellular transportation. The cytoskeleton also makes extracellular com-

plexes with other proteins forming a matrix so that cells can "stick" together. This is called cellular adhesion.

The components of the cytoskeleton in increasing order of size are: microfilaments, intermediate filaments, and microtubules. Microfilaments are important for cell movement and contraction (i.e. actin and myosin. See Contractile Cells and Tissues, BIO 5.2). Microfilaments, also known as actin filaments, are composed of actin monomer (G actin) linked into a double helix. They display polarity (= having distinct and opposite poles), with polymerization and depolymerization occuring preferentially at the barbed end [also called the plus (+) end which is where ATP is bound to G actin; BIO 5.2]. Microfilaments squeeze the membrane together in phagocytosis and cytokinesis. They are also important for muscle contraction and microvilli movement.

Intermediate filaments and microtubules extend along axons and dendrites of neurons acting like railroad tracks, so organelles or protein particles can shuttle to or from the cell body. Microtubules also form:

(i)   the core of cilia and flagella (see the 9 doublet + 2 structure in BIO 1.5);
(ii)   the mitotic spindles which we shall soon discuss; and
(iii) centrioles.

A flagellum is an organelle of locomotion found in sperm and bacteria. Eukaryotic flagella are made from microtubule configurations while prokaryotic flagella are thin strands of a single protein called flagellin. Thus, eukaryotic flagella move in a whip-like motion while prokaryotic flagella rotate. Cilia are hair-like vibrating organelles which can be used to move particles along the surface of the cell (e.g., in the fallopian tubes cilia can help the egg move toward the uterus). Microtubules are composed of tubulin subunits. They display polarity, with polymerization and depolymerization occuring preferentially at the plus end where GTP is bound to the tubulin subunit. Microtubules are involved in flagella and cilia construction, and the spindle apparatus. Centrioles are cylinder-shaped complexes of microtubules associated with the mitotic spindle (MTOC, see later). At the

base of flagella and cilia, two centrioles can be found at right angles to each other: this is called a basal body.

Microvilli are regularly arranged finger-like projections with a core of cytoplasm (see BIO 9.5). They are commonly found in the small intestine where they help to increase the absorptive and digestive surfaces (= brush border).

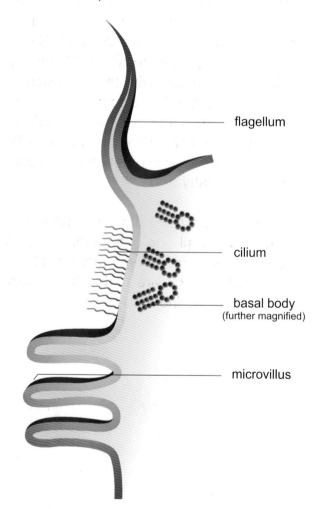

flagellum

cilium

basal body
(further magnified)

microvillus

Figure IV.A.1.6: Cytoskeletal elements and the plasma membrane. The core of cilia and flagella is composed of 9 doublet or pairs of microtubules with another *doublet* in the center (= *axoneme*; see BIO 1.5).

1.2.1 Membrane Bound Organelles

Mitochondrion: The Power House

Mitochondria produce energy (i.e. ATP) for the cell through aerobic respiration (BIO 4.4). It is a double membraned organelle whose inner membrane has shelf-like folds which are called cristae. The matrix, the fluid within the inner membrane, contains the enzymes for the Krebs cycle and circular DNA. The latter is the only cellular DNA found outside of the nucleus with the exception of chloroplasts which will be discussed in Chapter 17. There are numerous mitochondria in muscle cells. Mitochondria synthesize ATP via the Krebs cycle via oxidation of glucose, amino acids or fatty acids.

Mitochondria have their own DNA and ribosomes and replicate independently from eukaryotic cells. However, most proteins used in mitochondria are coded by nuclear DNA, not mitochondrial DNA.

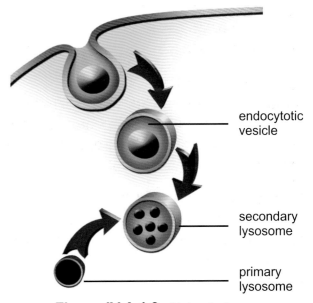

Figure IV.A.1.8: Heterolysis.

Lysosomes: Suicide Sacs

In a diseased cell, lysosomes may release their powerful acid hydrolases to digest away the cell (autolysis). In normal cells, a primary (normal) lysosome can fuse with an endocytotic vesicle to form a secondary lysosome where the phagocytosed particle (i.e. a bacterium) can be digested. This is called heterolysis. There are numerous lysosomes in phagocytic cells of the immune system (i.e. macrophages, neutrophils).

Endoplasmic Reticulum: Synthesis Center

The endoplasmic reticulum (ER) is an interconnected membraned system resembling flattened sacs and extends from the cell membrane to the nuclear membrane.

Figure IV.A.1.7: Mitochondria.

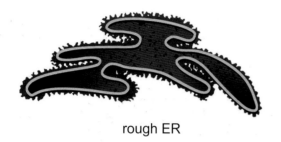

rough ER

smooth ER

Figure IV.A.1.9: The endoplasmic reticulum.

There are two kinds: (i) dotted with ribosomes on its surface which is called rough ER and (ii) without ribosomes which is smooth ER.

The ribosomes are composed of ribosomal RNA (rRNA) and numerous proteins. It may exist freely in the cytosol or bound to the rough ER or outer nuclear membrane. The ribosome is a site where mRNA is translated into protein.

Rough ER is important in protein synthesis and is abundant in cells synthesizing secretory proteins. It is associated with the synthesis of secretory protein, plasma membrane protein, and lysosomal protein. Smooth ER is abundant in cells synthesizing steroids, triglycerides and cholesterol. It is associated with the synthesis and transport of lipids such as steroid hormone and detoxification of a variety of chemicals. It is also common in skeletal muscle cells involving muscle contraction and relaxation. It is a factor in phospholipid and fatty acid synthesis and metabolism.

Golgi Apparatus: The Export Department

The Golgi apparatus forms a stack of smooth membranous sacs or *cisternae* that function in protein modification, such as the addition of polysaccharides (i.e. glycosylation). The Golgi also packages secretory proteins in membrane bound vesicles which can be exocytosed.

The Golgi apparatus has a distinct polarity with one end being the "cis" face and the other being "trans". The cis face lies close to a separate vesicular-tubular cluster (VTC) also referred to as the ER-Golgi intermediate compartment (ERGIC) which is an organelle. The ERGIC mediates trafficking between the ER and Golgi complex, facilitating the sorting of 'cargo'. The medial (middle) compartment of the Golgi lies between the cis and trans faces. The trans face is oriented towards vacuoles

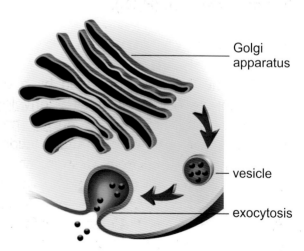

Golgi apparatus

vesicle

exocytosis

Figure IV.A.1.10: Golgi apparatus.

and secretory granules. The trans Golgi network separates from the trans face and sorts proteins for their final destination.

An abundant amount of rER and Golgi is found in cells which produce and secrete protein. For example, *B-cells* of the immune system which secrete antibodies, *acinar cells* in the pancreas which secrete digestive enzymes into the intestines, and *goblet cells* of the intestine which secrete mucus into the lumen.

Peroxisomes (Microbodies)

Peroxisomes are membrane bound organelles that contain enzymes whose functions include oxidative deamination of amino acids, oxidation of long chain fatty acids and synthesis of cholesterol.

The name "*perox*isome" comes from the fact that it is an organelle with enzymes that can transfer hydrogen from various substrates to oxygen, producing and then degrading hydrogen *perox*ide (H_2O_2).

The Nucleus

The nucleus is surrounded by a double membrane called the nuclear envelope. Throughout the membrane are nuclear pores which selectively allow the transportation of large particles to and from the nucleus. The nucleus is responsible for protein synthesis in the cytoplasm via ribosomal RNA (rRNA), messenger RNA (mRNA), and transfer RNA (tRNA).

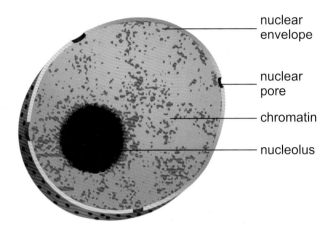

nuclear envelope

nuclear pore

chromatin

nucleolus

Figure IV.A.1.11: The nucleus.

DNA can be found within the nucleus as chromatin (DNA complexed to proteins like *histones*) or as chromosomes which are more clearly visible in a light microscope. The nucleolus is not membrane bound. It contains mostly ribosomal RNA and protein as well as the DNA necessary to synthesize ribosomal RNA.

The nucleolus is associated with the synthesis of ribosomal RNA (rRNA) and its assembly into ribosome precursors.

Chromosomes are basically extensively folded chromatin maintained by histone proteins. Each chromosome is composed of DNA and associated proteins, forming a nucleosome, the basic structural unit of chromatin. Chromatin exists as heterochromatin and euchromatin. Heterochromatin is a transcriptionally inactive form of chromatin while euchromatin is a transcriptionally active form of chromatin. Chromatin is responsible for RNA synthesis.

Deoxyribonucleic Acid (DNA) and ribonucleic acid (RNA) are essential components in constructing the proteins which act as the cytoskeleton, enzymes, membrane channels, antibodies, etc. It is the DNA which contains the genetic information of the cell.

DNA and RNA are both important nucleic acids. Nucleotides are the subunits which attach in sequence or in other words polymerize via phosphodiester bonds to form nucleic acids. A nucleotide (also called a *nucleoside phosphate*) is composed of a five carbon sugar, a nitrogen base, and an inorganic phosphate.

The sugar in RNA is ribose but for DNA an oxygen atom is missing in the second position of the sugar thus it is 2-deoxyribose.

There are two categories of nitrogen bases: *purines* and *pyrimidines*. The purines have two rings and include adenine (A) and guanine (G). The pyrimidines contain one ring and include thymine (T), cytosine (C), and uracil (U).

DNA contains the following four bases: adenine, guanine, thymine, and cytosine. RNA contains the same bases except uracil is substituted for thymine.

Watson and Crick's model of DNA has allowed us to get insight into what takes shape as the nucleotides polymerize to form this special nucleic acid. The result is a double *helical* or *stranded* structure.

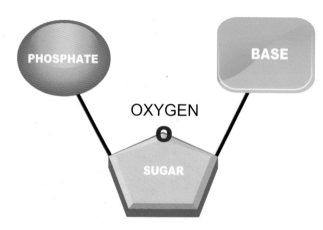

Figure IV.A.1.12: Nucleotide.

The DNA double helix is composed of two complementary and anti-parallel DNA strands held together by hydrogen bonds between base pairing A-T and G-C.

DNA is made from deoxyribose while RNA is made from ribose. DNA is double stranded while RNA is single stranded. DNA contains thymine while RNA contains uracil.

The backbone of each helix is the 2-deoxyribose phosphates. The nitrogen bases project to the center of the double helix in order to hydrogen bond with each other (imagine the double helix as a winding staircase: each stair would represent a pair of bases binding to keep the shape of the double helix intact).

There is specificity in the binding of the bases: one purine binds one pyrimidine. In fact, adenine only binds thymine (through two hydrogen bonds) and guanine only binds cytosine (through three hydrogen bonds).

enzymes including DNA polymerase, and the parent strand as a template. The preceding is termed "DNA <u>S</u>ynthesis" and occurs in the <u>S</u> stage of interphase during the cell cycle.

Each nucleotide has a hydroxyl or phosphate group at the 3rd and 5th carbons designated the 3′ and 5′ positions (see BIO 20.3.2, 20.5). Phosphodiester bonds can be formed between a free 3′ hydroxyl group and a free 5′ phosphate group. Thus the DNA strand has *polarity* since one end of the molecule will have a free 3′ hydroxyl while the other terminal nucleotide will have a free 5′ phosphate group. Polymerization of the two strands occurs in opposite directions (= *antiparallel*). In other words, one strand runs in the 5′ - 3′ direction, while its partner runs in the 3′ - 5′ direction.

DNA replication is <u>semi-discontinuous</u>. DNA polymerase can only synthesize DNA in the 5′ to 3′ direction. As a result of the anti-parallel nature of DNA, the 5′ - 3′ strand is replicated continuously (the *leading strand*), while the 3′ - 5′ strand is replicated discontinuously (the *lagging strand*) in the <u>reverse direction</u>. The short, newly synthesized DNA fragments that are formed on the lagging strand are called *Okazaki fragments*. DNA synthesis begins at a specific site called the replication origin (*replicon*) and proceeds in both directions. Eukaryotic chromosomes contain multiple origins while prokaryotic chromosomes contain a single origin. The parental strand is always read in the 3′ - 5′ direction and the daughter strand is always synthesized in the 5′ - 3′ direction.

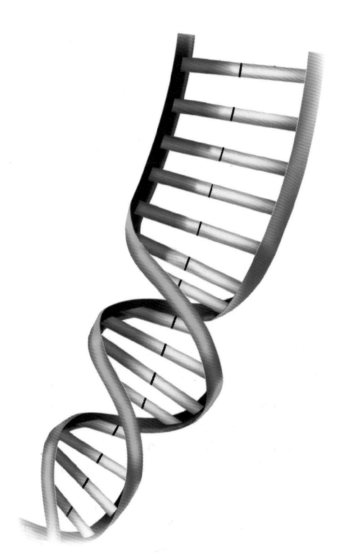

The more the H-bonds (i.e. the more G-C), the more stable the helix will be.

The *replication* (duplication) of DNA is <u>semi-conservative</u>: each strand of the double helix can serve as a template to generate a complementary strand. Thus for each double helix there is one parent strand (*old*) and one daughter strand (*new*). The latter is synthesized using one nucleotide at a time,

Previous knowledge of recombinant DNA techniques, restriction enzymes, hybridization, DNA repair mechanisms, etc., is not normally required for the DAT. However, because these topics do occasionally show up on the exam, they are discussed here and in BIO 2.2.1, 15.7 and the Appendix to Chapter 15. The following is an overview regarding DNA repair.

Because of environmental factors including chemicals and UV radiation, any one of the trillions of cells in our bodies may undergo as many as 1 million individual molecular "injuries" per day. Structural damage to DNA may result and could have many effects such as inducing mutation. Thus our DNA repair system is constantly active as it responds to damage in DNA structure.

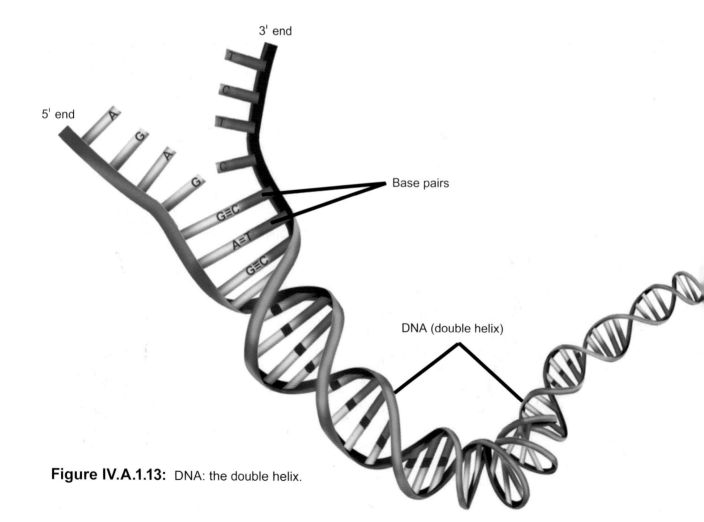

Figure IV.A.1.13: DNA: the double helix.

A cell that has accumulated a large amount of DNA damage, or one that no longer effectively repairs damage to its DNA, can: (1) become permanently dormant; (2) exhibit unregulated cell division which could lead to cancer; (3) succumb to cell suicide, also known as *apoptosis* or programmed cell death.

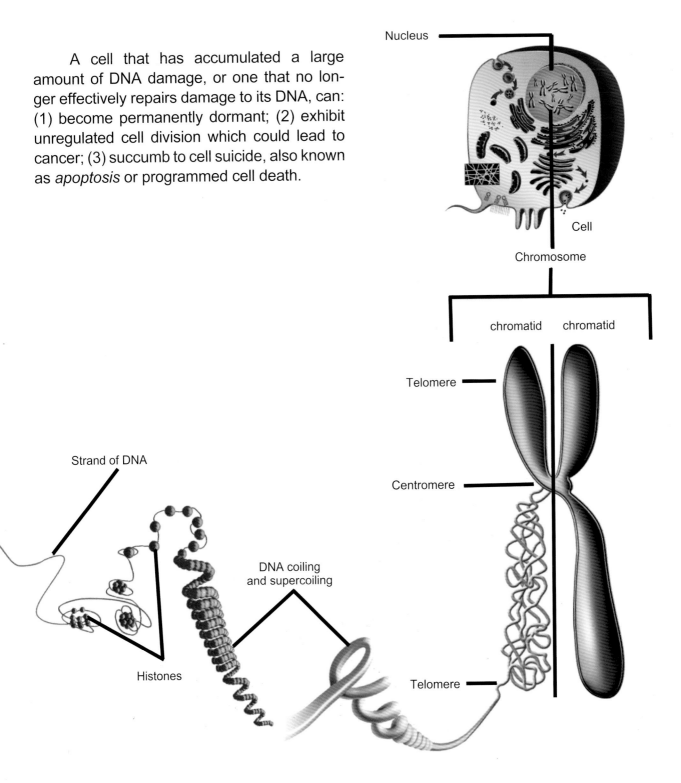

The cell cycle is a period of approximately 18 - 22 hours during which the cell can synthesize new DNA and partition the DNA equally; thus the cell can divide. Mitosis involves nuclear division (*karyokinesis*) which is usually followed by cell division (*cytokinesis*). Mitosis and cytokinesis together define the mitotic (M) phase of the cell cycle - the division of the mother cell into two daughter cells, genetically identical to each other and to their parent cell. The cell cycle is divided into a number of phases: interphase (G_1, S, G_2) and mitosis (prophase, metaphase, anaphase and telophase).

The cell cycle is temporarily suspended in resting cells. These cells stay in the G_0 state but may reenter the cell cycle and start to divide again. The cell cycle is permanently suspended in non-dividing differentiated cells such as cardiac muscle cells.

Interphase occupies about 90% of the cell cycle. During interphase, the cell prepares for DNA synthesis (G_1), synthesizes or replicates DNA (S) resulting in duplication of chromosomes, and ultimately begins preparing for mitosis (G_2). During interphase, the DNA is not folded and the individual chromosomes are not visible. Also, centrioles grow to maturity, RNA and protein for mitosis are synthesized. Mitosis begins with prophase.

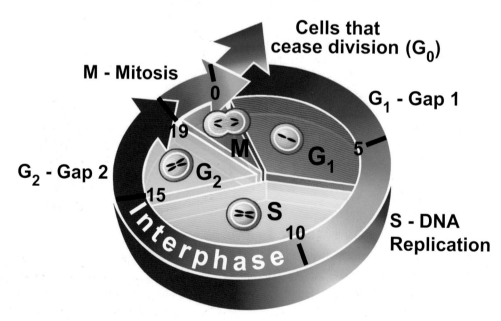

Figure IV.A.1.14: The cell cycle.
The numbers represent time in hours. Note how mitosis (M) represents the shortest period of the cycle.

Figure IV.A.1.15: Prophase.

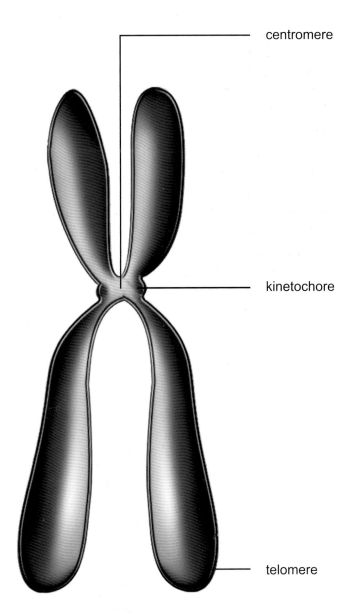

centromere

kinetochore

telomere

Figure IV.A.1.16: Chromosome Anatomy. Each chromosome has two arms separated by the centromere, labeled p (the shorter, named for 'petit' meaning 'small') and q (the longer of the two). The telomeres contain repetitive nucleotide sequences which protect the end of the chromosome. Over time, due to each cell division, the telomeres become shorter.

Prophase: pairs of centrioles migrate away from each other while microtubules appear in between forming a spindle. Other microtubules emanating from the centrioles give a radiating star-like appearance; thus they are called asters. Therefore, centrioles form the core of the Microtubule Organizing Centers (MTOC). The MTOC is a structure found in eukaryotic cells from which microtubules emerge and associated with the protein tubulin.

Simultaneously, the diffuse nuclear chromatin condenses into the visible chromosomes which consist of two sister chromatids - each being identical copies of each other. Each chromatid consists of a complete double stranded DNA helix. The area of constriction where the two chromatids are attached is the *centromere*. Kinetochores develop at the centromere region and function as MTOC. Just as centromere refers to the center, *telomere* refers to the ends of the chromosome (note: as cells divide and we age, telomeres progressively shorten). Ultimately, the nuclear envelope disappears at the end of prophase.

Figure IV.A.1.17: Metaphase.

Figure IV.A.1.19: Telophase.

Metaphase: centromeres line up along the equatorial plate. At or near the centromeres are the *kinetochores* which are proteins that face the spindle poles (asters). Microtubules, from the spindle, attach to the kinetochores of each chromosome.

Anaphase: sister chromatids are pulled apart such that each migrates to opposite poles being guided by spindle microtubules. At the end of anaphase, a cleavage furrow forms around the cell due to contraction of actin filaments called the contractile ring.

Telophase: new membranes form around the daughter nuclei; nucleoli reappear; the chromosomes uncoil and become less distinct (decondense). At the end of telophase, the cleavage furrow becomes deepened, facilitating the division of cytoplasm into two new daughter cells - each with a nucleus and organelles.

Finally, *cytokinesis* (cell separation) occurs. The cell cycle continues with the next interphase. {Mnemonic for the sequence of phases: P. MATI}

Figure IV.A.1.18: Anaphase.

Figure IV.A.1.20: Interphase.

1.4 Cell Junctions

Multicellular organisms (i.e. animals) have cell junctions or intercellular bridges. They are especially abundant in epithelial tissues and serve as points of contact between cells and/or the extracellular matrix (BIO 4.3, 4.4). The multiprotein complex that comprise cell junctions can also build up the barrier around epithelial cells (*paracellular*) and control paracellular transport.

The molecules responsible for creating cell junctions include various cell adhesion molecules (CAMs). CAMs help cells stick to each other and to their surroundings. There are four main types: selectins, cadherins, integrins, and the immunoglobulin superfamily.

1.4.1 Types of Cell Junctions

There are three major types of cell junctions in vertebrates:

1. **Anchoring junctions**: (note: "adherens" means "to adhere to"): (i) <u>Adherens junctions</u>, AKA "belt desmosome" because they can appear as bands encircling the cell (= zonula adherens); they link to the actin cytoskeleton; (ii) <u>desmosomes</u>, AKA macula (= "spot") adherens analogous to spot welding. Desmosomes include cell adhesion proteins like cadherins which can bind intermediate filaments and provide mechanical support and stability; and (iii) <u>hemidesmosomes</u> ("hemi" = "half"), whereas desmosomes link two cells together, hemidesmosomes attach one cell to the extracellular matrix (usually anchoring the 'bottom' or basal aspect of the epithelial cell or keratinocyte to the basement membrane; see Fig. IV.A.1.21 and BIO 5.3).

2. **Communicating junctions**: <u>Gap junctions</u> which are narrow tunnels which allow the free passage of small molecules and ions. One gap junction channel is composed of two connexons (or hemichannels) which connect across the intercellular space.

3. **Occluding junctions**: <u>Tight junctions</u>, AKA zonula occludens, as suggested by the name, are a junctional complex that join together forming a virtually impermeable barrier to fluid. These associate with different peripheral membrane proteins located on the intracellular side of the plasma membrane which anchor the strands to the actin component of the cytoskeleton. Thus, tight junctions join together the cytoskeletons of adjacent cells. Often tight junctions form narrow belts that circumferentially surround the upper part of the lateral (i.e. "side") surfaces of adjacent epithelial cells.

Invertebrates have several other types of specific junctions; for example, the septate junction which is analogous to the tight junction in vertebrates.

In multicellular plants, the structural functions of cell junctions are instead provided for by cell walls. The analogues of communicating cell junctions in plants are called plasmodesmata (BIO 17.6.4).

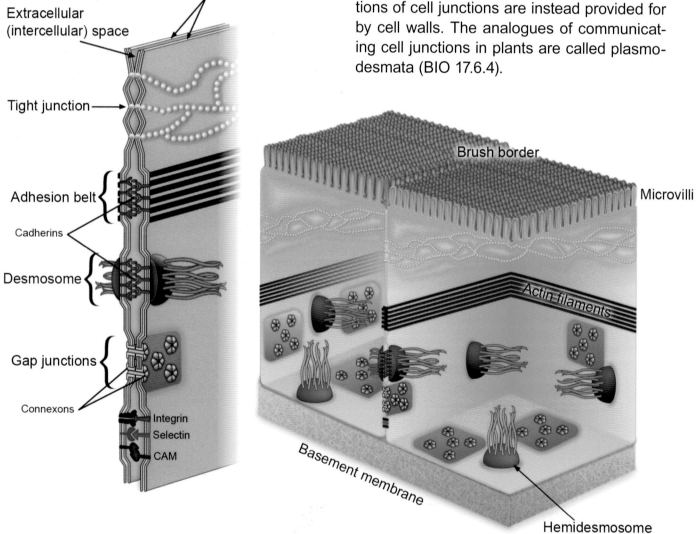

Figure IV.A.1.21: Various cell junctions in epithelia with microvilli at the surface (brush border, BIO 9.5).

1.5 Microscopy

A natural question about cells would be: if they are so small, how do we know what the inside of a cell really looks like? The story begins with the instrument used to produce magnified images of objects too small to be seen by the naked eye: the microscope.

Let us compare the basic principles of two popular methods of microscopy utilized by the vast majority of molecular biology research scientists: (1) the optical or light microscope; and (2) the electron microscope (the transmission electron microscope or TEM and the scanning electron microscope or SEM).

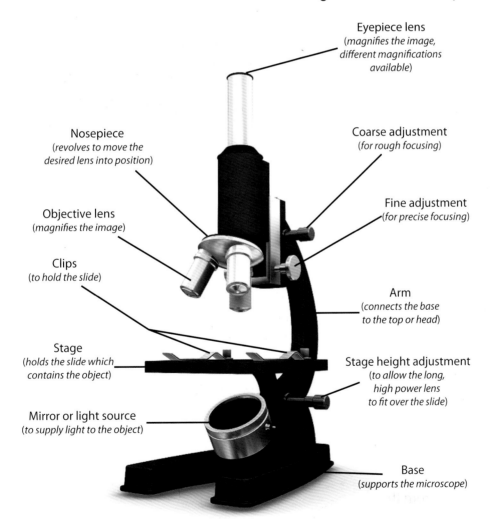

Eyepiece lens
(*magnifies the image, different magnifications available*)

Nosepiece
(*revolves to move the desired lens into position*)

Objective lens
(*magnifies the image*)

Clips
(*to hold the slide*)

Stage
(*holds the slide which contains the object*)

Mirror or light source
(*to supply light to the object*)

Coarse adjustment
(*for rough focusing*)

Fine adjustment
(*for precise focusing*)

Arm
(*connects the base to the top or head*)

Stage height adjustment
(*to allow the long, high power lens to fit over the slide*)

Base
(*supports the microscope*)

Figure IV.A.1.21: Compound light microscope. Typical magnification for the eyepiece is 10x and for the objective: 10x, 40x or 100x.

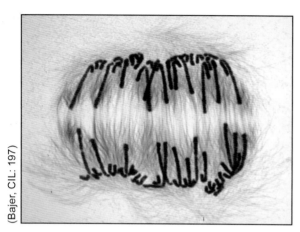

Figure IV.A.1.22: Light microscope image of a cell from the endosperm (BIO 17.2.1) of an African lily. Staining shows microtubules in red and chromosomes in blue during late anaphase (BIO 1.3).

Light microscopy involves the use of an external or internal light source. The light first passes through the *iris* which controls the amount of light reaching the specimen. The light then passes through a *condenser* which is a lens that focuses the light beam through the specimen before it ultimately meets the *objective lens* which magnifies the image depending on your chosen magnification factor. Two terms you should be familiar with are *magnification* (how much bigger the image appears) and *resolution* (the ability to distinguish between two points on an image).

Magnification is the ratio between the apparent size of an object (or its size in an image) and its true size, and thus it is a dimensionless number usually followed by the letter "x". A compound microscope uses multiple lenses to collect light from the sample or specimen (this lens is the objective with a magnification of up to 100x), and then a separate set of lenses to focus the light into the eye or camera (the eyepiece, magnification up to 10x). So the total magnification can be 100 x 10 = 1000 times the size of the specimen (1000x makes a 100 nanometer object visible).

Light microscopes enjoy their popularity thanks to their relative low cost and ease of use. A very important feature is that they can be used to view live specimens. Their shortfall is that the magnification is limited.

Common Units of Length in Biology
For details on units, see QR Chapter 3

- m = meter(s)
- cm = centimeter(s) (1 cm = 10^{-2} m)
- mm = millimeter(s) (1 mm = 10^{-3} m)
- μm = micrometer(s) (1 μm = 10^{-6} m)
        NOT micron or μ
- nm = nanometer(s) (1 nm = 10^{-9} m)
- Å = angstrom(s) (1 Å = 10^{-10} m)
- pm = picometer(s) (1 pm = 10^{-12} m)

The term "micron" is no longer in technical use.

Electron microscopy is less commonly used due to its high price and associated scarcity. It also cannot observe live organisms as a vacuum is required and the specimen is flooded with electrons. All images being produced are in black and white though color is sometimes added to the raw images. Its primary advantage lies in the fact that it is possible to achieve a magnification up to 10,000,000x and it is the obvious choice when a high level of detail is required using an extremely small specimen. In fact, an object as tiny as a small fraction of a nanometer becomes visible with an incredible 50 picometer resolution. TEM shows the interior of the cell while SEM shows the surface of the specimen.

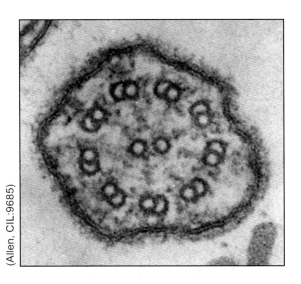

(Allen, CIL:9685)

Figure IV.A.1.23: TEM of the cross section of a cilium (BIO 1.2) showing an axoneme consisting of 9 doublet and 2 central microtubules (= 9x2 + 2). Each doublet is composed of 2 subfibers: a complete A subfiber with dynein and an attached B subfiber. Eukaryotic flagella are also 9x2 + 2.

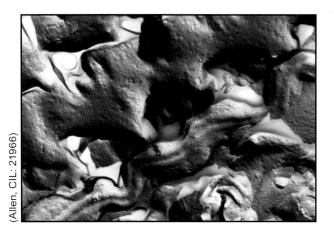

(Allen, CIL: 21966)

Figure IV.A.1.24: TEM freeze fracture of the plasma membrane which is cleaved between the acyl tails of membrane phospholipids (BIO 1.1, 20.4), leaving a monolayer on each half of the specimen. The "E" face is the inner face of the outer lipid monolayer. The complementary surface is the "P" face (the inner surface of the inner leaflet of the bilayer shown above). The 2 large ribbons are intrinsic proteins.

1.5.1 Fluorescent Microscopy and Immunofluorescence

Lastly, you should be familiar with <u>fluorescent microscopy</u> which is commonly used to identify cellular components (organelles, cytoskeleton, etc.) and microbes with a high degree of specificity and color. The fluorescent microscope makes use of a special filter that only permits certain radiation wavelengths that matches the fluorescing material being analyzed. It is an optical microscope and very similar to the light microscope except that a highly intensive light source is used to excite a fluorescent species in the sample of interest.

<u>Immunofluorescence</u> is a technique that uses the specificity of the antibody-antigen interaction (BIO 8.2) to target fluorescent dyes to specific molecules in a cell. Immunofluorescence can be used on tissue sections, cultured cell lines or individual cells. This can be called *immunostaining*, or specifically, *immunohistochemistry* where the location of the antibodies can be seen using fluorophores (= a fluorescent chemical that can re-emit light upon light excitation; CHM 11.5, 11.6).

There are two classes of immunofluorescence: direct (= primary) and indirect (= secondary).

<u>Direct immunofluorescence</u> uses a single antibody linked to a fluorophore. The antibody binds to the target molecule (antigen),

and the fluorophore attached to the antibody can be detected with a microscope. This technique is cheaper, faster but less sensitive than indirect immunofluorescence.

Indirect immunofluorescence uses two antibodies: (1) the unlabeled first, or primary, antibody binds the antigen; and (2) the secondary antibody, which carries the fluorophore and recognizes the primary antibody and binds to it.

Photobleaching is the photochemical destruction of a dye or a fluorophore. Thus the fluorescent molecules are sometimes destroyed by the light exposure necessary to stimulate them into fluorescing. On the other hand, photobleaching can be fine tuned to improve the signal-to-noise ratio (like seeing the tree from the forest). Photobleaching can also be used to study the motion of molecules (i.e. FRAP).

Immunofluorescence samples can be seen through a simple fluorescent microscope (*epifluorescence*) or through the more complex *confocal* microscope.

A confocal microscope is a state-of-the-art fluorescent microscope which uses a laser as the light source. The confocal microscope is used in FRAP, fluorescence recovery after photobleaching, which is an optical technique used to "view" the movement of proteins or molecules. FRAP is capable of quantifying the 2D diffusion of a thin film of molecules containing fluorescently labeled probes, or to examine single cells. FRAP has had many uses including: studies of cell membrane diffusion and protein binding; determining if axonal transport is retrograde or anterograde, meaning towards or away from the neuron's cell body (soma), respectively.

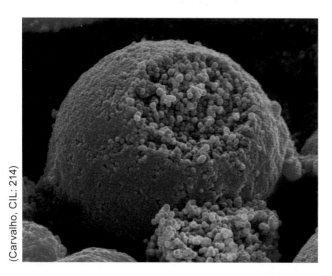

(Carvalho, CIL: 214)

Figure IV.A.1.25: SEM colorized image of a neuron's presynaptic terminal (BIO 5.1) that has been broken open to reveal the synaptic vesicles (orange and blue) beneath the cell membrane.

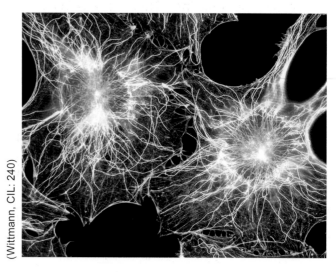

(Wittmann, CIL: 240)

Figure IV.A.1.26: Fluorescence microscopy of two interphase cells with immunofluorescence labeling of actin filaments (purple), microtubules (yellow), and nuclei (green).

GOLD STANDARD WARM-UP EXERCISES

CHAPTER 1: Generalized Eukaryotic Cell

1) Proteins in the plasma membrane can diffuse laterally, however, the specific orientations maintained by integral membrane proteins with respect to the bilayer suggest that rotation of these molecules through the plane of the bilayer very rarely occurs. The most likely reason for this is:

A. the carbohydrate attachments to many of the proteins makes rotation impossible.
B. rotation of these proteins would affect their ability to channel specific ions and molecules.
C. rotation of these proteins would affect the permeability of the plasma membrane.
D. since most integral proteins have some hydrophilic surface area, a transverse rotation would be energetically unfavorable.

2) Some peripheral proteins are bound to the membrane due to interactions with the integral membrane proteins. These interactions are likely:

A. hydrophobic in nature.
B. electrostatic in nature.
C. covalent in nature.
D. due to Van Der Waal's bonds.

3) Proteins are frequently adorned by straight/chain or branched oligosaccharides, in which case they are called glycoproteins. This type of modification can serve a variety of functions including to provide the protein with surface characteristics that facilitate its recognition. In which of the following cellular components would the greatest proportion of glycoproteins be expected?

A. Lysosomes
B. Microfilaments
C. Mitochondria
D. Phospholipid bilayer

4) Oligosaccharide modification most likely occurs in the:

A. smooth endoplasmic reticulum.
B. Golgi apparatus.
C. lysosomes.
D. cytosol.

5) Sweat is less concentrated than blood plasma and is secreted by the activity of sweat glands under the control of pseudomotor neurons. The transport of electrolytes in sweat from blood plasma to the sweat glands is best accounted for by which of the following processes?

A. Osmosis
B. Simple diffusion
C. Active transport
D. All of the above

6) Microfilaments and microtubules would have an important locomotive function in all but which of the following organelles?

A. Flagella
B. Endocytotic vesicles
C. Lysosomes
D. None of the above

7) All of the following are closely associated with microtubules EXCEPT:

A. flagella.
B. cilia.
C. villi.
D. centrioles.

8) Fas/APO-1 is a transmembrane receptor which, when stimulated, may activate intracellular mechanisms leading to cell death. Fas/APO-1 is likely:

A. a phospholipid.
B. a complex carbohydrate.
C. synthesized in the nucleus.
D. synthesized by rough endoplasmic reticulum.

9) The ATP-dependent dopamine transporter can be found at the presynaptic terminal of nerve cells. By which of the following mechanisms would the dopamine transporter most likely work?

A. Simple diffusion
B. Facilitated transport
C. Passive co-transport
D. Active transport

10) An effect of UV radiation on DNA is the formation of harmful covalent bonds among bases. For example, adjacent thymines form thymine dimers. Which of the following is most likely true of the bonds which create the dimers?

A. They consist of two carbon-carbon bonds between purines.
B. They consist of two carbon-carbon bonds between pyrimidines.
C. They consist of one carbon-carbon bond and one oxygen-sulfur bond between pyrimidines.
D. They consist of one carbon-carbon bond and one nitrogen-sulfur bond between pyrimidines.

11) Which of the following statements could be held LEAST accountable for DNA maintaining its helical structure?

A. Unwinding the helix would separate the base pairs enough for water molecules to enter between the bases, making the structure unstable.
B. The helix is stabilized by hydrogen bonds between bases.
C. The sugar phosphate backbone is held in place by hydrophilic interactions with the solvent.
D. C-G pairs have 3 hydrogen bonds between them but A-T pairs only have 2.

12) Apo-X is a drug which blocks prophase from occurring. When Apo-X is added to a tissue culture, in which phase of the cell cycle would most cells be arrested?

A. Mitosis
B. G_1
C. G_2
D. Synthesis

13) Evidence that DNA replication occurs in a bidirectional manner would be that shortly after initiation:

A. each gene in the E. coli genome would be represented only once.
B. each gene in the E. coli genome would be represented twice.
C. DNA duplication would begin on both sides of the origin of replication.
D. gene frequencies should be very high for regions symmetrically disposed about the origin.

14) If E. coli was allowed to replicate in the presence of ^{3}H-thymidine, during the second round of replication, what would an autoradiograph, which detects irradiation, show proving that the replication was semi-conservative?

A. A uniformly unlabeled structure

B. A uniformly labeled structure

C. One branch of the growing replication eye would be half as strongly labeled as the remainder of the chromosome

D. One branch of the growing replication eye would be twice as strongly labeled as the remainder of the chromosome

15) Colchicine is a plant alkaloid that inhibits normal mitosis by delaying the formation of daughter cells by inhibiting chromatid segregation. The advantage of colchicine treatment in this experiment is that in tissue so treated many cells become arrested in the state where the sister chromatids are paired. Colchicine might act by:

A. disrupting mitotic spindle formation.

B. inhibiting DNA synthesis.

C. inhibiting the replication of chromosomes.

D. preventing the degeneration of the nuclear envelope.

16) The Sanger method for sequencing DNA uses newly synthesized DNA that is randomly terminated. The method employs chain-terminating dideoxynucleotide triphosphates (ddXTPs) to produce a continuous series of fragments during catalyzed reactions. The ddXTPs act as terminators because while they can add to a growing chain during polymerization, they cannot be added onto because they must lack a:

A. hydroxyl group on their phosphoric acid component.

B. hydroxyl group on C1 of their ribose component.

C. hydroxyl group on C3 of their ribose component.

D. hydroxyl group on C5 of their ribose component.

17) When DNA is being sequenced, the appropriate enzymes are added to make a complementary copy of a primed single-stranded DNA fragment. Which of the following enzymes would have to be included in the Sanger method in order for it to work?

A. DNA gyrase

B. DNA polymerase

C. Reverse transcriptase

D. DNA helicase

18) The least likely of the following radioactive deoxynucleoside triphosphates to be used to label DNA fragments is:

A. dATP

B. dGTP

C. dUTP

D. dCTP

19) E. coli bacteriophages were added to E. coli cells in a medium containing inorganic ^{32}P-labelled phosphate and ^{35}S-labelled inorganic sulfate. After infection of the cells had occurred, examination of the progeny would show that:

A. the phosphorus had been incorporated into both the DNA and the protein components of the bacteriophages

B. the sulfur became incorporated into both the DNA and protein components of the bacteriophages.

C. the phosphorus became incorporated into the DNA component of the phages and the sulfur into their protein component.

D. the sulfur became incorporated into the DNA component of the phages and the phosforus into their protein component.

20) If increasing the concentration gradient across the plasma membrane increases the rate of transport until a maximum rate is reached, this would be convincing evidence for:

A. simple diffusion.
B. carrier-mediated transport.
C. osmosis.
D. the Fluid Mosaic model.

21. Receptor-mediated endocytosis is usually associated with:

A. clathrin.
B. selectin.
C. integrin.
D. tubulin.

22. In desmosomes, cadherins link to what aspect of an adjacent cell?

A. Intermediate filaments
B. Connexons
C. Actin
D. Integrins

23. Which of the following surrounds the cell like a belt and prevents the passage of substances between the cells?

A. Hemidesmosome
B. Tight junction
C. Desmosome
D. Gap junction

24. If the ocular of a light microscope is 10x and the objective is set at 40x, then what is the total magnification of the microscope?

A. 400x
B. 50x
C. 40x
D. 10x

25. A microscope used to visualize specific fluoro-phore-labeled proteins in a living cell is the:

A. compound light microscope.
B. transmission electron microscope (TEM).
C. scanning electron microscope (SEM).
D. confocal microscope.

GS ANSWER KEY

CHAPTER 1

Cross-Reference

1.	D	BIO 1.1, ORG 12.1.1
2.	B	BIO 1.1, ORG 12.1-12.2.2, CHM 4.2
3.	D	BIO 1.1
4.	B	BIO 1.2.1
5.	B	BIO 1.1.1
6.	D	BIO 1.2, 1.2.1, 7.5F
7.	C	BIO 1.2
8.	D	BIO 1.1, 1.2.1
9.	D	BIO 1.2.2
10.	B	BIO 1.2.2, ORG 12.2.2
11.	A	BIO 1.2.2
12.	C	BIO 1.3
13.	C	BIO 1.2.2, 3.0

Cross-Reference

14.	D	BIO 1.2.2
15.	A	BIO 1.2, 1.3
16.	C	BIO 1.2.2, ORG 12.5
17.	B	BIO 1.2.2
18.	C	BIO 1.2.2
19.	C	BIO 1.2.2, ORG 12.2.2
20.	B	BIO 1.2.2
21.	A	BIO 1.1.3
22.	A	BIO 1.4.1
23.	B	BIO 1.4.1
24.	A	BIO 1.5
25.	D	BIO 1.5, 1.5.1

* Explanations can be found at the back of the book.

Go online to DAT-prep.com for additional chapter review Q&A and forum.

Go online to DAT-prep.com for additional chapter review Q&A and forum.

GOLD NOTES

MICROBIOLOGY

Chapter 2

DAT-Prep.com

Introduction

Microbiology is the study of microscopic organisms including viruses, bacteria and fungi. It is important to be able to focus on the differences and similarities between these microorganisms and the generalized eukaryotic cell you have just studied. Classification of these microorganisms will be done in Chapter 16.

Additional Resources

Free Online Q&A + Forum　　　Video: Online or DVD　　　Flashcards　　　Special Guest

Unlike cells, viruses are too small to be seen directly with a light microscope. Viruses infect all types of organisms, from animals and plants to bacteria and archaea (BIO 2.2). Only a very basic and general understanding of viruses is required for the DAT.

Viruses are obligate intracellular parasites; in other words, in order to replicate their genetic material and thus multiply, they must gain access to the inside of a cell. Replication of a virus takes place when the virus takes control of the host cell's synthetic machinery. Viruses are often considered non-living for several reasons:

(i) they do not grow by increasing in size

(ii) they cannot carry out independent metabolism

(iii) they do not respond to external stimuli

(iv) they have no cellular structure.

The genetic material for viruses may be either DNA or RNA, never both. Viruses do not have organelles or ribosomes. The nucleic acid core is encapsulated by a protein coat (capsid) which together forms the head region in some viruses. The tail region helps to anchor the virus to a cell. An extracellular viral particle is called a *virion*.

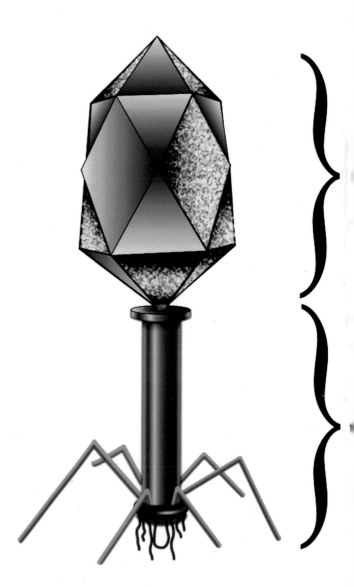

Figure IV.A.2.1: A virus.

Viruses are much smaller than prokaryotic cells (i.e. bacteria) which, in turn, are much smaller than eukaryotes (i.e. animal cells, fungi). A virus which infects bacteria is called a <u>bacteriophage</u> or simply a <u>phage</u>.

The life cycle of viruses has many variants; the following represents the main themes for DAT purposes. A virus attaches to a specific receptor on a cell. Some viruses may now enter the cell; others, as in the diagram, will simply inject their nucleic acid. Either way, viral molecules induce the metabolic machinery of the host cell to produce more viruses.

The new viral particles may now exit the cell by lysing (bursting). This is also a feature of many bacteria. The preceding is deemed <u>lytic</u> or virulent. Some virus lie latent for long periods of time without lysing the host and its genome becomes incorporated by genetic recombination into the host's chromosome. Therefore, whenever the host replicates, the viral genome is also replicated. These are called <u>lysogenic</u> or temperate viruses. Eventually, at some point, the virus may become activated and lyse the host cell.

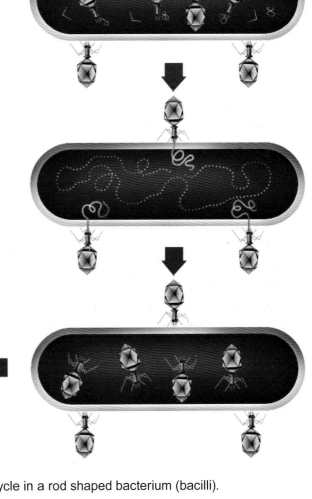

Figure IV.A.2.2: Lytic viral life cycle in a rod shaped bacterium (bacilli).

A retrovirus uses RNA as its genetic material. It is called a retrovirus because of an enzyme (reverse transcriptase) that gives these viruses the unique ability of transcribing RNA (their RNA) into DNA (see Biology Chapter 3 for the central dogma regarding protein synthesis). The retroviral DNA can then integrate into the chromosomal DNA of the host cell to be expressed there. The human immunodeficiency virus (HIV), the cause of AIDS, is a retrovirus.

Retroviruses are used, in genetics, to deliver DNA to a cell (= a vector); in medicine, they are used for gene therapy.

2.2 Prokaryotes

Prokaryotes (= pre-nucleus) are organisms without a membrane bound nucleus which includes 2 types of organisms: bacteria (= Eubacteria) and archaea (= bacteria-like organisms that live in extreme environments). For the purposes of the DAT, we will focus on bacteria. They are haploid and have a long circular strand of DNA in a region called the nucleoid.

The nucleoid is a region in a bacterium that contains DNA but is not surrounded by a nuclear membrane. Because bacterial DNA is not surrounded by a nuclear membrane, transcription and translation can occur at the same time, that is, protein synthesis can begin while mRNA is being produced. Bacteria also have smaller circular DNA called plasmid, which is extra chromosomal genetic element that can replicate independently of the bacterial chromosome and helps to confer resistance to antibiotics.

Bacteria do not have mitochondria, Golgi apparatus, lysosomes, nor endoplasmic reticulum. Instead, metabolic processes can

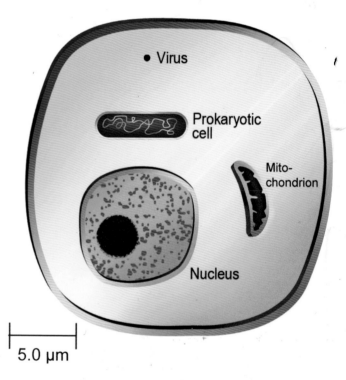

Typical eukaryotic cell

Figure IV.A.2.3

Comparing the size of a typical eukaryote, prokaryote and virus. Note that both the prokaryote and mitochondrion are similar in size and both contain circular DNA suggesting an evolutionary link.

be carried out in the cytoplasm or associated with bacterial membranes. Bacteria have ribosomes (smaller than eukaryotes), plasma membrane, and a cell wall. The cell wall, made of peptidoglycans, helps to prevent the hypertonic bacterium from bursting. Some bacteria have a slimy polysaccharide mucoid-like capsule on the outer surface for protection.

Bacteria can achieve movement with their flagella. Bacterial flagella are helical filaments, each with a rotary motor at its base which can turn clockwise or counterclockwise.

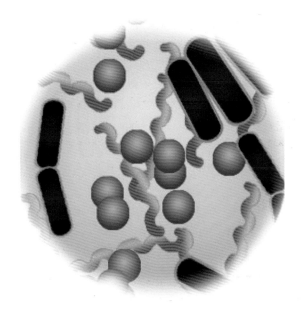

Figure IV.A.2.5

Schematic representation of bacteria colored for the purpose of identification: cocci (spherical, green), bacilli (cylindrical, purple) and spirilli (helical, orange).

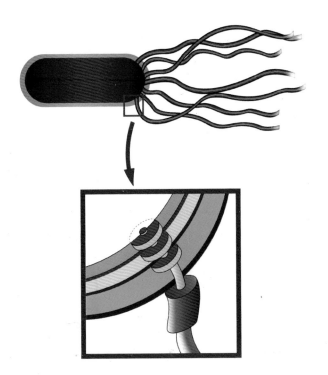

Figure IV.A.2.4

Schematic representation of the basis for flagellar propulsion. The flagellum, similar to a flexible hook, is anchored to the membrane and cell wall by a series of protein rings forming a motor. Powered by the flow of protons, the motor can rotate the flagellum more than 100 revolutions per second.

The form and rotary engine of flagella are maintained by proteins (i.e. flagellin) which interact with the plasma membrane and the basal body (BIO 1.2). Power is generated by a proton motive force similar to the proton pump in metabolism (Biology, Chapter 4).

Bacteria also have short, hairlike filaments called pili (also called fimbriae) arising from the bacterial cell wall. These pili are much shorter than flagella. Common pili can serve as adherence factors which promote binding of bacteria to host cells. Sex pili, encoded by a self-transmissible plasmid, are involved in transferring of DNA from one bacterium to another via conjugation.

Bacteria are partially classified according to their shapes: <u>cocci</u> which are spheri-

Prokaryotic Cells	Eukaryotic Cells
Small cells (1-10 μm)	Larger cells (10-100 μm)
Always unicellular	Often multicellular
No nuclei or any membrane-bound organelles, such as mitochondria	Always have nuclei and other membrane-bound organelles
DNA is circular, without proteins	DNA is linear and associated with proteins to form chromatin
Ribosomes are small (70S)	Ribosomes are large (80S)
No cytoskeleton	Always has a cytoskeleton
Motility by rigid rotating flagellum made of flagellin)	Motility by flexible waving cilia or flagellae (made of tubulin)
Cell division is by binary fission	Cell division is by mitosis or meiosis
Reproduction is always asexual	Reproduction is asexual or sexual
Great variety of metabolic pathways	Common metabolic pathways

Table IV.A.2.1: Summary of the differences between prokaryotic and eukaryotic cells.

cal or sometimes elliptical; bacilli which are rod shaped or cylindrical (Fig. IV.A.2.2 in BIO 2.1 showed phages attacking a bacillus bacterium); spirilli which are helical or spiral. They are also classified according to whether or not their cell wall reacts to a special dye called a Gram stain; thus they are gram-positive if they retain the stain and gram-negative if they do not.

Most bacteria engage in a form of asexual reproduction called binary fission. Two identical DNA molecules migrate to opposite ends of a cell as a transverse wall forms, dividing the cell in two. The cells can now separate and enlarge to the original size. Under ideal conditions, a bacterium can undergo fission every 10-20 minutes producing over 10^{30} progeny in a day and a half. If resources are unlimited, exponential growth would be expected. The doubling time of bacterial populations can be calculated as follows:

$$b = B \times 2^n$$

where b is the number of bacteria at the end of the time interval, B is the number of bacteria at the beginning of the time interval and n is the number of generations. Thus if we start with 2 bacteria and follow for 3 generations then we get:

$$b = B \times 2^n = 2 \times 2^3 = 2 \times 8 = 16$$
bacteria after 3 generations.

{Note: bacterial doubling time is a relatively popular question type.}

Bacteria do not produce gametes nor zygotes, nor do they undergo meiosis; however, four forms of genetic recombination do occur: <u>transduction</u>, <u>transformation</u>, <u>conjugation</u> and <u>transposon</u> <u>insertion</u>.

In transduction, fragments of bacterial chromosome accidentally become packaged into virus during a viral infection. These viruses may then infect another bacterium. A piece of bacterial DNA that the virus is accidentally carrying will be injected and incorporated into the host chromosome if there is homology between the newly injected piece of DNA and the recipient bacterial genome.

In transformation, a foreign chromosome fragment (plasmid) is released from one bacterium during cell lysis and enters into another bacterium. The DNA can then become incorporated into the recipient's genome if there is homology between the newly incorporated genome and the recipient one.

In conjugation, DNA is transferred directly by cell-to-cell contact formed by a conjugation bridge called the sex pilus. For conjugation to occur, one bacterium must have the sex factor called F plasmid. Bacteria that carry F plasmids are called F^+ cells. During conjugation, a F^+ cell replicates its F factor and will pass its F plasmid to an F^- cell, converting it to an F^+ cell. This type of exchange is the major mechanism for transfer of antibiotic resistance.

In transposon insertion, mobile genetic elements called transposons move from one position to another in a bacterial chromosome or between different molecules of DNA without having DNA homology.

Most bacteria cannot synthesize their own food and thus depend on other organisms for it; such a bacterium is heterotrophic. Most heterotrophic bacteria obtain their food from dead organic matter; this is called saprophytic. Some bacteria are autotrophic meaning they can synthesize organic compounds from simple inorganic substances. Thus some are photosynthetic producing carbohydrate and releasing oxygen, while others are chemoautotrophic obtaining energy via chemical reactions including the oxidation of iron, sulfur, nitrogen, or hydrogen gas.

Bacteria can be either aerobic or anaerobic. The former refers to metabolism in the presence of oxygen and the latter in the absence of oxygen (i.e. fermentation).

Based on variations in the oxygen requirement, bacteria are divided into four types:

1) Obligate aerobes: require oxygen for growth

2) Facultative anaerobes: are aerobic; however, can grow in the absence of oxygen by undergoing fermentation

3) Aerotolerant anaerobes: use fermentation for energy; however, can tolerate low amounts of oxygen

4) Obligate anaerobes: are anaerobic, can be damaged by oxygen

Symbiosis generally refers to close and often long term interactions between different biological species. Bacteria have various symbiotic relationships with, for example, humans. These include mutualism (both benefit: GI tract bacteria, BIO 9.5), parasitism (parasite benefits over the host: tuberculosis, appendicitis) and commensalism (one benefits and the other is not significantly harmed or benefited: some skin bacteria).

2.2.1 Operons

E. coli is a gram-negative, rod-shaped intestinal bacterium with DNA sequences called *operons* that direct biosynthetic pathways. Operons are composed of:

1. A repressor which can bind to an operator and prevent gene expression by blocking RNA polymerase. However, in the presence of an inducer, a repressor will be bound to the inducer instead, forming an inducer-repressor complex. This complex cannot bind to an operator and thus gene expression is permitted.

2. A promoter which is a sequence of DNA where RNA polymerase attaches to begin transcription.

3. Operators which can block the action of RNA polymerase if there is a repressor present.

4. A regulator which codes for the synthesis of a repressor that can bind to the operator and block gene transcription.

5. Structural genes that code for several related enzymes that are responsible for production of a specific end product.

The *lac operon* controls the breakdown of lactose and is the simplest way of illustrating how gene regulation in bacteria works. In the lac operon system there is an active repressor that binds to the operator. In this scenario RNA polymerase is unable to transcribe the structural genes necessary to control the uptake and subsequent breakdown of lactose. When the repressor is inactivated (in the presence of lactose) the RNA polymerase is now able to transcribe the genes that code for the required enzymes. These enzymes are said to be *inducible* as it is the lactose that is required to turn on the operon.

Lac Operon

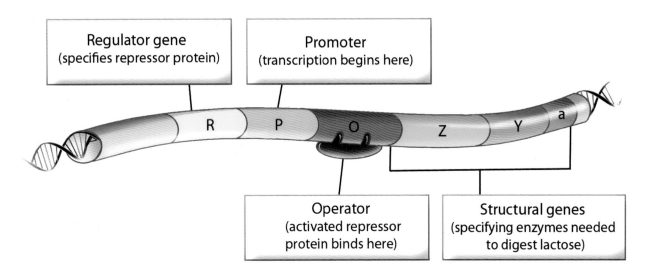

Regulator gene
(specifies repressor protein)

Promoter
(transcription begins here)

R P O Z Y a

Operator
(activated repressor
protein binds here)

Structural genes
(specifying enzymes needed
to digest lactose)

2.3 Fungi

Fungi are eukaryotic (= true nucleus) organisms which absorb their food through their chitinous cell walls. They may either be unicellular (i.e. yeast) or filamentous (i.e. mushrooms, molds) with individual filaments called hyphae which collectively form a mycelium. Fungal cell membranes contain ergosterol rather than cholesterol found in cell membranes of other eukaryotes.

Fungi often reproduce asexually. In molds, spores can be produced and then liberated from outside of a sporangium; or, as in yeast, a simple asexual budding process may be used. Sexual reproduction can involve the fusion of opposite mating types to produce asci (singular: ascus), basidia (singular: basidium), or zygotes. All of the three preceding diploid structures must undergo meiosis to produce haploid spores. If resources are unlimited, exponential growth would be expected.

Fungi are relatively important for humans as a source of disease and a decomposer of both food and dead organic matter. On the lighter side, they also serve as food (mushrooms, truffles), for alcohol and food production (cheese molds, bread yeast) and they have given us the breakthrough antibiotic, penicillin (from penicillium molds).

2.4 Vectors

A vector can be a person, animal or microorganism that carries and transmits an infectious organism (i.e. bacteria, viruses, etc.) into another living organism. Examples: the mosquito is a vector for malaria; bats are vectors for rabies and a SARS-like virus.

2.5 The Scientific Method

The scientific method could be used in conjunction with any DAT Biology experiment but microbiology is most common.

The point of the experiment is to test your ability to read scientific material, understand what is being tested, and determine if the hypothesis has been proved, refuted or neither. When a hypothesis survives rigorous testing, it graduates to a *theory*.

Observation, formulation of a theory, and testing of a theory by additional observation is called the scientific method. In biology, a key aspect to evaluate the validity of a trial or experiment is the presence of a *control group*. Generally, treatment is withheld from the control group but given to the *experimental group*.

First we will make an observation and then use deductive reasoning to create an appropriate hypothesis which will result in an experimental design. Consider the following: trees grow well in the sunlight. Hypothesis: exposure to light is directly related to tree growth. Experiment: two groups of trees are grown in similar conditions except one group (*experimental*) is exposed to light while the other group (*control*) is not exposed to light. Growth is carefully measured and the two groups are compared. Note that tree growth (*dependent variable*) is dependent on light (*independent variable*).

There are experiments where it is important to expose the control group to some factor different from the factor given to the experimental group (= *positive control*); as opposed to not giving the control group any exposure at all (= *negative control*). Exposure for a control group is used in medicine and dentistry because of the "Placebo Effect."

Experiments have shown that giving a person a pill that contains no biologically active material will cure many illnesses in up to 30% of individuals. Thus if Drug X is developed using a traditional control group, and the "efficacy" is estimated at 32%, it may be that the drug is no more effective than a sugar pill! In this case, the control group must be exposed to an unmedicated preparation to negate the Placebo Effect. To be believable the experiment must be well-grounded in evidence (= *valid,* based on the scientific method) and then one must be able to reproduce the results.

2.5.1 The Experiment

A lab in Boston reports 15% cell death when maximally stimulating the APO-1 receptor. In order to appropriately interpret the results, it must first be compared to:

A. data from other labs.

B. the attrition rate of other cell types.

C. the actual number of APO-1 cells dying in the tissue culture.

D. the rate of cell death without stimulation of APO-1.

● The experiment: stimulating a specific receptor on cells led to a 15% rate of cell death.

● Treatment is the stimulation of a receptor.

● The control (*group without treatment*): under the same conditions, do not stimulate the receptor (choice **D.**).

Choice **C.** does not answer the question. Choices **A.** and **B.** are most relevant if the initial data is shown to be significant. To prove that the data is significant or valid, one must first compare to a control group (choice **D.**).

GOLD STANDARD WARM-UP EXERCISES

CHAPTER 2: Microbiology

1) The blood of hepatitis B chronically infected people contains numerous particles of a harmless protein component of the virus called HBsAg. HBsAg is likely a component of:

   A. the capsid of the virus.
   B. the nucleic acid core of the virus.
   C. the tail of the virus.
   D. the slimy mucoid-like capsule on the outer surface of the virus.

2) Both bacteria and eukaryotic cells may share all of the following features EXCEPT:

   A. phospholipid bilayer.
   B. cell wall.
   C. ribosomes.
   D. nuclear membrane.

3) What features does the HIV virus share in common with all viruses?

   I. RNA as genetic material
   II. The ability to infect lymphocytes
   III. Obligate intracellular parasite

   A. I only
   B. III only
   C. II and III only
   D. I, II and III

4) Once teeth appear, the bacteria comprising the microbial flora of the tissues surrounding the teeth are mainly:

   A. gram-negative, aerobes.
   B. gram-positive, aerobes.
   C. gram-positive, facultative anaerobes.
   D. gram-negative, obligate anaerobes.

5) Streptococcus mutans is associated with the tooth surface and appears to be the major causative agent of dental caries, or tooth decay. Streptococcus mutans produces glucan, a sticky polymer of glucose that acts like a cement and binds the bacterial cells together and to the tooth surface. The enzyme which catalyzes the formation of glucan is likely located:

   A. in the cytosol of the cocci.
   B. in lysosomes within the cytoplasm of the cocci.
   C. in the nuclei of the cocci.
   D. on the cell surface membrane of the cocci.

6) The difference between the bacterium E. coli and the fungus Aspergillus is:

   A. Aspergillus contains ribosomes.
   B. E. coli has a cell wall.
   C. Aspergillus can undergo anaerobic metabolism.
   D. E. coli does not have a nucleus.

7) Streptococcus mutans and Lactobacillus are, respectively:

   A. spherical and helical.
   B. spherical and cylindrical.
   C. cylindrical and helical.
   D. helical and cylindrical.

8) The high number of bacteria in dental plaque result from the proliferation of bacteria by all of the following methods, EXCEPT:

   A. translocation.
   B. transduction.
   C. transformation.
   D. binary fission.

9) Given that the time for one TS type E. coli to divide at 30 °C is approximately 15 minutes, if 10 bacteria should begin dividing in ample culture media, approximately how many would be present 2 hours later?

A. 500
B. 1000
C. 2500
D. 5000

10) Given unlimited resources, which of the following graphs shows the population growth curve for the yeast Candida albicans once infection occurs?

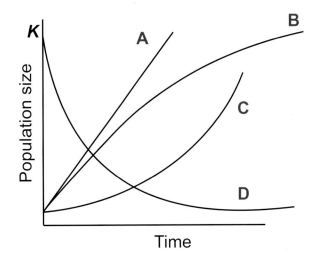

11) Yeast cells used for cloning the gene for HBsAg could be propagated by all but which of the following methods?

A. Budding
B. Transduction
C. Fusion
D. Meiotic division

12) Nitrogen fixation is accomplished by:

A. plants.
B. animals.
C. bacteria.
D. viruses.

GS ANSWER KEY

CHAPTER 2

			Cross-Reference					Cross-Reference
1.	A	BIO 2.1			7.	B	BIO 2.2	
2.	D	BIO 2.2			8.	A	BIO 2.2, 15.5	
3.	B	BIO 2.1			9.	C	BIO 1.3, 2.2	
4.	C	BIO 2.2, 4.5			10.	C	Ap A.4.2, BIO 2.3	
5.	D	BIO 1.1, 2.2, 4.1			11.	B	BIO 2.3	
6.	D	BIO 2.2-2.3			12.	C	BIO 2.2	

* Explanations can be found at the back of the book.

APPENDIX
CHAPTER 2

Introduction to Advanced DAT-30 Topics

Most students will be accepted to dental school without coming near to a perfect score; and frankly, no student is going to obtain a perfect scaled score of 30/30. However, for students who have the time and the will to aim for a perfect score, we have added a number of advanced topics in the form of passages, followed by questions so that the material can be learned in an interactive way. As per usual, explanations are at the back of the book. You should decide if you wish to read these sections based on the requirements of the dental program(s) you wish to attend.

Advanced DAT-30 Topic: Chimeric Plasmid

Muscular dystrophy is one of the most frequently encountered genetic diseases, affecting one in every 4000 boys (but much less commonly girls) born in America. Muscular dystrophy results in the progressive degeneration of skeletal and cardiac muscle fibers, weakening the muscle and leading ultimately to death from respiratory or cardiac failure.

The gene responsible for a major form of muscular dystrophy has been identified. This gene codes for a protein known as dystrophin, which is absent or present in a nonfunctional form in patients with the disease. Dystrophin is located on the inner surface of the plasma membrane in normal muscle protein.

The cloning of a fragment of DNA allows indefinite amounts of dystrophin to be produced from even a single original molecule. An insertion generates a hybrid or chimeric plasmid or phage, consisting in part of the additional "foreign" sequences. These chimeric elements replicate in bacteria just like the original plasmid or phage and so can be obtained in large amounts. Copies of the original foreign fragment can be retrieved from the progeny. Since the properties of the chimeric species usually are unaffected by the particular foreign sequences that are involved, almost any sequence of DNA can be cloned in this way. Because the phage or plasmid is used to "carry" the foreign DNA as an inert part of the genome, it is often referred to as the cloning vector.

13) The functions of dystrophin likely include all of the following EXCEPT one. Which is the EXCEPTION?

 A. Recognition of protein hormones important to the functioning of the cells
 B. Maintenance of the structural integrity of the plasma membrane
 C. Keeping ion channels within the cells open
 D. Protection of elements within the membrane during contraction of the cells

14) In order for cloning of foreign DNA to take place:

A. plasmids must incorporate the foreign DNA into the DNA in their capsids.

B. there must be several sites at which DNA can be inserted.

C. bacteria must be able to resume their usual life cycle after additional sequences of DNA have been incorporated into their genomes.

D. bacteria must divide meiotically, so no two daughter cells are exactly alike.

15) Plasmid genomes are circular and a single cleavage converts the DNA into a linear molecule. The two ends can be joined to the ends of a linear foreign DNA to regenerate a circular chimeric plasmid. Which of the following rules would be most important in allowing this process to occur?

A. DNA replication occurs in a semi-conservative manner.

B. The genetic code is composed of triplets of bases which correspond to the 20 amino acids used in protein structure.

C. The stability of the DNA helix is dependent on the number of C-G bonds present.

D. Phosphodiester bonds must link the plasmid DNA to the foreign DNA.

16) One possible method of treating muscular dystrophy using cloning techniques would be to:

A. Splice the nonfunctional genes out of dystrophic muscle cells and clone them in bacterial plasmids.

B. Determine the amino acid sequence of dystrophin and introduce the protein into muscle cells artificially.

C. Clone the gene responsible for coding dystrophin and insert the normal gene into dystrophic muscle cells.

D. Prevent skeletal and cardiac muscle tissue degradation by cloning and inserting the genes for troponin and tropomyosin into dystrophic muscle cells.

17) If the gene which codes for troponin was absent from muscle cells, all of the following processes would be inhibited EXCEPT one. Which is the EXCEPTION?

A. The movement of tropomyosin to a new position on the actin molecules

B. The uncovering of the active sites for the attachment of actin to the cross bridges of myosin

C. The hydrolysis of ATP in the myosin head to produce ADP, P_i, and energy

D. The release of Ca^{2+} ions from the sarcoplasmic reticulum

---

ANSWER KEY

ADVANCED TOPICS - CHAPTER 2

Cross-Reference

13.	A	P2, S3
14.	C	P3, S3, S5; BIO 2.2, BIO 15.7
15.	D	BIO 1.2.2, BIO 20.5, BIO 15.7
16.	C	deduce, BIO 15.7
17.	D	BIO 5.2

P = paragraph; S = sentence; E = equation; T = table; F = figure

Go online to DAT-prep.com for additional chapter review Q&A and forum.

GOLD NOTES

PROTEIN SYNTHESIS

Chapter 3

Memorize	Understand	Importance
The genetic code (triplet) Central Dogma: DNA ➡ RNA ➡ protein Definitions: mRNA, tRNA, rRNA Codon-anticodon relationship Initiation, elongation and termination	* Mechanism of transcription * Mechanism of translation * Roles of mRNA, tRNA, rRNA * Role and structure of ribosomes	**0 to 2 out of the 40 Biology** DAT questions are based on content in this chapter (in our estimation). * Note that between 25% and 50% of the questions in DAT Biology are from 5 chapters: 1, 2, 14, 15, and 16.

DAT-Prep.com

Introduction

Protein synthesis is the creation of proteins using DNA and RNA. Individual amino acids are connected to each other in peptide linkages in a specific order given by the sequence of nucleotides in DNA. Thus the process occurs through a precise interplay directed by the genetic code and involving mRNA, tRNA and amino acids - all in an environment provided by a ribosome.

Additional Resources

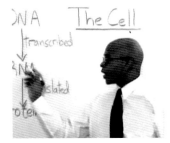

Free Online Q&A + Forum   Video: Online or DVD   Flashcards   Special Guest

Building Proteins

Proteins (which comprise many hormones, enzymes, antibodies, etc.) are long chains formed by peptide bonds between combinations of twenty amino acid subunits. Each amino acid is encoded in a sequence of three nucleotides (a triplet code = the *genetic code*). A gene is a conglomeration of such codes and thus is a section of DNA which encodes for a protein (or a polypeptide which is exactly like a protein but much smaller).

DNA Transcription

The information in DNA is rewritten (transcribed) into a messenger composed of RNA (= mRNA); the reaction is catalyzed by the enzyme RNA polymerase. The newly synthesized mRNA is elongated in the 5′ to 3′ direction. It carries the complement of a DNA sequence.

Transcription can be summarized in 4 or 5 steps for prokaryotes or eukaryotes, respectively:

1. RNA polymerase moves the transcription bubble, a stretch of unpaired nucleotides, by breaking the hydrogen bonds between complementary nucleotides (see BIO 1.2.2 for nucleoside phosphates - nucleotides - and the binding of nitrogen bases).

2. RNA polymerase adds matching RNA nucleotides that are paired with complementary DNA bases.

3. The extension of the RNA sugar-phosphate backbone is catalyzed by RNA polymerase.

4. Hydrogen bonds of the untwisted RNA +

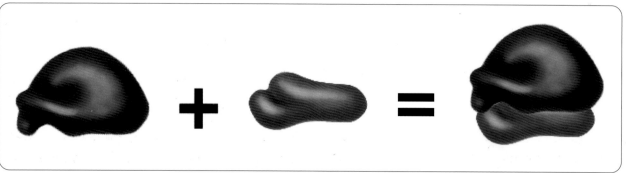

Figure IV.A.3.1: A ribosome provides the environment for protein synthesis. Ribosomes are composed of a large and a small subunit. The unit of measurement used is called the "Svedberg unit" (S) which is a measure of the rate of sedimentation in a centrifuge as opposed to a direct measurement of size. For this reason, fragment names do not add up (70S is made of 50S and 30S). Prokaryotes have 70S ribosomes, each comprised of a small (30S) and a large (50S) subunit. Eukaryotes have 80S ribosomes, each comprised of a small (40S) and large (60S) subunit. The ribosomes found in chloroplasts and mitochondria of eukaryotes also consist of large and small subunits bound together with proteins into one 70S ribosome. These organelles are believed to be descendants of bacteria ("Endosymbiotic theory") thus their ribosomes are similar to those of bacteria (see BIO 16.6.3).

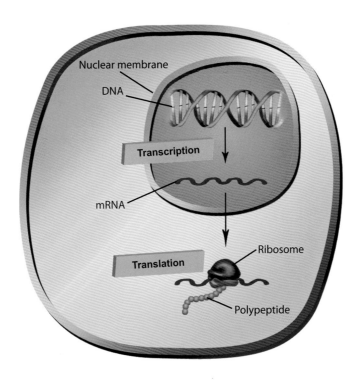

Figure IV.A.3.2: The central dogma of protein synthesis.

DNA helix break, freeing the newly synthesized RNA strand.

5. If the cell has a nucleus, the RNA is further processed [addition of a 5′ cap and a 3′ poly(A) tail] and then exits through the nuclear pore to the cytoplasm.

The mRNA synthesis in eukaryotes begins with the binding of RNA polymerase at a specific DNA sequence known as promoters. Elongation continues until the RNA polymerase reaches a termination signal. The initially formed primary mRNA transcript, also called pre-mRNA, contains regions called introns that are not expressed in the synthesized protein. The introns are removed and the regions that are expressed (exons) are spliced together to form the final functional mRNA molecule. {EXons EXpressed; INtrons IN the garbage!}

Post-transcriptional processing of mRNA occurs in the nucleus. Even before transcription is completed, a 7-methylguanosine cap is added to the 5′ end of the growing mRNA serving as attachment site for protein synthesis and protection against degradation. The 3′ end is added with a poly(A) tail consisting of 20 to 250 adenylate residues as protection. Of course, "A" refers to adenine and the nucleotide is thus adenosine monophosphate or AMP (BIO 1.2.2, ORG 12.5) which *polymerizes* to create the tail of residues. The mes-

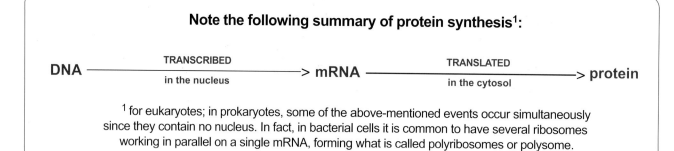

Note the following summary of protein synthesis[1]:

DNA ———— TRANSCRIBED / in the nucleus ————> mRNA ———— TRANSLATED / in the cytosol ————> protein

[1] for eukaryotes; in prokaryotes, some of the above-mentioned events occur simultaneously since they contain no nucleus. In fact, in bacterial cells it is common to have several ribosomes working in parallel on a single mRNA, forming what is called polyribosomes or polysome.

senger then leaves the nucleus with the information necessary to make a protein.

RNA Translation

The mRNA is constantly produced and degraded, which is the main method through which cells regulate the amount of a particular protein they synthesize. It attaches to a small subunit of a ribosome which will then attach to a larger ribosomal subunit thus creating a full ribosome. A ribosome is composed of a complex of protein and ribosomal RNA (= rRNA). The rRNA is the most abundant of all RNA types.

Floating in the cytoplasm is yet another form of RNA; this RNA specializes in taking amino acids and transfering them onto other amino acids when contained within the environment of the ribosome. More specifically, this transfer RNA (tRNA) molecule can be charged with a specific amino acid by aminoacyl-tRNA synthetase enzyme, bring the amino acid to the environment of ribosome, recognize the triplet code (= codon) on mRNA via its own triplet code anticodon, which is a three nucleotide sequence on tRNA that recognizes the complementary codon

in mRNA; and finally, tRNA can transfer its amino acid onto the preceding one thus elongating the polypeptide chain. In a way, tRNA translates the code that mRNA carries into a sequence of amino acids which can produce a protein.

Translation of mRNA into a protein involves three stages: initiation, elongation and termination. The direction of synthesis of the protein chain proceeds from the amino end/terminus to the carboxyl end/terminus. Synthesis begins when the ribosome scans the mRNA until it binds to a start codon (AUG), which specifies the amino acid methionine. During elongation, a peptide bond is formed between the existing amino acid in the protein chain and the incoming amino acid. Following peptide bond formation, the ribosome shifts by one codon in the 5′ to 3′ direction along mRNA and the uncharged tRNA is expelled and the peptidyl-tRNA grows by one amino acid. Protein synthesis terminates when the ribosome binds to one of the three mRNA termination codons (UAA, UAG or UGA; notice the similarity with the DNA stop codons in Table IV.A.3.1 except that U replaces T in this RNA molecule).

The 20 Amino Acids	The 64 DNA Codons
Alanine	GCT, GCC, GCA, GCG
Arginine	CGT, CGC, CGA, CGG, AGA, AGG
Asparagine	AAT, AAC
Aspartic acid	GAT, GAC
Cysteine	TGT, TGC
Glutamic acid	GAA, GAG
Glutamine	CAA, CAG
Glycine	GGT, GGC, GGA, GGG
Histidine	CAT, CAC
Isoleucine	ATT, ATC, ATA
Leucine	CTT, CTC, CTA, CTG, TTA, TTG
Lysine	AAA, AAG
Methionine	ATG
Phenylalanine	TTT, TTC
Proline	CCT, CCC, CCA, CCG
Serine	TCT, TCC, TCA, TCG, AGT, AGC
Threonine	ACT, ACC, ACA, ACG
Tyrosine	TAT, TAC
Tryptophan	TGG
Valine	GTT, GTC, GTA, GTG
Stop codons	TAA, TAG, TGA

Table IV.A.3.1: The 20 standard amino acids.

The 20 standard amino acids are encoded by the genetic code of 64 codons. Notice that since there are 4 bases (A, T, G, C), if there were only two bases per codon, then only 16 amino acids could be coded for ($4^2=16$). However, since at least 21 codes are required (20 amino acids plus a stop codon) and the next largest number of bases is three, then 4^3 gives 64 possible codons, meaning that some degeneracy exists.

Degeneracy is the redundancy of the genetic code. Degeneracy occurs because there are more codons than encodable amino acids. This makes the genetic code more tolerant to point mutations (BIO 15.5). For example, in theory, fourfold degenerate codons can tolerate any point mutation at the third position (see valine, alanine, glycine, etc. in Table IV.A.3.1 and notice that any 3rd base codes for the same amino acid). The structure of amino acids will be discussed in ORG 12.1.

A nonsense mutation is a point mutation (BIO 15.5) in a sequence of DNA that results in a premature stop codon (UAA, UAG, UGA), or a nonsense codon in the transcribed mRNA. Either way, an incomplete, and usually nonfunctional protein is the result. A missense mutation is a point mutation where a single nucleotide is changed to cause substitution of a different amino acid. Some genetic disorders (i.e. thalassemia) result from nonsense mutations.

Protein made on free ribosomes in the cytoplasm may be used for intracellular purposes (i.e. enzymes for glycolysis, etc.). Whereas proteins made on rER ribosomes are usually modified by both rER and the Golgi apparatus en route to the plasma membrane or exocytosis (i.e. antibodies, intestinal enzymes, etc.).

Key Points

Note the following: i) the various kinds of RNA are single stranded molecules which are produced using DNA as a template; ii) hormones can have a potent regulatory effect on protein synthesis (esp. enzymes); iii) allosteric enzymes (= proteins with two different configurations - each with different biological

DNA	Coding Strand (codons)	5′ → → ------ T T C ------ → → 3′
	Template Strand (anticodons)	3′ ← ← ------ A A G ------ ← ← 5′
mRNA	The Message (codons)	5′ → → ------ U U C ------ → → 3′
tRNA	The Transfer (anticodons)	3′ ← ← A A G ← ← 5′
Protein	Amino Acid	N-terminus → → Phenylalanine → → C-terminus

Table IV.A.3.2. DNA, RNA and protein strands with directions of synthesis. For both DNA and RNA, strands are synthesized from the **5′** ends → → to the **3′** ends. Protein chains are synthesized from the **N-terminus** → → to the **C-terminus**. Color code: the **old** end is **cold blue**; the **new** end is **red hot** where new residues are added. As shown in the table, mRNA is synthesized complementary and antiparallel to the **template strand (anticodons)** of DNA, so the resulting mRNA consists of codons corresponding to those in the coding strand of DNA. The **anticodons of tRNA** read each three-base mRNA codon and thus transfers the corresponding **amino acid** to the growing **polypeptide chain** or **protein** according to the genetic code.

properties) are important regulators of transcription; iv) there are many protein factors which trigger specific events in the <u>initiation</u> (using a start codon, AUG), <u>elongation</u> and <u>termination</u> (using a stop codon) of the synthesis of a protein; v) one end of the protein has an amine group (-NH$_2$, which projects from the first amino acid), while the other end has a carboxylic acid group (-COOH, which projects from the last amino acid). {Amino acids and protein structure will be explored in ORG 12.1 and 12.2}

Note that the free amine group end, the start of the protein, is also referred to as: N-terminus, amino-terminus, NH$_2$-terminus, N-terminal end or amine-terminus. The free carboxylic acid end, which is the end of the protein, is also referred to as: C-terminus, carboxyl-terminus, carboxy-terminus, C-terminal tail, C-terminal end, or COOH-terminus.

Differences in translation between prokaryotes and eukaryotes:

1) Ribosomes: in prokaryotes it is 70S, in eukaryotes it is 80S

2) Start codon: the start codon AUG specifies formyl-methionine [f-Met] in prokaryotes, in eukaryotes it is methionine

3) Location of translation: in prokaryotes translation occurs at the same compartment and same time as transcription, in eukaryotes transcription occurs in the nucleus while translation occurs in the cytosol.

Because of the incredible variety of organisms that use the genetic code, it was thought to be a *truly* 'universal' code but that is not quite accurate. Variant codes have evolved. For example, protein synthesis in human mitochondria relies on a genetic code that differs from the standard genetic code.

Furthermore, not all genetic information is stored using the genetic code. DNA also has regulatory sequences, chromosomal structural areas and other non-coding DNA that can contribute greatly to phenotype. Such elements operate under sets of rules that are different from the codon-to-amino acid standard underlying the genetic code.

GOLD STANDARD WARM-UP EXERCISES

CHAPTER 3: Protein Synthesis

1) Which of the following enzymes is most important in RNA synthesis during transcription?

   A. DNA polymerase
   B. RNA replicase
   C. RNA polymerase
   D. Reverse transcriptase

2) The last step in translation, termination, in addition to the termination codon, requires release factors (RFs). Where would the RFs be expected to be found in the cell?

   A. Within the nuclear membrane
   B. Floating in the cytosol
   C. In the matrix of the mitochondria
   D. Within the lumen of the smooth endoplasmic reticulum

3) During the period of time that primary oocytes remain in prophase I of meiosis, they undergo an extended period of growth, including accelerated synthesis and accumulation of rRNA. The increased rate of rRNA synthesis is accompanied by:

   A. disassembly of ribosomes into their component parts.
   B. thickening of the nuclear membrane.
   C. an increase in the size and/or number of nucleoli.
   D. a decrease in nuclear chromatin material.

4) The 3 base pair sequence found on an mRNA strand is called which of the following?

   A. Codon
   B. Anticodon
   C. Genome
   D. Gene

5) A ribosome is:

   A. one of three binding sites for tRNA during translation.
   B. a sequence of nucleotides in DNA that marks the end of a gene and signals RNA polymerase to release the newly made RNA molecule and detach from the DNA.
   C. a noncoding, intervening sequence within a primary transcript that is removed from the transcript during RNA processing.
   D. a complex of rRNA and protein molecules that functions as a site of protein synthesis.

6) The triplet code of CAT in DNA is represented as _____ in mRNA and _____ in tRNA.

   A. GUA, CAU
   B. CAT, CAT
   C. GAA, CAT
   D. GTA, CAU

7) Transcription occurs along a _____ template forming an mRNA in the _____ direction.

   A. 3' to 5'; 3' to 5'
   B. 5' to 3'; 3' to 5'
   C. 5' to 3'; 5' to 3'
   D. 3' to 5'; 5' to 3'

8) What is the meaning of the degeneracy of the genetic code?

   A. A single codon may specify more than one amino acid.
   B. A single amino acid may have more than one codon.
   C. AUG is a single start codon.
   D. The first two bases specify the amino acid.

GS ANSWER KEY

CHAPTER 3

		Cross-Reference				Cross-Reference
1.	C	BIO 3.0	5.	D	BIO 3.0
2.	B	BIO 1.2.1, 3.0	6.	A	BIO 1.2.2, 3.0
3.	C	BIO 3.0, 1.2.1	7.	D	BIO 1.2.2, 3.0
4.	A	BIO 3.0	8.	B	BIO 3.0

* Explanations can be found at the back of the book.

APPENDIX

CHAPTER 3: Protein Synthesis

Advanced DAT-30 Topic: Release Factor Recognition

The last step in translation involves the cleavage of the ester bond that joins the complete peptide chain to the tRNA corresponding to its C-terminal amino acid. This process of termination, in addition to the termination codon, requires release factors (RFs). The freeing of the ribosome from mRNA during this step requires the participation of a protein called ribosome releasing factor (RRF).

Cells usually do not contain tRNAs that can recognize the three termination codons. In E. coli, when these codons arrive on the ribosome they are recognized by one of three release factors. RF-1 recognizes UAA and UAG, while RF-2 recognizes UAA and UGA. The third release factor, RF-3, does not itself recognize termination codons but stimulates the activity of the other two factors.

The consequence of release factor recognition of a termination codon is to alter the peptidyl transferase center on the large ribosomal subunit so that it can accept water as the attacking nucleophile rather than requiring the normal substrate, aminoacyl-tRNA.

Figure 1

9) The alteration to the peptidyl transferase center during the termination reaction serves to convert peptidyl transferase into a(n):

A. exonuclease

B. lyase.

C. esterase.

D. ligase.

10) Sparsomycin is an antibiotic that inhibits peptidyl transferase activity. The effect of adding this compound to an in vitro reaction in which E. coli ribosomes are combined with methionine aminoacyl-tRNA complex, RF-1 and the nucleotide triplets, AUG and UAA, would be to:

A. inhibit hydrolysis of the amino acid, allowing polypeptide chain extension.

B. inhibit peptide bond formation causing the amino acid to be released.

C. induce hydrolysis of the aminoacyl-tRNA complex.

D. inhibit both hydrolysis of the aminoacyl-tRNA complex and peptide bond formation.

11) If the water in the reaction in Fig. 1 was labeled with ^{18}O, which of the following molecules would contain ^{18}O at the end of the reaction?

A. The free amino acid

B. The phosphate group of the tRNA molecule

C. Oxygen-containing molecules in the cytoplasm.

D. The ribose moiety of the tRNA molecule

ANSWER KEY

ADVANCED TOPICS - CHAPTER 3

Cross-Reference

9. C   P1; E; BIO 4.1, ORG 9.4
10. D   P3; E; BIO 3.0, 4.2, 20.2.1
11. A   BIO 20.2.1, ORG 8.1, 9.4

P = paragraph; S = sentence; E = equation; T = table; F = figure

ENZYMES AND CELLULAR METABOLISM

Chapter 4

Memorize	Understand	Importance
fine: catabolism, anabolism, ivation energy fine: metabolism, active/allosteric s strates/products, especially: tyl CoA, pyruvate ymes: kinase, phosphatase	* Feedback, competitive, non-competitive inhibition * Krebs cycle, electron transport chain: main features * Oxidative phosphorylation, substrates and products, general features * Metabolism: carbohydrates (glucose), fats and proteins	**0 to 3 out of the 40 Biology** DAT questions are based on content in this chapter (in our estimation). * Note that between 25% and 50% of the questions in DAT Biology are from 5 chapters: 1, 2, 14, 15, and 16.

DAT-Prep.com

Introduction

Cells require energy to grow, reproduce, maintain structure, respond to the environment, etc. Biochemical reactions and other energy producing processes that occur in cells, including cellular metabolism, are regulated in part by enzymes. Pathways specific to plants will be discussed on Chapter 17.

Additional Resources

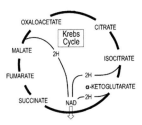

Free Online Q&A + Forum   Video: Online or DVD   Flashcards   Special Guest

In an organism or an individual many biochemical reactions take place. All these biochemical reactions are collectively termed metabolism. In general, metabolism can be broadly divided into two main categories. They are:

(a) Catabolism which is the breakdown of macromolecules (larger molecules) such as glycogen to micromolecules (smaller molecules) such as glucose.

(b) Anabolism which is the building up of macromolecules such as protein using micromolecules such as amino acids.

As we all know, chemical reactions in general involve great energy exchanges when they occur. Similarly most catabolic and anabolic reactions would involve massive amounts of energy if they were to occur in vitro (outside the cell). However, all these reactions could be carried out within an environment of less free energy exchange, using molecules called enzymes.

What is an enzyme?

An enzyme is a protein catalyst. A protein is a large polypeptide made up of amino acid subunits. A catalyst is a substance that alters the rate of a chemical reaction without itself being permanently changed into another compound. A catalyst accelerates a reaction by decreasing the free energy of activation (see diagrams in CHM 9.5, 9.7).

Enzymes fall into two general categories:

(a) Simple proteins which contain only amino acids like the digestive enzymes ribonuclease, trypsin and chymotrypsin.

(b) Complex proteins which contain amino acids and a non-amino acid cofactor. Thus the complete enzyme is called a holoenzyme and it is made up of a protein portion (apoenzyme) and a cofactor.

> Holoenzyme = Apoenzyme + Cofactor.

A metal may serve as a cofactor. Zinc, for example, is a cofactor for the enzymes carbonic anhydrase and carboxypeptidase. An organic molecule such as pyridoxal phosphate or biotin may serve as a cofactor. Cofactors such as biotin, which are covalently linked to the enzyme are called prosthetic groups or ligands.

In addition to their enormous catalytic power which accelerates reaction rates, enzymes exhibit exquisite specificity in the types of reactions that each catalyzes as well as specificity for the substrates upon which they act. Their specificity is linked to the concept of an active site. An active site is a cluster of amino acids within the tertiary (i.e. 3-dimensional) configuration of the enzyme where the actual catalytic event occurs. The active site is often similar to a pocket or groove with properties (chemical or structural) that accommodate the intended substrate with high specificity.

Examples of such specificity are as follows: Phosphofructokinase catalyzes a reaction between ATP and fructose-6-phosphate. The enzyme does not catalyze a reaction between other nucleoside triphosphates. It is worth mentioning the specificity of trypsin and chymotrypsin though both of them are proteolytic (i.e. they degrade or hydrolyse proteins). Trypsin catalyzes the hydrolysis of peptides and proteins only on the carboxyl side of polypeptidic amino acids lysine and arginine. Chymotrypsin catalyzes the hydrolysis of peptides and proteins on the carboxyl side of polypeptidic amino acids phenylalanine, tyrosine and tryptophan. The degree of specificity described in the previous examples originally led to the **Lock and Key Model** which has been generally replaced by the **Induced Fit Hypothesis**. While the former suggests that the spatial structure of the active site of an enzyme fits exactly that of the substrate, the latter is more widely accepted and describes a greater flexibility at the active site and a conformational change in the enzyme to strengthen binding to the substrate.

4.2 Enzyme Kinetics and Inhibition

There is an increase in reaction velocity (= reaction rate) with an increase in the concentration of substrate. At increasingly higher substrate concentrations the increase in activity is progressively smaller. From this, it could be inferred that enzymes exhibit saturation kinetics. The mechanism of the preceding lies largely with saturation of the enzyme's active sites. As substrate concentration increases, more and more enzymes are converted to the substrate bound enzyme complex until all the enzyme active sites are bound to substrate. After this point, further increase in substrate concentration will not increase reaction rate.

Enzyme inhibitors are classified as: competitive inhibitor, noncompetitive inhibitor and irreversible inhibitor. In competitive inhibition, the inhibitor and the substrate are analogues that compete for binding to the active site, forming an unreactive enzyme-inhibitor complex. However, at higher substrate concentration, the inhibition can be reversed. In noncompetitive inhibition, the inhibitor can bind to the enzyme at a site different from the active site where the substrate binds to, thus forming either an unreactive enzyme-inhibitor complex or enzyme-substrate-inhibitor complex. However, a higher substrate concentration does not reverse the inhibition. In irreversible inhibition, the inhibitor binds permanently to the enzyme and inactivates it (e.g. heavy metals, aspirin, organophosphates). The effects caused by irreversible inhibitors are only overcome by synthesis of new enzyme.

The activity of enzymes in the cell is subject to a variety of regulatory mechanisms. The amount of enzyme can be altered by increasing or decreasing its synthesis or degradation. Enzyme induction refers to an enhancement of its synthesis. Repression refers to a decrease in its biosynthesis.

Enzyme activity can also be altered by covalent modification. Phosphorylation of specific serine residues by protein kinases increases or decreases catalytic activity depending upon the enzyme. Proteolytic cleavage of proenzymes (e.g., chymotrypsinogen, trypsinogen, protease and clotting factors) converts an inactive form to an active form (e.g., chymotrypsin, trypsin, etc.).

Enzyme activity can be greatly influenced by its environment (esp. pH and temperature). For example, most enzymes exhibit optimal activity at a pH in the range 6.5 to 7.5. However, pepsin (an enzyme found in the stomach) has an optimum pH

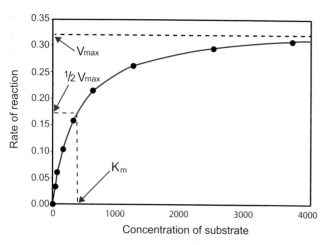

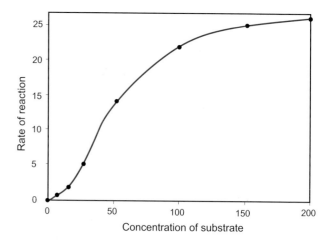

Michaelis-Menten Kinetics: Enzymes with single-substrate mechanisms usually follow the Michaelis-Menten model, in which the plot of velocity vs. substrate concentration [S] produces a rectangular hyperbola. Initially, the reaction rate [V] increases as substrate concentration [S] increases over a range of substrate concentration. However, as [S] gets higher, the enzyme becomes saturated with substrate and eventually the reaction rate [V] reaches maximum velocity V_{max} when the enzyme is fully saturated with substrate. Compare the diagram above with the curve of carrier-mediated transport (i.e. showing saturation kinetics) for solutes crossing the plasma membrane in BIO 1.1.2. The K_m is the substrate concentration at which an enzyme-catalyzed reaction occurs at half its maximal velocity, $V_{max}/2$. K_m is called the Michaelis constant. Each enzyme has a unique K_m value.

Non-Michaelis-Menten Kinetics: Some enzymes with multiple-substrate mechanisms exhibit the non-Michaelis-Menten model, in which the plot of velocity vs. substrate concentration [S] produces a sigmoid curve. This characterizes cooperative binding of substrate to the active site, which means that the binding of one substrate to one subunit affects the binding of subsequent substrate molecules to other subunits. This behavior is most common in multimeric enzymes with several active sites. Positive cooperativity occurs when binding of the first substrate increases the affinity of the other active sites for the following substrates. Negative cooperativity occurs when binding of the first substrate decreases the affinity of the other active site for the following substrates.

Fig. IV. A. 4.1 Enzyme Kinetic Curve Plot.

of ~ 2.0. Thus it cannot function adequately at a higher pH (i.e. in the small intestine). Likewise, enzymes function at an optimal temperature. When the temperature is lowered, kinetic energy decreases and thus the rate of reaction decreases. If the temperature is raised too much then the enzyme may become denatured and thus non-functional.

Enzyme activity can also be modified by an *allosteric* mechanism which involves binding to a site other than the active site. Isocitrate dehydrogenase is an enzyme in the Krebs Tricarboxylic Acid Cycle, which is activated by ADP. ADP is not a substrate or substrate analogue. It is postulated to bind a site *distinct* from the active site called the *allosteric site.* Positive effectors stabilize the

more active form of enzyme and enhance enzyme activity while negative effectors stabilize the less active form of enzyme and inhibit enzyme activity.

Some enzymes fail to behave by simple saturation kinetics. In such cases a phenomenon called positive cooperativity is explained in which binding of one substrate or ligand shifts the enzyme from the less active form to the more active form and makes it easier for the second substrate to bind. Instead of a hyperbolic curve of velocity vs. substrate concentration [S] that many enzymes follow, sigmoid curve of velocity vs. [S] characterizes cooperativity (i.e. see the Enzyme Kinetic Curve Plot in this section as well as hemoglobin and myoglobin, BIO 7.5.1).

4.4 Bioenergetics

Biological species must transform energy into readily available sources in order to survive. ATP (adenosine triphosphate) is the body's most important short term energy storage molecule. It can be produced by the breakdown or oxidation of protein, lipids (i.e. fat) or carbohydrates (esp. glucose). If the body is no longer ingesting sources of energy it can access its own stores: glucose is stored in the liver as glycogen, lipids are stored

throughout the body as fat, and ultimately, muscle can be catabolized to release protein (esp. amino acids).

We will be examining four key processes that can lead to the production of ATP: glycolysis, Krebs Citric Acid Cycle, the electron transport chain (ETC), and oxidative phosphorylation. Figure IV.A.4.2 is a schematic summary.

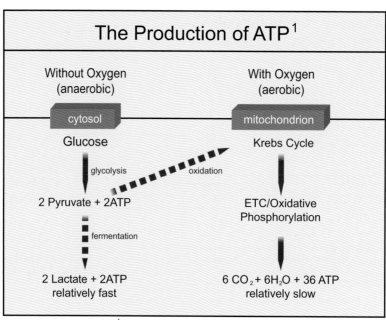

Figure IV.A.4.2: Summary of ATP production.

4.5 Glycolysis

The initial steps in the catabolism or *lysis* of D-glucose constitute the Embden - Meyerhof glyco*lytic* pathway. This pathway can occur in the absence of oxygen (anaerobic). The enzymes for glycolysis are present in all human cells and are located in the cytosol. The overall reaction can be depicted as follows (ADP: adenosine diphosphate, NAD: nicotinamide adenine dinucleotide, P_i: inorganic phosphate):

$$Glucose + 2ADP + 2 NAD^+ + 2P_i \longrightarrow 2Pyruvate + 2ATP + 2NADH + 2H^+$$

The first step in glycolysis involves the phosphorylation of glucose by ATP. The enzyme that catalyzes this irreversible reaction is either hexokinase or glucokinase. Phosphohexose isomerase then catalyzes the conversion of glucose-6-phosphate to fructose-6-phosphate. Phosphofructokinase (PFK) catalyzes the second phosphorylation. It is an irreversible reaction. This reaction also utilizes 1 ATP. This step, which produces fructose-1,6-diphosphate, is said to be the rate limiting or pacemaker step in glycolysis. Aldolase then catalyzes the cleavage of fructose-1,6-diphosphate to glyceraldehyde-

3-phosphate and dihydroxyacetone phosphate (= 2 triose phosphates). Triose phosphate isomerase catalyzes the interconversion of the two preceding compounds. Glyceraldehyde-3-phosphate dehydrogenase mediates a reaction between the designated triose, NAD^+ and P_i to yield 1,3-diphosphoglycerate.

Next, phosphoglycerate kinase catalyzes the reaction of the latter, an energy rich compound, with ADP to yield ATP and phosphoglycerate. This reaction generates 2 ATP per glucose molecule. Phosphoglycerate mutase catalyzes the transfer of the phosphoryl group to carbon two to yield 2-phosphoglycerate. Enolase catalyzes a dehydration reaction to yield phosphoenolpyruvate and water. The enzyme enolase is inhibited by fluoride at high, nonphysiological concentrations. This is why blood samples that are drawn for estimation of glucose are added to fluoride to inhibit glycolysis. Phosphoenolpyruvate is then acted upon by pyruvate kinase to yield pyruvate which is a three carbon compound and 2 ATP.

NADH produced in glycolysis must regenerate NAD^+ so that glycolysis can continue. Under **aerobic** conditions (i.e. in the presence of oxygen) pyruvate is converted to Acetyl CoA which will enter the Krebs Cycle followed by oxidative phosphorylation producing a total of 38 ATP per molecule of glucose (i.e. 2 pyruvate). Electrons from NADH are transferred to the electron transfer chain located on the inside of the inner mitochondrial membrane and thus NADH produced during glycolysis in the cytosol is converted back to NAD^+.

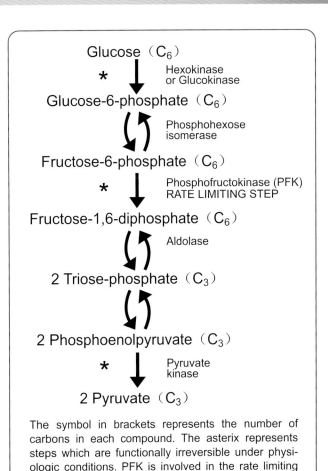

The symbol in brackets represents the number of carbons in each compound. The asterix represents steps which are functionally irreversible under physiologic conditions. PFK is involved in the rate limiting step which is activated by ADP and inhibited by ATP.

Figure IV.A.4.3: Summary of glycolysis.

Under **anaerobic conditions**, pyruvate is quickly reduced by NADH to lactic acid using the enzyme lactate dehydrogenase and NAD^+ is regenerated. A net of only 2 ATP is produced per molecule of glucose (this process is called *fermentation*).

Oxygen Debt: after running a 100m dash you may find yourself gasping for air even if you have completely ceased activity. This is because during the race you could not get an adequate amount of oxygen to your muscles and your muscles needed energy quickly; thus the anaerobic pathway was used. The lactic acid which built up during the race will require you to *pay back* a certain amount of oxygen in order to oxidize lactate to pyruvate and continue along the more energy efficient aerobic pathway.

4.6 Glycolysis: A Negative Perspective

An interesting way to summarize the main events of glycolysis is to follow the fate of the phosphate group which contains a negative charge. Note that *kinases* and *phosphatases* are enzymes that can add or subtract phosphate groups, respectively.

The first event in glycolysis is the phosphorylation of glucose. Thus glucose becomes negatively charged which prevents it from leaking out of the cell. Then glucose-6-phosphate becomes its isomer (= *same* molecular formula, *different* structure) fructose-6-phosphate which is further phosphorylated to fructose-1,6-diphosphate. Imagine that this six carbon sugar (*fructose*) now contains two large negatively charged ligands which repel each other! The six carbon sugar (*hexose*) sensibly breaks into two three-carbon compounds (*triose phosphates*).

A triose phosphate is ultimately converted to 1,3-diphosphoglycerate which is clearly an unstable compound (i.e. *two negative phosphate groups*). Thus it transfers a high energy phosphate group onto ADP to produce ATP. When ATP is produced from a substrate (i.e. 1,3-diphosphoglycerate), the reaction is called *substrate level phosphorylation*.

A closer look at ATP and glycolysis: from one molecule of glucose, 2 molecules of pyruvate are obtained. During the glycolytic reaction, 2 ATP are used (one used in the phosphorylation of glucose to glucose 6-phosphate and one used in the phosphorylation of fructose 6-phosphate to fructose 1,6-bisphosphate) and 4 ATP are generated (two in the conversion of 1,3-bisphophoglycerate to 3-phosphoglycerate and two in the conversion of phosphoenolpyruvate to pyruvate).

4.7 Krebs Citric Acid Cycle

Aerobic conditions: for further breakdown of pyruvate it has to enter the mitochondria where a series of reactions will cleave the molecule to water and carbon dioxide. All these reactions (which were discovered by Hans. A. Krebs) are collectively known as the Tricarboxylic Acid Cycle (TCA) or Krebs Citric Acid Cycle. Not only carbohydrates but also lipids and proteins use the TCA for channelling their metabolic pathways. This is why

TCA is often called the final common pathway of metabolism.

The glycolysis of glucose (C_6) produces 2 pyruvate (C_3) which in turn produces 2 CO_2 and 2 acetyl CoA (C_2). Pyruvate is oxidized to acetyl CoA and CO_2 by the pyruvate dehydrogenase complex (PDC). The PDC is a complex of 3 enzymes located in the mitochondria of eukaryotic cells (and of course, in the cytosol of prokaryotes). This step is also known as the *link reaction* or *transition step* since it links glycolysis and the TCA cycle.

The catabolism of both glucose and fatty acids yield acetyl CoA. Metabolism of amino acids yields acetyl CoA or actual intermediates of the TCA Cycle. The Citric Acid Cycle provides a pathway for the oxidation of acetyl CoA. The pathway includes eight discrete steps. Seven of the enzyme activities are found in the mitochondrial matrix; the eighth (succinate dehydrogenase) is associated with the Electron Transport Chain (ETC) within the inner mitochondrial membrane.

The following includes key points to remember about the TCA Cycle: i) glucose → 2 acetyl CoA → 2 turns around the TCA Cycle; ii) 2 CO_2 per turn is generated as a waste product which will eventually be blown off in the lungs; iii) one GTP (guanosine triphosphate) per turn is produced by substrate level phosphorylation; one GTP is equivalent to one ATP (*GTP + ADP → GDP + ATP*); iv) *reducing equivalents* are <u>hydrogens</u> which are carried by NAD^+ ($→$ $NADH + H^+$) three times per turn and FAD ($→$ $FADH_2$) once per turn; v) for each molecule of glucose, 2 pyruvates are produced and oxidized to acetyl CoA in the "fed" state (as opposed to the "fasting" state). The acetyl CoA then enters the TCA cycle, yielding 3 NADH, 1 $FADH_2$, and 1 GTP per acetyl CoA. These reducing equivalents will eventually be oxidized to produce ATP (*oxidative phosphorylation*) and eventually produce H_2O as a waste product (the last step in the ETC); vi) the hydrogens (*H*) which are reducing equivalents are not protons (H^+) - quite the contrary! Often the reducing equivalents are simply called electrons.

4.8 Oxidative Phosphorylation

The term oxidative phosphorylation refers to reactions associated with oxygen consumption and the phosphorylation of ADP to yield ATP. The synthesis of ATP is coupled to the flow of electrons from NADH and $FADH_2$ to O_2 in the electron transport chain. Oxidative phosphorylation is associated with an Electron Transport Chain or Respiratory Chain which is found in the inner mitochondrial membrane of eukaryotes. A similar process occurs within the plasma membrane of prokaryotes such as *E.coli*.

The importance of oxidative phosphorylation is that it accounts for the reoxidation of reducing equivalents generated in the reac-

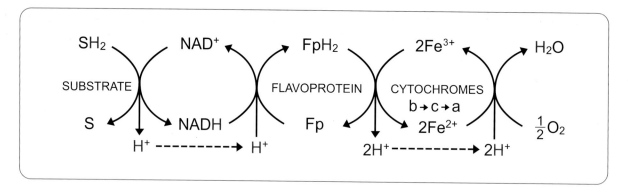

Figure IV.A.4.4: Transport of reducing equivalents through the respiratory chain. Examples of substrates (S) which provide reductants are isocitrate, malate, etc. Cytochromes contain iron (Fe).

tions of the Krebs Cycle as well as in glycolysis. This process accounts for the preponderance of ATP production in humans. The electron flow from NADH and $FADH_2$ to oxygen by a series of carrier molecules located in the inner mitochondrial membrane (IMM) provides energy to pump hydrogens from the mitochondrial matrix to the intermembrane space against the proton electrochemical gradient. The proton motive force then drives the movement of hydrogen back into the matrix thus providing the energy for ATP synthesis by ATP synthase. A schematic summary is in Figure IV.A.4.4.

The term *chemiosmosis* refers to the movement of protons across the IMM (a selectively permeable membrane) down their electrochemical gradient using the kinetic energy to phosphorylate ADP making ATP. The generation of ATP by chemiosmosis occurs in chloroplasts and mitochondria as well as in some bacteria.

4.9 Electron Transport Chain (ETC)

The following are the components of the ETC: iron - sulphur proteins, cytochromes c, b, a and coenzyme Q or *ubiquinone*. The respiratory chain proceeds from NAD specific dehydrogenases through flavoprotein, ubiquinone, then cytochromes and ultimately molecular oxygen. Reducing equivalents can enter the chain at two locations. Electrons from NADH are transferred to NADH dehydrogenase. In reactions involving iron - sulphur proteins electrons are transferred to coenzyme Q; protons are translocated from the mitochondrial matrix to the exterior of the inner membrane during this process. This creates a proton gradient, which is coupled to the production of ATP by ATP synthase.

Electrons entering from succinate dehydrogenase (FADH$_2$) are donated directly to coenzyme Q. Electrons are transported from reduced coenzyme Q to cytochrome b and then cytochrome c. Electrons are then carried by cytochrome c to cytochrome a.

Cytochrome a is also known as *cytochrome oxidase*. It catalyzes the reaction of electrons and protons with molecular oxygen to produce water. Cyanide and carbon monoxide are powerful inhibitors of cytochrome oxidase.

4.10 Summary of Energy Production

Note the following: i) 1 NADH produces 3 ATP molecules while 1 FADH$_2$ produces only 2 ATP; ii) there is a cost of 2 ATP to get the two molecules of NADH generated in the cytoplasm (see the preceding point # 2.) to enter the mitochondrion, thus the *net yield for eukaryotes is 36 ATP.*

The efficiency of ATP production is far from 100%. Energy is lost from the system primarily in the form of heat. Under standard conditions, less than 40% of the energy generated from the complete oxidation of glucose is converted to the production of ATP. As a comparison, a gasoline engine fairs much worse with an efficiency rating generally less than 20%. Further inefficiencies reduce the net theoretical yield in the (non-DAT!) real world.

Process of reaction	ATP yield
1. Glycolysis (Glucose → 2 Pyruvate)	2
2. Glycolysis (2NADH from glyceraldehyde-3-phosphate dehydrogenase)	6
3. Pyruvate dehydrogenase (2NADH)	6
4. Isocitrate dehydrogenase (2NADH)	6
5. Alpha-ketoglutarate dehydrogenase (2NADH)	6
6. Succinate thiokinase (2GTP)	2
7. Succinate dehydrogenase (2FADH$_2$)	4
8. Malate dehydrogenase (2NADH)	6
TOTAL	38 ATP yield per hexose.

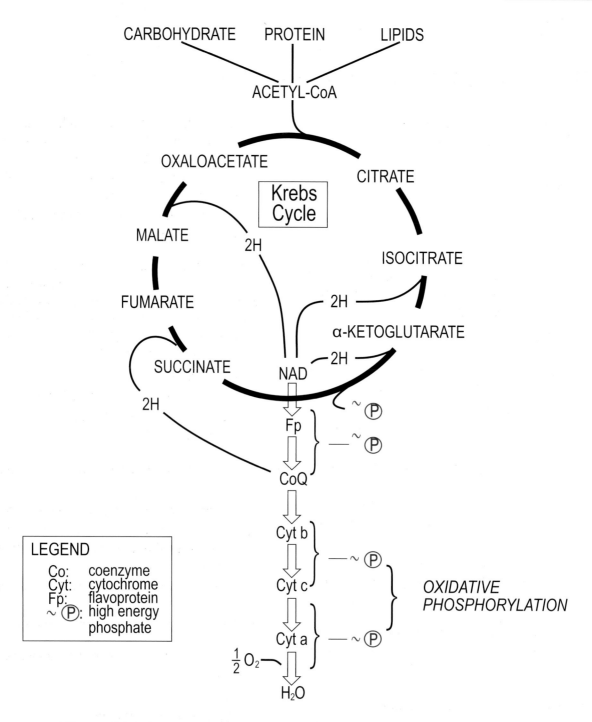

Figure IV.A.4.5: Summary of the Krebs Cycle and the Electron Transport Chain.

Note: Acetyl CoA can be the product of carbohydrate, protein, or lipid metabolism. Thick black arrows represent the Krebs Cycle while white arrows represent the Electron Transport Chain. High energy phosphate groups are transferred from ADP to produce ATP. Ultimately, oxygen accepts electrons and hydrogen from Cyt a to produce water.

GOLD STANDARD WARM-UP EXERCISES

CHAPTER 4: Enzymes and Cellular Metabolism

1) Oxidation of fats and carbohydrates within a cell would be an example of:

   A. biosynthesis.

   B. catabolism.

   C. anabolism.

   D. positive co-operativity.

2) If individuals with PKU disease lack the protein phenylalanine hydroxylase, what would best explain their being able to metabolize small amounts of phenylalanine?

   A. Non-specific enzymes cleave phenylalanine.

   B. Phenylalanine catalyzes reactions in the liver.

   C. Phenylalanine is broken down mechanically in the formation of chyme in the stomach.

   D. Phenylalanine is defecated from the body.

3) Phenylalanine hydroxylase most likely:

   A. cleaves a -OCH$_3$ group from phenylalanine.

   B. adds a -OCH$_3$ group to phenylalanine.

   C cleaves a -OH$_2$ group from phenylalanine.

   D. adds a -OH group to phenylalanine.

4) Prostaglandins are complex lipid molecules, some of which mediate the sensation of pain. Aspirin, a common pain reliever, likely works by:

   A. acting like a non-competitive reversible inhibitor and binding to the active site on the prostaglandin molecule.

   B. acting like a competitive inhibitor and binding to a site other than the active site on the prostaglandin molecule.

   C. acting like an allosteric inhibitor of the prostaglandin molecule.

   D. inhibiting the synthesis of the prostaglandin molecule.

5) The symmetry model describes a form of cooperative binding. Most enzymes do not engage in cooperative binding. The predicted shape of a graph representing the addition of substrate to most enzymes over a period of time would be expected to be:

   A. a hyperbola.

   B. a straight line with a positive slope.

   C. a straight line with a negative slope.

   D. sigmoidal.

6) Allosteric enzymes differ from other enzymes in that they:

   A. are not denatured at high temperatures.

   B. are regulated by compounds which are not their substrates and which do not bind to their active sites.

   C. they operate at an optimum pH of about 2.0.

   D. they are not specific to just one substrate.

7) What controls the steps in the respiration of glucose?

   A. Enzymes

   B. Rate of photosynthesis

   C. Amount of water present

   D. Absence of NAD

8) Which of the following is NOT a product of glycolysis?

A. A net 2 ATP

B. Acetyl-CoA

C. Pyruvate

D. Reducing equivalents

9) Most body heat, under normal conditions, is produced by:

A. the reduction of foods.

B. the oxidation of foods.

C. the breakdown of skeletal muscle.

D. the release of thyroid stimulating hormone.

10) What is the role of electron transfer in ATP synthesis?

A. Pump protons to create an electrochemical potential

B. Create a pH gradient

C. Create a concentration gradient

D. Create a chemical gradient

11) Why do you think the inner mitochondrial membrane (IMM) is impermeable to protons?

A. Because the IMM is positively charged.

B. Because the IMM is negatively charged.

C. Because the IMM is polar.

D. Because the IMM is highly selective due to its complex structure generating a gradient.

12) The highest amount of ATP per molecule of glucose would be generated as a result of:

A. glycolysis.

B. the Krebs cycle.

C. the hydrolysis of glycogen.

D. the transamination of amino acids.

GS ANSWER KEY

CHAPTER 4

Cross-Reference

1. B   BIO 4.1, 4.4
2. A   BIO 4.1, 4.3
3. D   BIO 4.5-4.10
4. D   BIO 4.2
5. A   Ap A.3.3, CHM 9.7F, BIO 4.1, 7.5.1
6. B   BIO 4.1, 4.3

Cross-Reference

7. A   BIO 4.5, 4.6
8. B   BIO 4.5
9. B   BIO 4.4-4.10, 6.3.3
10. A   BIO 4.8, 4.9, 4.10
11. D   BIO 4.8, 4.9, 4.10
12. B   BIO 4.7, 4.10

⋆ Explanations can be found at the back of the book.

Go online to DAT-prep.com for additional chapter review Q&A and forum.

APPENDIX
CHAPTER 4: Enzymes and Cellular Metabolism

Advanced DAT-30 Passage: The Symmetry Model (MWC Model)

Several models have been developed for relating changes in dissociation constants to changes in the tertiary and quaternary structures of oligomeric proteins. One model suggests that the protein's subunits can exist in either of two distinct conformations, R and T. At equilibrium, there are few R conformation molecules: 10 000 T to 1 R and it is an important feature of the enzyme that this ratio does not change. The substrate is assumed to bind more tightly to the R form than to the T form, which means that binding of the substrate favors the transition from the T conformation to R.

The conformational transitions of the individual subunits are assumed to be tightly linked, so that if one subunit flips from T to R the others must do the same. The binding of the first molecule of substrate thus promotes the binding of the second and if substrate is added continuously, all of the enzyme will be in the R form and act on the substrate. Because the concerted transition of all of the subunits from T to R or back, preserves the overall symmetry of the protein, this model is called the symmetry model (= the concerted model or MWC model, an acronym for Monod-Wyman-Changeux). The model further predicts that allosteric activating enzymes make the R conformation even more reactive with the substrate while allosteric inhibitors react with the T conformation so that most of the enzyme is held back in the T shape.

13) What assumption is made about the T and R conformations and the substrate?

A. In the absence of any substrate, the T conformation predominates.

B. In the absence of any substrate, the R conformation predominates.

C. In the absence of any substrate, the T and R conformations are in equilibrium.

D. In the absence of any substrate, the enzyme exists in another conformation, S.

14) The substrate binds more tightly to R because:

A. T has a higher affinity for the substrate than R.

B. R has a higher affinity for the substrate than T.

C. there are 10 000 times more T conformation molecules than R conformation molecules.

D. the value of the equilibrium constant does not change.

15) The symmetry model describes a form of cooperative binding. Most enzymes do not engage in cooperative binding. The predicted shape of a graph representing the addition of substrate to most enzymes over a period of time would be expected to be:

A. a hyperbola.

B. a straight line with a positive slope.

C. a straight line with a negative slope.

D. sigmoidal.

16) The symmetry model would NOT account for an enzyme:

A. with many different biologically active conformations.

B. which engages in positive cooperativity.

C. with a complex metal cofactor.

D. which is a catalyst for anabolic reactions.

17) Allosteric enzymes differ from other enzymes in that they:

A. are not denatured at high temperatures.

B. are regulated by compounds which are not their substrates and which do not bind to their active sites.

C. they operate at an optimum pH of about 2.0.

D. they are not specific to just one substrate.

ANSWER KEY

ADVANCED TOPICS - CHAPTER 4

Cross-Reference

13.	A	P1
14.	B	BIO 4.1, 4.3
15.	A	BIO 4.3, 7.5.1
16.	A	Deduce; BIO 4.1, 4.2
17.	B	BIO 4.1, 4.3

P = paragraph; *S* = sentence; *E* = equation; *T* = table; *F* = figure

Go online to DAT-prep.com for additional chapter review Q&A and forum.

Memorize	Understand	Importance
Neuron: basic structure and function Reasons for the membrane potential Structural characteristics of striated, smooth, and cardiac muscle Basic structure/function: epithelial cells, sarcomeres, connective tissue cells	* Resting potential: electrochemical gradient/action potential, graph * Excitatory and inhibitory nerve fibers: summation, frequency of firing * Organization of contractile elements: actin and myosin filaments * Cross bridges, sliding filament model; calcium regulation of contraction	**0 to 2 out of the 40 Biology** DAT questions are based on content in this chapter (in our estimation). * Note that between 25% and 50% of the questions in DAT Biology are from 5 chapters: 1, 2, 14, 15, and 16.

DAT-Prep.com

Introduction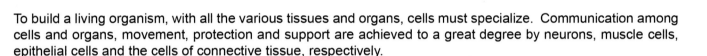

To build a living organism, with all the various tissues and organs, cells must specialize. Communication among cells and organs, movement, protection and support are achieved to a great degree by neurons, muscle cells, epithelial cells and the cells of connective tissue, respectively.

Additional Resources

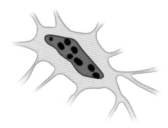

Free Online Q&A + Forum   Video: Online or DVD   Flashcards   Special Guest

The brain, spinal cord and peripheral nervous system are composed of nerve tissue. The basic cell types of nerve tissue is the *neuron* and the *glial cell*. Glial cells support and protect neurons and participate in neural activity, nutrition and defense processes. Neurons (= nerve cells) represent the functional unit of the nervous system. They conduct and transmit nerve impulses.

Neurons can be classified based on the shape or *morphology*. Unipolar neurons possess a single process. Bipolar neurons possess a single axon and a single dendrite. Multipolar neurons possess a single axon and more than one dendrite and are the most common type. Pseudounipolar neurons possess a single process that subsequently branches out into an axon and dendrite (note that in biology "pseudo" means "false"). Neurons can also be classified based on function. Sensory neurons receive stimuli from the environment and conduct impulses to the CNS. Motor neurons conduct impulses from the CNS to other neurons, muscles or glands. Interneurons connect other neurons and regulate transmitting signal between neurons.

Each neuron consists of a nerve cell body (*perikaryon or soma*), and its processes, which usually include multiple *dendrites* and a single *axon*. The cell body of a typical neuron contains a nucleus, *Nissl* material which is rough endoplasmic reticulum, free ribosomes, Golgi apparatus, mitochondria, many neurotubules, neurofilaments and pigment inclusions. The cell processes of neurons occur as axons and dendrites.

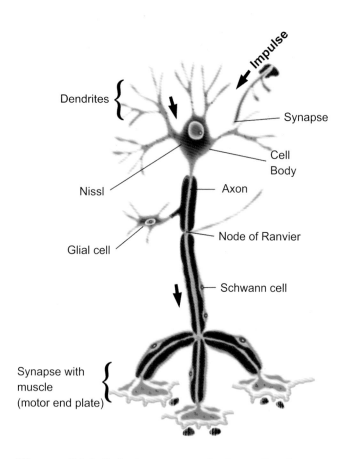

Figure IV.A.5.1: A neuron and other cells of nerve tissue, showing the neuromuscular junction, or motor end plate.

Dendrites contain most of the components of the cell, whereas axons contain major structures found in dendrites except for the Nissl material and Golgi apparatus. As a rule, dendrites receive stimuli from sensory cells, axons, or other neurons and conduct these impulses to the cell body of neurons and ultimately through to the axon. Axons are long cellular processes that conduct impulses away from the cell body of neurons. These originate from the axon hillock, a specialized region that contains many microtubules and neurofilaments. At the synaptic (terminal) ends of axons, the presynaptic process contains vesicles from which are elaborated excitatory or inhibitory substances.

Unmyelinated fibers in peripheral nerves lie in grooves on the surface of the neurolemma (= plasma membrane) of a type of glial cell (*Schwann cell*). **Myelinated** peripheral neurons are invested by numerous layers of plasma membrane of Schwann cells or oligodendrocytes that constitute a *myelin sheath*, which allows axons to conduct impulses faster. The myelin sheath is produced by oligodendrocytes in the CNS and by Schwann cells in the PNS. In junctional areas between adjacent Schwann cells or oligodendrocytes there is a lack of myelin. These junctional areas along the myelinated process constitute the nodes of Ranvier.

The neurons of the nervous system are arranged so that each neuron stimulates or inhibits other neurons and these in turn may stimulate or inhibit others until the functions of the nervous system are performed. The area between a neuron and the successive cell (i.e. another neuron, muscle fiber or gland) is called a *synapse*. Synapses can be classified as either a chemical synapse or an electrical synapse. A chemical synapse involves the release of a neurotransmitter by the presynaptic cell which then diffuses across the synapse and can act on the postsynaptic cell to generate an action potential. Signal transmission is delayed due to the time required for diffusion of the neurotransmitter across the synapse onto the membrane of the postsynaptic cell. An electrical synapse involves the movement of ions from one neuron to another via gap junctions (BIO 1.4.1). Signal transmission is immediate. Electrical synapses are often found in neural systems that require the fastest possible response, such as defensive reflexes.

When a neuron makes a synapse with muscle, it is called a *motor end plate* (see Fig. IV.A.5.1). The terminal endings of the nerve filament that synapse with the next cell are called presynaptic terminals, synaptic knobs, or more commonly - synaptic boutons. The postsynaptic terminal is the membrane part of another neuron or muscle or gland that is receiving the impulse. The synaptic cleft is the narrow space between the presynaptic and postsynaptic membrane.

At the synapse there is no physical contact between the two cells. The space between the dendrite of one neuron and the axon of another neuron is called the synaptic cleft and it measures about 200 - 300 angstroms (1 angstrom = 10^{-10} m) in a chemical synapse and about a tenth of that distance in an electrical synapse. The mediators in a chemical synapse, known as neurotransmitters, are housed in the presynaptic terminal and are exocytosed in response to an increase in intracellular Ca^{2+} concentration. The mediators or transmitters diffuse through the synaptic cleft when an impulse reaches the terminal and bind to receptors in the postsynaptic membrane. This transmitter substance may either excite the *postsynaptic* neuron or inhibit it. They are therefore called either excitatory or inhibitory transmitters (examples include *acetylcholine* and *GABA*, respectively).

5.1.1 The Membrane Potential

A membrane or resting potential (V_m) occurs across the plasma membranes of all cells. In large nerve and muscle cells this potential amounts to about 70 millivolts with positivity outside the cell membrane and negativity inside (V_m = -70 mV). The development of this potential occurs as follows: every cell membrane contains a Na^+ - K^+ ATPase that pumps each ion to where its concentration is highest. The concentration of K^+ is higher inside the neuron and the concentration of Na^+ is higher outside; therefore, Na^+ is pumped to the outside of the cell and K^+ to the inside. However, more Na^+ is pumped outward than K^+ inward ($3Na^+$ per $2K^+$). Also, the membrane is relatively permeable to K^+ so that it can leak out of the cell with relative ease. Therefore, the net effect is a loss of positive charges from inside the membrane and a gain of positive charges on the outside. The resulting membrane potential is the basis of all conduction of impulses by nerve and muscle fibers.

5.1.2 Action Potential

The action potential is a sequence of changes in the electric potential that occurs within a small fraction of a second when a nerve or muscle membrane impulse spreads over the surface of the cell. An excitatory stimulus on a postsynaptic neuron depolarizes the membrane and makes the membrane potential less negative. Once the membrane potential reaches a critical threshold, the voltage-gated Na^+ channels become fully open, permitting the inward flow of Na^+ into the cell. The membrane potential is at the critical threshold when it is in a state where an action potential is inevitable. As a result, the positive sodium ions on the outside of the membrane now flow rapidly to the more negative interior. Therefore, the membrane potential suddenly becomes reversed with positivity on the inside and negativity on the outside. This state is called *depolarization* and is caused by an inward Na^+ current.

Depolarization also leads to the inactivation of the Na^+ channel and slowly opens the K^+ channel. The combined effect of the two preceding events repolarizes the membrane back to its resting potential. This is called *repolarization*. In fact, the neuron may shoot past the resting membrane potential and become even more negative, and this is called hyperpolarization. The depolarized nerve goes on depolarizing the adjacent nerve membrane in a wavy manner which is called an impulse. In other words, an impulse is a wave of depolarization. Different axons can propagate impulses at different speeds. The increasing diameter of a nerve fiber or degree of myelination results in a faster impulse. The impulse is fastest in myelinated fibers since the wave of depolarization "jumps" from node to node of Ranvier: this is called *saltatory* conduction because an action potential can be generated only at nodes of Ranvier.

Immediately following an action potential, the neuron will pass through three stages in the following order: a) it can no longer elicit

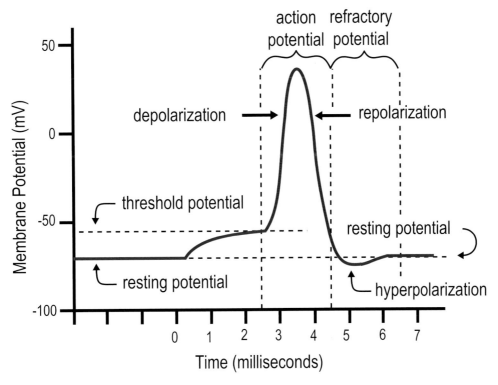

Figure IV.A.5.2: Action potential.

another action potential no matter how large the stimulus is = *absolute refractory period*; b) it can elicit another action potential only if a larger than usual stimulus is provided = *relative refractory period*; c) it returns to its original resting potential and thus can depolarize as easily as it originally did.

The action potential is an all-or-none event. The magnitude or strength of the action potential is not graded according to the strength of the stimulus. It occurs with the same magnitude each time it occurs, or it does not occur at all.

5.1.3 Action Potential: A Positive Perspective

To better understand the action potential it is useful to take a closer look at what occurs to the positive ions Na^+ and K^+. To begin with, there are protein channels in the plasma membrane that act like gates which guard the passage of specific ions. Some gates open or close in response to V_m and are thus called *voltage gated channels.*

Once a threshold potential is reached, the voltage gated Na^+ channels open allowing the permeability or *conductance* of Na^+ to increase. The Na^+ ions can now diffuse across their chemical gradient: from an area of high concentration (*outside the membrane*) to an area of low concentration (*inside the membrane*). The Na^+ ions will also diffuse across their electrical gradient: from an area of relative positivity (*outside the membrane*) to an area of relative negativity (*inside the membrane*). Thus the inside becomes positive and the membrane is depolarized. Repolarization occurs as the Na^+ channels close and the voltage gated K^+ channels open. As K^+ conductance increases to the outside (where K^+ concentration is lowest), the membrane repolarizes to once again become relatively negative on the inside.

5.2 Contractile Cells and Tissues

There are three types of muscle tissue: smooth, skeletal and cardiac. All three types are composed of muscle cells (fibers) that contain myofibrils possessing contractile filaments of actin and myosin.

Smooth muscle:- Smooth muscle cells are spindle shaped and are organized chiefly into sheets or bands of smooth muscle tissue. They contain a single nucleus and actively divide and regenerate. This tissue is found in blood vessels and other tubular visceral structures (i.e. intestines). Smooth muscles contain both actin and myosin filaments but actin predominates. The filaments are not organized into patterns that give cross striations as in cardiac and skeletal muscle. Filaments course obliquely in the cells and attach to the plasma membrane. Contraction of smooth muscle is involuntary and is innervated by the autonomic nervous system.

Skeletal muscle:- Skeletal muscle fibers are characterized by their peripherally located multiple nuclei and striated myofibrils. Myofibrils are longitudinally arranged bundles of thick and thin myofilaments. Myofilaments are composed of thick and thin filaments present in an alternating arrangement responsible for the cross-striation pattern. The striations in a sarcomere consists of an A-band (dark), which contains both thin and thick filaments. These are bordered toward the Z-lines by I-bands (light), which contain thin filaments only. The mid-region of the A-band contains an H-band (light), which contains thick filaments only and is bisected by an M-line. The Z lines are dense regions bisecting each I-band and anchor the thin filaments. The filaments interdigitate and are cross-bridged in the A-band with myosin filaments forming a hexagonal pattern of one myosin filament surrounded by six actin filaments. In the contraction of a muscle fiber,

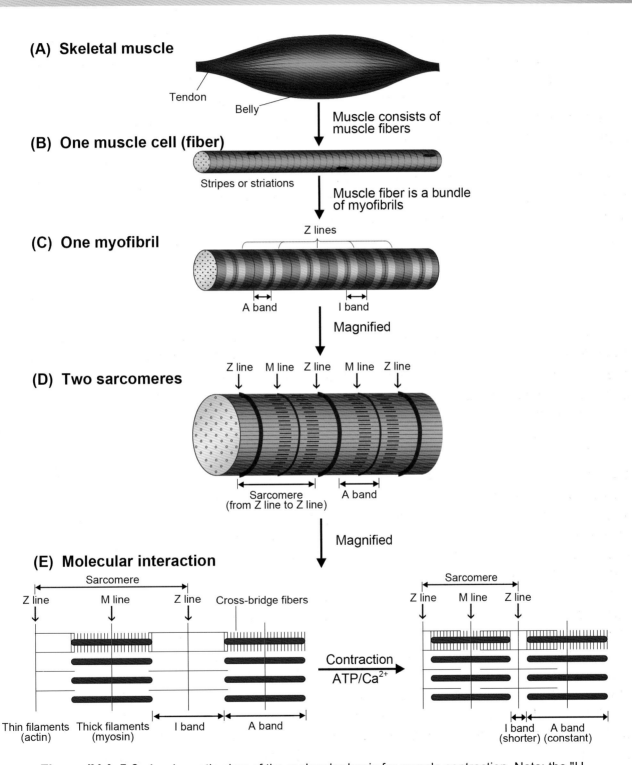

(A) Skeletal muscle

Tendon

Belly

Muscle consists of muscle fibers

(B) One muscle cell (fiber)

Stripes or striations

Muscle fiber is a bundle of myofibrils

(C) One myofibril

Z lines

A band   I band

Magnified

(D) Two sarcomeres

Z line   M line   Z line   M line   Z line

Sarcomere
(from Z line to Z line)   A band

Magnified

(E) Molecular interaction

Sarcomere

Z line   M line   Z line   Cross-bridge fibers

Thin filaments   Thick filaments   I band   A band
(actin)   (myosin)

Contraction
ATP/Ca^{2+}

Sarcomere

Z line   M line   Z line

I band   A band
(shorter)   (constant)

Figure IV.A.5.3: A schematic view of the molecular basis for muscle contraction. Note: the "H zone" is the central portion of an A band and is characterized by the presence of myosin filaments.

thick and thin filaments do not shorten but increase their overlap. The actin filaments of the I-bands move more deeply into the A-band, resulting in a shortening of the H-band and the I-bands as Z disks are brought closer. However, the A-band remains constant in length. {Mnemonic: "HI" bands shorten}

Each skeletal muscle fiber is invested with a sarcolemma (= plasmalemma = plasma membrane) that extends into the fiber as numerous small transverse tubes called T-tubules. These tubules ring the myofibrils at the A-I junction and are bounded on each side by terminal cisternae of the endoplasmic (sarcoplasmic) reticulum. The T-tubules, together with a pair of terminal cisternae form a triad. The triad helps to provide a uniform contraction throughout the muscle cell as it provides channels for ions to flow freely and helps to propagate action potentials. There are thousands of triads per skeletal muscle fiber.

The sarcoplasmic reticulum is a modified endoplasmic reticulum that regulates muscle contraction by either transporting Ca^{2+} into storage (muscle relaxation) or releasing Ca^{2+} during excitation-contraction coupling (muscle contraction).

The thick filaments within a myofibril are composed of about 250 myosin molecules arranged in an antiparallel fashion and some associated proteins. The myosin molecule is composed of two identical heavy chains and two pairs of light chain. The heavy chain consists of two "heads" and one "tail". The head contains an actin binding site which is involved in muscle contraction. The thin filaments within a myofibril are composed of actin and to a lesser degree two smaller proteins: *troponin and tropomyosin*. An action potential in the muscle cell membrane initiates depolarization of the T tubules, which causes the nearby sarcoplasmic reticulum to release its Ca^{2+} ions and thus an increase in intracellular $[Ca^{2+}]$. Calcium then attaches to a subunit of troponin resulting in the movement of tropomyosin and the uncovering of the active sites for the attachment of actin to the cross bridging heads of myosin. Due to this attachment, ATP in the myosin head hydrolyses, producing energy, Pi and ADP which results in a bending of the myosin head and a pulling of the actin filament into the A-band. These actin-myosin bridges detach again when myosin binds a new ATP molecule and attaches to a new site on actin toward the plus end as long as Ca^{2+} is bound to troponin. Finally, relaxation of muscle occurs when Ca^{2+} is sequestered by the sarcoplasmic reticulum. Thus calcium is pumped out of the cytoplasm and calcium levels return to normal, tropomyosin again binds to actin, preventing myosin from binding.

There are three interesting consequences to the preceding:

i) neither actin nor myosin change length during muscle contraction; rather, shortening of the muscle fiber occurs as the filaments slide over each other increasing the area of overlap.

ii) initially a dead person is very stiff (*rigor mortis*) since they can no longer produce the ATP necessary to detach the actin-myosin bridges thus their muscles remain locked in position.

iii) Ca^{2+} is a critical ion both for muscle contraction and for transmitter release from presynaptic neurons.

Cardiac muscle:- Cardiac muscle contains striations and myofibrils that are similar to those of skeletal muscle. Contraction of cardiac muscle is involuntary and is innervated by the autonomic nervous system. It differs from skeletal muscle in several major ways. Cardiac muscle fibers branch and contain centrally located nuclei (characteristically, one nucleus per cell) and large numbers of mitochondria. Individual cardiac muscle cells are attached to each other at their ends by *intercalated* disks. These disks contain several types of membrane junctional complexes, the most important of which is the *gap junction* (BIO 1.4.1). Cardiac muscle cells do not regenerate: injury to cardiac muscle is repaired by fibrous connective tissue.

The gap junction electrically couples one cell to its neighbor (= *syncytium*) so that electric depolarization is propagated throughout the heart by cell-to-cell contact rather than by nerve innervation to each cell. The sarcoplasmic reticulum - T-tubule system is arranged differently in cardiac muscle than in skeletal muscle. In cardiac muscle each T-tubule enters at the Z-line and forms a diad with only one terminal cisterna of sarcoplasmic reticulum.

5.3 Epithelial Cells and Tissues

Epithelia have the following characteristics:

1. they cover all body surfaces (i.e. skin, organs, etc.)
2. they are the principal tissues of glands
3. their cells are anchored by a nonliving layer (= the basement membrane)
4. they lack blood vessels and are thus nourished by diffusion.

Epithelial tissues are classified according to the characteristics of their cells. Tissues with elongated cells are called *columnar*, those with thin flattened cells are *squamous*, and those with cube-like cells are *cuboidal*. They are further classified as **simple** if they have a single layer of cells and **stratified** if they have multiple layers of cells. As examples of the classification, skin is composed of a stratified squamous epithelium while various glands (i.e. thyroid, salivary, etc.) contain a simple cuboidal epithelium. The former epithelium serves to protect against microorganisms, loss of water or heat, while the latter epithelium functions to secrete glandular products.

5.4 Connective Cells and Tissues

Connective tissue connects and joins other body tissue and parts. It also carries substances for processing, nutrition, and waste release. Connective tissue is characterized by the presence of relatively few cells surrounded by an extensive network of extracellular matrix, consisting of ground substance, extracellular fluid, and fibers.

The adult connective tissues are: connective tissue proper, cartilage, bone and blood (see *The Circulatory System*, section 7.5). Connective tissue proper is further classified into loose connective tissue, dense connective tissue, elastic tissue, reticular tissue and adipose tissue.

5.4.1 Loose Connective Tissue

Loose connective tissue is found in the superficial fascia. It is generally considered as the *packaging material* of the body, in part, because it frequently envelopes muscles. Fascia - usually a clear or white sheet (or band) of fibrous connective tissue - helps to bind skin to underlying organs, to fill spaces between muscles, etc. Loose connective tissue contains most of the cell types and all the fiber types found in the other connective tissues. The most common cell types are the fibroblast, macrophage, adipose cell, mast cell, plasma cell and wandering cells from the blood (which include several types of white blood cells).

Fibroblasts are the predominant cell type in connective tissue proper and have the capability to differentiate into other types of cells under certain conditions.

Macrophages are part of the *reticulo-endothelial system* (tissue which predominately destroys foreign particles). They are responsible for phagocytosing foreign bodies and assisting the immune response. They possess large lysosomes containing digestive enzymes which are necessary for the digestion of phagocytosed materials. Mast cells reside mostly along blood vessels and contain granules which include *heparin* and *histamine*. Heparin is a compound which prevents blood clotting and histamine is associated with allergic reactions. Mast cells mediate type I hypersensitivity.

Plasma cells are part of the immune system in that they produce circulatory antibodies (BIO 7.5, 8.2). They contain extensive amounts of rough endoplasmic reticulum (rER).

Adipose cells are found in varying quantities, when they predominate, the tissue is called adipose (fat) tissue.

Fibers are long protein polymers present in different types of connective tissue. Common types of fibers include collagen fiber, reticular fiber and elastic fiber.

Collagen fibers are usually found in bundles and provide **strength** to the tissue. Many different types of collagen fibers are identified on the basis of their molecular structure. Of the five most common types, collagen type I is the most abundant, being found in dermis, bone, dentine, tendons, organ capsules, fascia and sclera. Type II is located in hyaline and elastic cartilage. Type III is probably the collagenous component of reticular fibers. Type IV is found in a specific part (*the basal lamina*) of basement membranes. Type V is a component of placental basement membranes. **Reticular fibers** are smaller, more delicate fibers that form the basic framework of reticular connective tissue. **Elastic fibers** branch and provide elasticity and support to connective tissue.

Ground substance is the gelatinous material that fills most of the space between the cells and the fibers. It is composed of acid mucopolysaccharides and structural glycoproteins and its properties are important in determining the permeability and consistency of the connective tissue.

5.4.2 Dense Connective Tissue

Dense irregular connective tissue is found in the dermis, periosteum, perichondrium and capsules of some organs. All of the fiber types are present, but collagenous fibers predominate. Dense regular connective tissue occurs as aponeuroses, ligaments and tendons. In most ligaments and tendons collagenous fibers are most prevalent and are oriented parallel to each other. Fibroblasts are practically the only cell type present.

5.4.3 Cartilage

Cartilage is composed of chondrocytes (= cartilage cells) embedded in an intercellular (= extracellular) matrix, consisting of fibers and an amorphous firm ground substance. In cases of injury, cartilage repairs slowly since it has no direct blood supply. Three types of cartilage are distinguished on the basis of the amount of ground substance and the relative abundance of collagenous and elastic fibers. They are hyaline, elastic and fibrous cartilage.

Hyaline Cartilage is found as costal (rib) cartilage, articular cartilage and cartilage of the nose, larynx, trachea and bronchi. The extracellular matrix consists primarily of collagenous fibers and a ground substance rich in chondromucoprotein, a copolymer of a protein and chondroitin sulphates.

Elastic Cartilage is found in the pinna of the ear, auditory tube and epiglottis, and some laryngeal cartilage. Elastic fibers predominate and thus provide greater flexibility. Calcification of this type of cartilage is rare.

Fibrous Cartilage occurs in the anchorage of tendons and ligaments, in intervertebral disks, in the symphysis pubis, and in some interarticular disks and in some ligaments. Chondrocytes occur singly or in rows between large bundles of collagenous fibers. Compared with hyaline cartilage, only small amounts of hyaline matrix surround the chondrocytes of fibrous cartilage.

5.4.4 Bone

Bone tissue consists of three **cell types** and a calcified **extracellular matrix** that contains organic and inorganic components. The three cell types are: *osteoblasts* which synthesize the organic components of the matrix (osteoid) and become embedded in lacunae; *osteocytes* which are mature bone cells entrapped in their own lacunae within the matrix and maintain communication with each other via gap junctions; and *osteoclasts* which are large multinucleated cells functioning in resorption and remodeling of bone.

The organic matrix consists of dense collagenous fibers (primarily type I collagen) which is important in providing flexibility and tensile strength to bone. The inorganic component is responsible for the *rigidity* of the bone and is composed chiefly of calcium phosphate and calcium carbonate with small amounts of magnesium, fluoride, hydroxide, sulphate and hydroxyapatite.

Compact bone contains <u>haversian systems</u> (osteons), interstitial lamellae and circumferential lamellae. The Haversian system is the structural unit for bone and each osteon consists of a central Haversian canal surrounded by a number of concentric deposits of bony matrix called lamellae. Haversian systems consist of extensively branching haversian canals that are oriented chiefly longitudinally in long bones. Each canal contains blood vessels and is surrounded by 8 to 15 concentric lamellae and osteocytes.

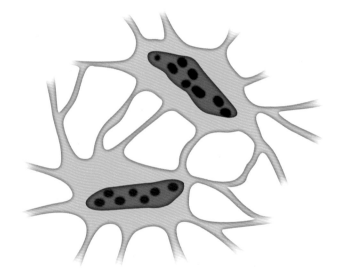

Figure IV.A.5.4: Osteocytes.

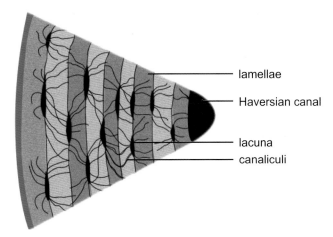

Figure IV.A.5.5: Schematic drawing of part of a haversian system.

Nutrients from blood vessels in the haversian canals pass through canaliculi and lacunae to reach all osteocytes in the system. Volkmann's canals traverse the bone transversely and interconnect the haversian systems. They enter through the outer circumferential lamellae and carry blood vessels and nerves which are continuous with those of the haversian canals and the periosteum. The periosteum is the connective tissue layer which envelopes bone. The endosteum is the connective tissue layer which lines the marrow cavities and supplies osteoprogenitor cells and osteoblasts for bone formation.

Figure IV.A.5.6
Schematic drawing of the wall of a long bone.

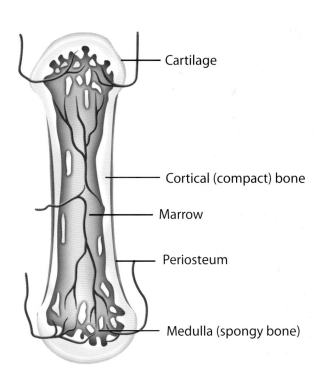

Figure IV.A.5.7
Schematic drawing of adult bone structure.

Bones are supplied by a loop of blood vessels that enter from the periosteal region, penetrate the cortical bone, and enter the medulla before returning to the periphery of the bone. Long bones are specifically supplied by arteries which pass to the marrow through diaphyseal, metaphyseal and epiphyseal arteries (for bone structure, see BIO 11.3.1).

Bone undergoes extensive remodelling, and harvesian systems may break down or be resorbed in order that calcium can be made available to other parts of the body. Bone resorption occurs by osteocytes engaging in osteolysis or by osteoclastic activity.

GOLD STANDARD WARM-UP EXERCISES

CHAPTER 5: Specialized Eukaryotic Cells and Tissues

1) Which of the following is NOT part of a neuron?

   A. Synapse

   B. Dendrite

   C. Axon

   D. Nissl bodies

2) The ATP-dependent dopamine transporter can be found at the presynaptic terminal of nerve cells. The dopamine transporter is most likely a:

   A. protein in the neurolemma.

   B. protein in the outer membrane of mitochondria.

   C. protein in the neural nuclear membranes.

   D. phospholipid in the plasma membrane.

3) Consider the following Table.

   Table 1: Concentration of Na^+, K^+, and Cl^- inside and outside mammalian motor neurons.

Ion	Concentration (mmol/L H_2O)		Equilibrium potential (mV)
	Inside cell	Outside cell	
Na^+	15.0	150.0	+60
K^+	150.0	5.5	−90
Cl^-	9.0	125.0	−75
Resting membrane potential (V_m) = −70 mV			

At resting membrane potential, in what direction will K^+ ions move spontaneously in a cell?

   A. From the cytosol to the nucleus

   B. From the cytosol to the cell exterior

   C. From the cell exterior to the cytosol

   D. From the mitochondria to the cytosol

4) All of the following explain the ionic concentrations in Table 1 EXCEPT:

   A. Na^+ and Cl^- ions passively diffuse more quickly into the extracellular fluid than K^+ ions.

   B. Na^+ ions are actively pumped out of the intracellular fluid.

   C. the negative charge of the cell contents repels Cl^- ions from the cell.

   D. the cell membrane is more freely permeable to K^+ ions than to Na^+ and Cl^- ions.

5) At inhibitory synapses, a hyperpolarization of the membrane known as an inhibitory postsynaptic potential is produced rendering V_m more negative. This occurs as a result of (data from Table 1 can be considered):

   A. an increase in the postsynaptic membrane's permeability to Na^+ and K^+ ions.

   B. an increase in the permeability of the presynaptic membrane to Ca^{2+} ions.

   C. the entry of Cl^- ions into the synaptic knob.

   D. an increase in the permeability of the postsynaptic membrane to Cl^- ions.

6) Diisopropylfluorophosphate (DFP) acts as an irreversible inhibitor at the active site of acetyl-cholinesterase. This enzyme deactivates the chemical transmitter acetylcholine. The main effect of DFP would be to:

A. prevent the passage of nerve impulses along the postsynaptic neuron.
B. prevent the entry of Ca^{2+} into the synaptic knob.
C. initiate muscular tetany.
D. generate a very large action potential.

7) According to the following diagram, which ion channel opens and closes more quickly?

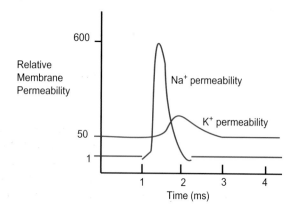

A. The K^+ channel because its relative membrane permeability is lower than for Na^+.
B. The Na^+ channel because its extracellular concentration is greater than for K^+.
C. The K^+ channel because it remains permeable for a longer period of time.
D. The Na^+ channel because its permeability increases and decreases at a faster rate.

8) An experiment is performed in which an inhibitor is applied to a single neuron. Upon stimulating the neuron and measuring both the intracellular and extracellular ion concentrations, it is found that the levels of K^+ and Na^+ have reached equilibrium. Based on these results, the inhibitor most likely inhibits the:

A. ATPase.
B. Cl^- channel.
C. K^+ channel.
D. Na^+ channel.

9) What would happen to the action potential in the previous diagram if K^+ channels were hindered but not completely blocked following depolarization?

A. The action potential would not repolarize.
B. The action potential would repolarize at a faster rate.
C. The duration of the action potential would be more than 1 ms.
D. The action potential would repolarize to less than -70 mV.

10) If cyanide was added to nerve cells, what would be expected to happen to the ionic composition of the cells?

A. Na^+ ions would be actively pumped into the cell and K^+ ions would be pumped out.
B. Intracellular Na^+ would increase since the sodium pump would stop functioning.
C. The potential of the cell membrane would not be reversed so that Cl^- ions would freely enter the cell.
D. The cell membrane would become freely permeable to Na^+ and Cl^- ions.

11) The temporary increase in the sarcolemma's permeability to Na^+ and K^+ ions that occurs at the motor end plate of a neuromuscular junction is immediately preceded by which of the following?

A. The release of acetylcholine from the motor neuron into the synaptic gap.
B. The release of adrenaline from the motor neuron into the synaptic gap.
C. The passage of a nerve impulse along the axon of a motor neuron.
D. The release of noradrenaline from a sensory neuron into the synaptic gap.

12) The overall reaction which takes place at the sodium pump is given by the equation:

$$3Na^+_{(inside)} + 2K^+_{(outside)} + ATP^{4-} + H_2O \rightarrow$$
$$3Na^+_{(outside)} + 2K^+_{(inside)} + ADP^{3-} + P_i + H^+$$

When a muscle is very active, at the end of glycolysis, pyruvate is converted to lactate by the addition of H^+ ions. During vigorous exercise, how many ions of K^+ could be pumped into a cell per molecule of glucose?

A. 2

B. 4

C. 8

D. 12

13) Stimulating electrodes were placed on a nerve and a recording electrode was placed near the motor end plate. First curare and then eserine were added to the solution bathing the muscle. The action potentials produced by stimulating the nerve were recorded and the results are shown.

(A) CONTROL

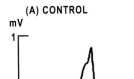

(B) EFFECT OF CURARE

Curare 10^{-5} M

(C) EFFECT OF ESERINE

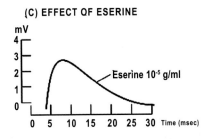

Eserine 10^{-5} g/ml

According to the results of the experiment, curare and eserine could act by, respectively:

A. blocking ion channels and binding to the receptors on ACh-activated channels.

B. blocking ion channels and preventing the hydrolysis of acetylcholinesterase.

C. initiating the entry of calcium ions into the synaptic knob and initiating the passage of a nerve impulse along the muscle cell.

D. binding to ACh receptor sites on the post-synaptic membrane and preventing the hydrolysis of acetylcholine.

14) In the control in the graph for the previous question, the part of the curve between 4 and 5 msec represents:

A. the absolute refractory period.

B. the relative refractory period.

C. the depolarization of the membrane.

D. saltatory conduction.

15) The depolarization across the muscle membrane triggers an all-or-none action potential in the muscle cell. This suggests that an increase in the amount of transmitter released at the neuromuscular junction would change:

A. the amplitude of the action potential.

B. the frequency of the nerve impulses.

C. the direction of the action potential.

D. the speed at which nerve impulses travel along the muscle cell.

16) Which of the following is true about muscle contraction?

A. Troponin and tropomyosin slide past one another allowing the muscle to shorten.

B. Decreased intracellular $[Ca^{++}]$ enhances the degree of muscular contraction.

C. Cardiac muscle fibers contain centrally located nuclei.

D. Neither actin nor myosin change length during muscle contraction.

17) In muscle cells, the actin filaments are:

   A. thin and associated with the proteins troponin and collagen.

   B. thin and associated with the proteins troponin and tropomyosin.

   C. thick and associated with the proteins troponin and collagen.

   D. thick and associated with the proteins troponin and tropomyosin.

18) If the gene which codes for troponin was absent from muscle cells, which of the following processes would NOT be inhibited?

   A. The movement of tropomyosin to a new position on the actin molecules

   B. The uncovering of the active sites for the attachment of actin to the cross bridges of myosin

   C. The hydrolysis of ATP in the myosin head to produce ADP, P_i, and energy

   D. The release of Ca^{2+} ions from the sarcoplasmic reticulum

19) Contraction of a muscle occurs when:

   A. myosin binds and releases actin.

   B. actin binds and releases myosin.

   C. tropomyosin binds and releases actin.

   D. actin binds and releases tropomyosin.

20) All of the following contain a phospholipid bilayer EXCEPT:

   A. sarcolemma.

   B. neurolemma.

   C. basement membrane.

   D. plasma membrane.

21) At the neuromuscular junction, the receptors on the acetylcholine-activated channels are likely located:

   A. on the tubule of the T system.

   B. in the sarcolemma.

   C. on the muscle surface.

   D. in the synaptic cleft.

22) Glycoproteins are found in all cellular compartments and are also secreted from the cell. Collagen, a secreted glycoprotein of the extracellular matrix, has simple carbohydrates - the disaccharide Glc beta (1,2) Gal linked to hydroxylysine. If a base mutation occurred in cells so that all the hydroxylysine residues were replaced by asparagine residues in the amino acid side chains, which of the following would result?

   A. Glycoprotein formation would cease.

   B. The strength of loose connective tissue might be affected.

   C. Protein folding could not occur.

   D. Protein recognition would be impossible.

23) What type of tissue is bone tissue?

   A. Muscle

   B. Epithelial

   C. Connective

   D. Nervous

24) Muscle is surrounded by what tough sheet of whitish connective tissue?

   A. Tendon

   B. Ligament

   C. Marrow

   D. Fascia

25) The organic portion of bone consists of which one of the following proteins?

   A. Collagen

   B. Fibrin

   C. Actin

   D. Myosin

GS ANSWER KEY

Chapter 5

		Cross-Reference				Cross-Reference
1.	A	BIO 5.1	14.	B		BIO 5.1.2
2.	A	BIO 5.1, 1.1, 1.1.3	15.	B		BIO 5.1.1-5.1.2
3.	B	BIO 5.1.1-5.1.3, deduce	16.	D		BIO 5.2
4.	A	BIO 1.2.2, 5.1.1-5.1.3, deduce	17.	B		BIO 5.2
5.	D	BIO 5.1.1-5.1.3, deduce	18.	D		BIO 5.2
6.	C	BIO 4.2, 5.1, 11.2	19.	A		BIO 5.2
7.	D	BIO 5.1.1-5.1.3, deduce	20.	C		BIO 1.1, 5.2-5.3
8.	A	BIO 4.2, 5.1.1-5.1.3, deduce	21.	B		BIO 1.1, 5.2 paragraph 4
9.	C	BIO 5.1.1, 5.1.2	22.	B		BIO 5.4.1
10.	B	BIO 4.4, 4.9, 5.1.1	23.	C		BIO 5.4
11.	A	BIO 5.1.1-5.1.3	24.	D		BIO 5.4.1, 5.4.2
12.	B	BIO 4.4, 5.1.1; CHM 1.5	25.	A		BIO 5.4.4
13.	D	BIO 5.1.2, deduce				

* Explanations can be found at the back of the book.

Go online to DAT-prep.com for additional chapter review Q&A and forum.

APPENDIX

CHAPTER 5: Specialized Eukaryotic Cells and Tissues

Advanced DAT-30 Passage: The Nernst Equation

When movement of ions is considered, two factors will influence the direction in which they diffuse: one is concentration, the other is electrical charge. An ion will usually diffuse from a region of its high concentration to a region of its low concentration. It will also generally be attracted towards a region of opposite charge, and move away from a region of similar charge. Thus ions are said to move down electrochemical gradients, which are the combined effects of both electrical and concentration gradients. Strictly speaking, active transport of ions is their movement against an electrochemical gradient powered by an energy source.

Consider the data in the following Table.

Table 1: Concentration of Na$^+$, K$^+$, and Cl$^-$ inside and outside mammalian motor neurons. The sign of the potential (mV) is inside relative to the outside of the cell.

Ion	Concentration (mmol/L H$_2$O)		Equilibrium potential (mV)
	Inside cell	Outside cell	
Na$^+$	15.0	150.0	+60
K$^+$	150.0	5.5	−90
Cl$^-$	9.0	125.0	−75
Resting membrane potential (V$_m$) = −70 mV			

The value of the equilibrium potential for any ion depends upon the concentration gradient for that ion across the membrane. The equilibrium potential for any ion can be calculated using the Nernst equation.

$$E_{cell} = E°_{cell} - (RT/nF)\ln Q$$

- E_{cell} = cell potential under nonstandard conditions (V); CHM 10.1
- $E°_{cell}$ = cell potential under standard conditions
- R = gas constant, which is 8.31 (volt-coulomb)/(mol-K); CHM 4.1.8
- T = temperature (K); CHM 4.1.1
- n = number of moles of electrons exchanged in the electrochemical reaction (mol)
- F = Faraday's constant (96,500 coulombs/mol); CHM 10.5
- Q = reaction quotient, which is the equilibrium expression with prevailing concentrations rather than, necessarilly, with equilibrium concentrations (= K$_{eq}$; CHM 9.8)
- ln = the natural logarithm which is log base e; CHM 6.5.1, QR Appendix

Once the relevant values have been

inserted, the Nernst equation can be simplified for specific ions. For example, the following is an approximation of the Nernst equation for the equilibrium potential for potassium (E_k in mV) at room temperature:

$$E_k = 60 \log_{10} \frac{[K^+]_o}{[K^+]_i}$$

- $[K^+]_o$ = extracellular K^+ concentration in mM
- $[K^+]_i$ = intracellular K^+ concentration in mM

The Goldman–Hodgkin–Katz voltage equation (= the Goldman equation) also determines the equilibrium potential across a cell's membrane. However, as opposed to the Nernst equation, the Goldman equation takes into account all of the ions that are permeant through that membrane.

26) If the concentration of potassium outside a mammalian motor neuron were changed to 0.55 mol/L, what would be the predicted change in the equilibrium potential for potassium?

A. 12 mV
B. 120 mV
C. 60 mV
D. 600 mV

27) A graph of E_k vs $\log_{10}[K^+]_o$ would be:

A. a straight line.
B. a logarithmic curve.
C. an exponential curve.
D. a sigmoidal curve.

Go online to DAT-prep.com for additional chapter review Q&A and forum.

Memorize	Understand	Importance
vous system: basic structure, major ctions c sensory reception and processing c ear, eye: structure and function ne: endocrine gland, hormone or endocrine glands: names, tions, major hormones	* Organization of the nervous system; sensor and effector neurons * Feedback loop, reflex arc: role of spinal cord, brain * Endocrine system: specific chemical control at cell, tissue, and organ level * Cellular mechanisms of hormone action, transport of hormones * Integration with nervous system: feedback control	**0 to 3 out of the 40 Biology** DAT questions are based on content in this chapter (in our estimation). * Note that between 25% and 50% of the questions in DAT Biology are from 5 chapters: 1, 2, 14, 15, and 16.

DAT-Prep.com

Introduction ▮▮▮▮

The nervous and endocrine systems are composed of a network of highly specialized cells that can communicate information about an organism's surroundings and itself. Thus together, these two systems can process incoming information and then regulate and coordinate responses in other parts of the body.

Additional Resources

Free Online Q&A + Forum   Video: Online or DVD   Flashcards   Special Guest

The role of the nervous system is to control and coordinate body activities in a rapid and precise mode of action. The nervous system is composed of central and peripheral nervous systems.

The **central nervous system** (CNS) is enclosed within the cranium (skull) and vertebral (spinal) canal and consists respectively of the brain and spinal cord. The **peripheral nervous system** (PNS) is outside the bony encasement and is composed of peripheral nerves, which are branches or continuations of the spinal or cranial nerves. The PNS can be divided into the **somatic nervous system** and the **autonomic nervous system** which are *anatomically* a portion of both the central and peripheral nervous systems.

The somatic nervous system contains sensory fibers that bring information back to the CNS and motor fibers that innervate skeletal muscles. The autonomic nervous system (ANS) contains motor fibers that innervate smooth muscle, cardiac muscle and glands. The ANS is then divided into *sympathetic* and *parasympathetic* divisions, which generally act against each other. The sympathetic division acts to prepare the body for an emergency situation (fight or flight) while the parasympathetic division acts to conserve energy and restore the body to resting level (rest and digest).

As a rule, a collection of nerve cell bodies in the CNS is called a *nucleus* and outside the CNS it is called a *ganglion*. Neurons that carry information from the environment to the brain or spinal cord are called *afferent neurons*. Neurons that carry motor commands from the brain or spinal cord to the different parts of body are called *efferent neurons*. Neurons that connect sensory and motor neurons in neural pathways are called *interneurons*.

The spinal cord is a long cylindrical structure whose hollow core is called the *central canal*. The central canal is surrounded by a gray matter which is in turn surrounded by a white matter (the reverse is true for the brain: outer gray matter and inner white matter). Basically, the gray matter consists of the cell bodies of neurons whereas the white matter consists of the nerve fibers (axons and dendrites). There are 31 pairs of spinal nerves each leaving the spinal cord at various levels: 8 cervical (neck), 12 thoracic (chest), 5 lumbar (abdomen), 5 sacral and 1 coccygeal (these latter 6 are from the pelvic region). The lower end of the spinal cord is cone shaped and is called the *conus medullaris*.

The brain can be divided into three main regions: the forebrain which contains the telencephalon and the diencephalon; the midbrain; and the hindbrain which contains the cerebellum, the pons and the medulla. The **brain stem** includes the latter two structures and the midbrain.

The telencephalon is the **cerebral hemispheres** (cerebrum) which contain an outer surface (cortex) of gray matter. Its function is in higher order processes (i.e. learning, memory, emotions, voluntary motor activity, processing sensory input, etc.). For

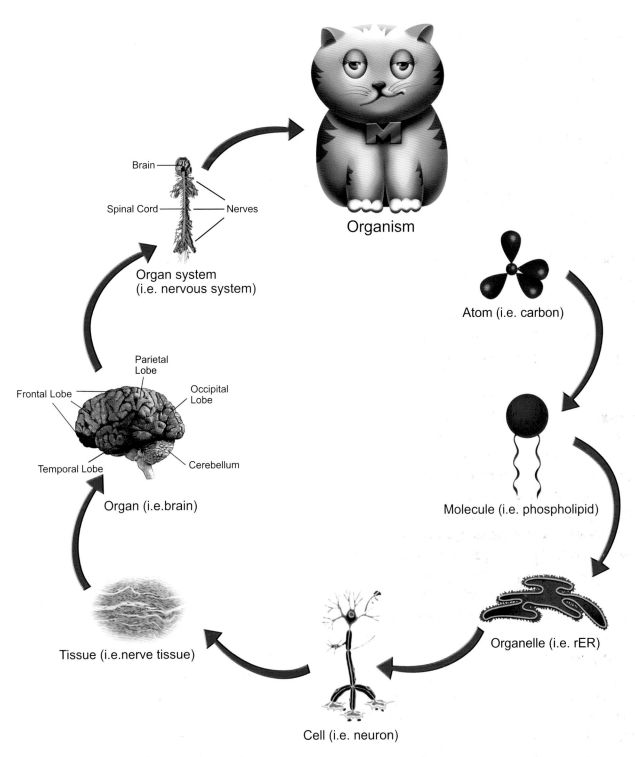

Brain

Spinal Cord — — Nerves

Organ system
(i.e. nervous system)

Organism

Atom (i.e. carbon)

Parietal
Lobe

Frontal Lobe

Occipital
Lobe

Temporal Lobe

Cerebellum

Organ (i.e.brain)

Molecule (i.e. phospholipid)

Tissue (i.e.nerve tissue)

Cell (i.e. neuron)

Organelle (i.e. rER)

Figure IV.A.6.0: Levels of organization.

most people, the left hemisphere specializes in language, while the right hemisphere specializes in patterns and spatial relationships.

Each hemisphere is subdivided into four lobes: *occipital* which receives input from the optic nerve for vision; *temporal* which receives auditory signals for hearing; *parietal* which receives somatosensory information from the opposite side of the body (= heat, cold, touch, pain, and the sense of body movement); and *frontal* which is involved in problem solving and controls voluntary movements for the opposite side of the body.

The diencephalon contains the **thalamus** which is a relay center for sensory input, and the **hypothalamus** which is crucial for homeostatic controls (heart rate, body temperature, thirst, sex drive, hunger, etc.). Protruding from its base and greatly influenced by the hypothalamus is the **pituitary** which is an endocrine gland. The limbic system, which functions to produce emotions, is composed of the diencephalon and deep structures of the cerebrum (esp. basal ganglia).

The midbrain is a relay center for visual and auditory input and also regulated motor function.

The hindbrain consists of the cerebellum, the pons and the medulla. The cerebellum plays an important role in coordination and the control of muscle tone. The pons acts as a relay center between the cerebral cortex and the cerebellum. The medulla controls many vital functions such as breathing, heart rate, arteriole blood pressure, etc.

There are 12 pairs of cranial nerves which emerge from the base of the brain (esp. the brain stem): *olfactory* (I) for smell; *optic* (II) for vision; *oculomotor* (III), *trochlear* (IV) and *abducens* (VI) for eye movements; *trigeminal* (V) for motor (i.e. *mastication* which is chewing) and sensory activities (i.e. pain, temperature, and pressure for the head and face); *facial* (VII) for taste (sensory) and facial expression (motor); *vestibulo-cochlear* (VIII) for the senses of equilibrium (vestibular branch) and hearing (cochlear branch); *glosso-pharyngeal* (IX) for taste and swallowing; *vagus* (X) for speech, swallowing, slowing the heart rate, and many sensory and motor innervations to smooth muscles of the viscera (internal organs) of the thorax and abdomen; *accessory* (XI) for head rotation and shoulder movement; and *hypoglossal* (XII) for tongue movement.

Both the brain and the spinal cord are surrounded by three membranes (= meninges). The outermost covering is called the dura mater, the innermost is called the pia mater (which is in direct contact with nervous tissue), while the middle layer is called the arachnoid mater. {DAP = **d**ura - **a**rachnoid - **p**ia, repectively, from out to in}.

6.1.1 The Sensory Receptors

The sensory receptors include any type of nerve ending in the body that can be stimulated by some physical or chemical stimulus either outside or within the body. These receptors include the rods and cones of the eye, the cochlear nerve endings of the ear, the taste endings of the mouth, the olfactory endings in the nose, sensory nerve endings in the skin, etc. Afferent neurons carry sense signals to the central nervous system.

6.1.2 The Effector Receptors

These include every organ that can be stimulated by nerve impulses. An important effector system is skeletal muscle. Smooth muscles of the body and the glandular cells are among the important effector organs. Efferent neurons carry motor signals from the CNS to effector receptors. {The term "effector" in biology refers to an organ, cell or molecule that *acts* in response to a stimulus (cause-effect).}

6.1.3 Reflex Arc

One basic means by which the nervous system controls the functions in the body is the reflex arc, in which a stimulus excites a receptor, appropriate impulses are transmitted into the CNS where various nervous reactions take place, and then appropriate effector impulses are transmitted to an effector organ to cause a reflex effect (i.e. removal of one's hand from a hot object, the knee-jerk reflex, etc.). The preceding can be processed at the level of the spinal cord.

Example of knee-jerk reflex: tapping on the patellar tendon causes the thigh muscle (quadriceps) to stretch. The stretching of muscle stimulates the afferent fibers, which synapse on the motoneuron (= motor neuron; BIO 5.1) in the spinal cord. The activation of the motoneuron causes contraction of the muscle that was stretched. This contraction makes the lower leg extend.

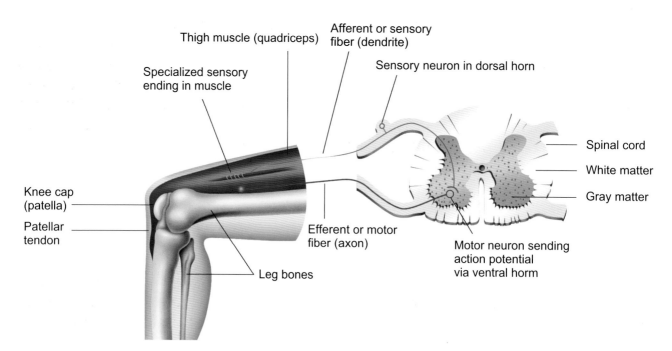

Figure IV.A.6.1: Schematic representation of the basis of the knee jerk reflex.

6.1.4 Autonomic Nervous System

While the Somatic Nervous System controls voluntary activities (i.e. innervates skeletal muscle), the Autonomic Nervous System (ANS) controls involuntary activities. The ANS consists of two components which often antagonize each other: the sympathetic and parasympathetic nervous systems.

The **Sympathetic Nervous System** originates in neurons located in the lateral horns of the gray matter of the spinal cord. Nerve fibers pass by way of anterior (ventral) nerve roots first into the spinal nerves and then immediately into the sympathetic chain. From here fiber pathways are transmitted to all portions of the body, especially to the different visceral organs and to the blood vessels.

The sympathetic nervous system uses norepinephrine as its primary neurotransmitter. This division of the nervous system is crucial in the "fight, fright or flight" responses (i.e. pupillary dilation, increase in breathing, blood pressure and heart rate, increase of blood flow to skeletal muscle, decrease of visceral function, etc.).

Parasympathetic Nervous System: The parasympathetic fibers pass mainly through the *vagus nerves*, though a few fibers pass through several of the other cranial nerves and through the anterior roots of the sacral segments of the spinal cord. Parasympathetic fibers do not spread as extensively through the body as do sympathetic fibers, but they do innervate some of the thoracic and abdominal organs, as well as the pupillary sphincter and ciliary muscles of the eye and the salivary glands.

The parasympathetic nervous system uses acetylcholine as its primary neurotransmitter. This division of the nervous system is crucial for vegetative responses (i.e. pupillary constriction, decrease in breathing, blood pressure and heart rate, increase in blood flow to the gastro-intestinal tract, etc.).

6.1.5 Autonomic Nerve Fibers

The nerve fibers from the ANS are primarily motor fibers. Unlike the motor pathways of the somatic nervous system, which usually include a single neuron between the CNS and an effector, those of the ANS involve *two* neurons. The first neuron has its cell body in the brain or spinal cord but its axon (= *preganglionic fiber*) extends outside of the CNS. The axon enters adjacent sympathetic chain ganglia, where they synapse with the cell body of a second neuron or travel up or down the chain to synapse with that of a remote second neuron (*recall: a ganglion is a collection of nerve cell bodies outside the CNS*). The axon of the second neuron (= *postganglionic fiber*) extends to a visceral effector.

The sympathetic ganglia form chains which, for example, may extend longitudinally along each side of the vertebral column. Conversely, the parasympathetic ganglia are located *near* or *within* various visceral organs (i.e. bladder, intestine, etc.) thus requiring relatively short postganglionic fibers. Therefore, sympathetic nerve fibers are characterized by short preganglionic fibers and long post-

ganglionic fibers while parasympathetic nerve fibers are characterized by long preganglionic fibers and short postganglionic fibers.

Both divisions of the ANS secrete *acetylcholine* from their preganglionic fibers. Most sympathetic postganglionic fibers secrete *norepinephrine* (= nor*adren*alin), and for this reason they are called **adren**ergic fibers. The parasympathetic postganglionic fibers secrete acetyl**choline** and are called ***cholinergic fibers.***

There are two types of acetylcholine receptors (AChR) that bind acetylcholine and transmit its signal: muscarinic AChRs and nicotinic AChRs, which are named after the agonists muscarine and nicotine, respectively. The two receptors are functionally different, the muscarinic type is a G-protein coupled receptor that mediates a slow metabolic response via second messenger cascades (involving cAMP), while the nicotinic type is a ligand-gated ionotropic channel that mediates a fast synaptic transmission of the neurotransmitter (no use of second messengers).

Each modality of sensation is detected by a particular nerve ending. The most common nerve ending is the free nerve ending. Different types of free nerve endings result in different types of sensations such as pain, warmth, pressure, touch, etc. In addition to free nerve endings, skin contains a number of specialized endings that are adapted to respond to some specific type of physical stimulus.

Sensory endings deep in the body are capable of detecting proprioceptive sensations such as joint receptors, which detect the degree of angulation of a joint, Golgi tendon organs which detect the degree of tension in the tendons, and muscle spindles which detect the degree of stretch of a muscle fiber (see diagram of reflex with muscle spindle in BIO 6.1.2).

6.2.1 Olfaction

Olfaction (the sense of smell) is perceived by the brain following the stimulation of the olfactory epithelium located in the nostrils. The olfactory epithelium contain large numbers of neurons with chemoreceptors called olfactory cells which are responsible for the detection of different types of smell. Odorant molecules bind to the receptors located on the cilia of olfactory receptor neurons and produce a depolarizing receptor potential. Once the depolarization passes threshold, an action potential is generated and is conducted into CNS. It is believed that there might be seven or more primary sensations of smell which combine to give various types of smell that we perceive in life.

6.2.2 Taste

Taste buds in combination with olfaction give humans the taste sensation. Taste buds are primarily located on the surface of the tongue with smaller numbers found in the roof of the mouth and the walls of the pharynx (throat). Taste buds contain chemoreceptors which are activated once the chemical is dissolved in saliva which is secreted by the salivary glands. Contrary to olfactory receptor cells, taste receptors are not true neurons: they are chemical receptors only.

Four different types of taste buds are known to exist, each of these responding principally to saltiness, sweetness, sourness and bitterness.

When a stimulus is received by either a taste bud or an olfactory cell for the second time, the intensity of the response is diminished. This is called sensory *adaptation*.

6.2.3 Ears: Structure and Function

Ears function in both hearing and balance. It consists of three parts: the *external ear* which receives sound waves; the air-filled *middle ear* which transmits and amplifies sound waves; and the fluid-filled *inner ear* which transduces sound waves into nerve impulse. The vestibular organ, located in the inner ear, is responsible for equilibrium.

The external ear is composed of the external cartilaginous portion, the pinna or *auricle*, and the external auditory meatus or canal. The external auditory meatus connects the auricle and the middle ear or *tympanic cavity*. The tympanic cavity is bordered on the outside by the tympanic membrane, and inside the air-filled cavity are the <u>auditory ossicles</u> - the *malleus* (hammer), *incus* (anvil), and *stapes* (stirrup). The stapes is held by ligaments to a part of inner ear called the *oval window*. The auditory ossicles function in amplifying the sound vibration and transmitting it from the tympanic membrane to the oval window.

The inner ear or *labyrinth* consists of an osseous (= bony) labyrinth containing a membranous labyrinth. The bony labyrinth houses the semicircular canals, the cochlea and the vestibule. The semicircular canals contain the semicircular ducts of the membranous labyrinth, which can detect angular acceleration. The vestibule contains the saccule and utricle, which are sac-like thin connective tissue lined by vestibular hair cells which are responsible for the detection of linear acceleration. Together, the semicircular canals and the vestibule, known as the vestibular system,

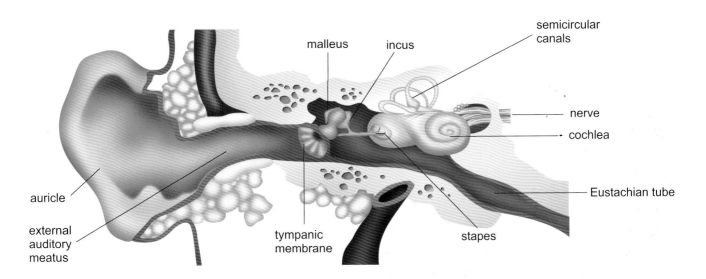

Figure IV.A.6.2: Structure of the external, middle and inner ear.

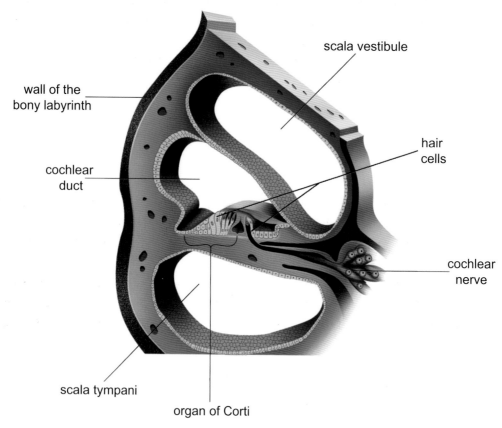

wall of the
bony labyrinth

scala vestibule

cochlear
duct

hair
cells

scala tympani

cochlear
nerve

organ of Corti

Figure IV.A.6.3: Cross-section of the cochlea.

are responsible for detection of linear and angular acceleration of the head. The cochlea is divided into three spaces: the scala vestibule, scala tympani and the scala media, or cochlear duct. The cochlear duct contains the spiral organ of Corti, which functions in the reception of sound and responds to different sound frequencies.

The eustachian tube connects the middle ear to the pharynx. This tube is important in maintaining equal pressure on both sides of the tympanic membrane. During ascent in an airplane, there is a decrease in cabin air pressure, leading to a relative increase in the pressure of the middle ear. Swallowing or yawning opens the eustachian tube allowing an equalization of pressure in the middle ear.

Mechanism of hearing: Sound is caused by the compression of waves that travel through the air. Each compression wave is funneled by the external ear to strike the tympanic membrane (ear drum). Thus the sound vibrations are transmitted through the osseous system which consists of three tiny bones (the malleus, incus, and stapes) into the cochlea at the oval window. Movement of the stapes at the oval window causes disturbance in the lymph of cochlea and stimulates the hair cells found in the basilar membrane which is called the *organ of Corti*. Bending of the hair cells causes depolarization of the basilar membrane. From here the auditory nerves carry the impulses to the auditory area of the brain (*temporal lobe*) where it is interpreted as sound.

6.2.4 Vision: Eye Structure and Function

The eyeball consists of three layers: i) an outer fibrous tunic composed of the sclera and cornea; ii) a vascular coat (uvea) of choroid, the ciliary body and iris; and iii) the retina formed of pigment and sensory (nervous) layers. The anterior chamber lies between the cornea anteriorly (in front) and the iris and pupil posteriorly (behind); the posterior chamber lies between the iris anteriorly and the ciliary processes and the lens posteriorly.

The transparent cornea constitutes the anterior one sixth of the eye and receives light from external environment. The sclera forms

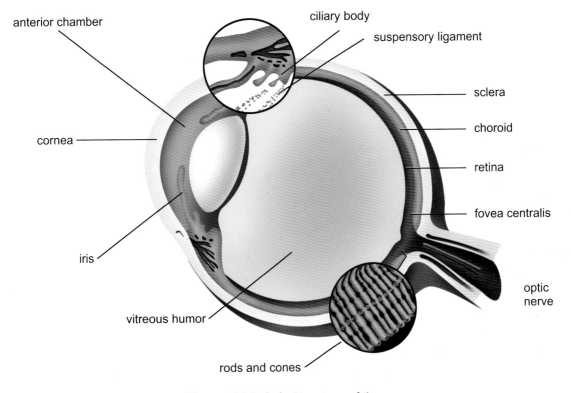

Figure IV.A.6.4: Structure of the eye.

the posterior five sixths of the fibrous tunic and is composed of dense fibrous connective tissue. The choroid layer consists of vascular loose connective tissue. The ciliary body is an anterior expansion of the choroid that encircles the lens. The lens can focus light on the retina by the contraction or relaxation of muscles in the ciliary body which transmit tension along suspensory ligaments to the lens.

Contraction of the ciliary muscle makes the lens become more convex, thereby allowing the eye to focus on nearby objects. Relaxation of the ciliary muscle allows the eye to focus on far objects. The iris separates the anterior and the posterior chamber and forms an aperture called the "pupil" whose diameter is continually adjusted by the pupillary muscles. This helps to control the intensity of light impinging on the retina.

The retina is divisible into ten layers. Layers two to five contain the rod and cone receptors of the light pathway.

Rods and Cones: The light sensitive receptors (*photoreceptors*) of the retina are millions of minute cells called rods and cones. The rods (*"night vision"*) distinguish only the black and white aspects of an image and are sensitive to light of low intensity (*"high sensitivity"*). The cones (*"day vision"*) are capable of distinguishing three colors: red, green and blue and are sensitive to light of high intensity (*"low sensitivity"*). From different combinations of these three colors, all colors can be seen.

Photoreceptors contain photosensitive pigments. For example, rods contain the membrane protein *rhodopsin* which is covalently linked to a form of vitamin A. Light causes an isomerization of *retinal* (an aldehyde form of vitamin A) which can affect Na^+ channels in a manner as to start an action potential.

The central portion of the retina which is called the fovea centralis has only cones, which allows this portion to have very sharp vision, while the peripheral areas, which contain progressively more and more rods, have progressively more diffuse vision. Since acuity and color vision are mediated by the same cells (cones), visual acuity is much better in bright light than dim light.

Each point of the retina connects with a discrete point in the visual cortex which is in the back of the brain (i.e. the occipital lobe). The image that is formed on the retina is upside down and reversed from left to right. This information leaves the eye via the optic nerve en route to the visual cortex which corrects the image.

Defects of vision

1. Myopia (short-sighted or nearsighted): In this condition, an image is formed in front of the retina because the lens converges light too much since the eyeballs are long. A diverging (concave) lens helps focus the image on the retina and it is used for the correction of myopia.

2. Hyperopia (long-sighted or farsighted): In this condition, an image is formed behind the retina since the eyeballs are too short. A converging (convex) lens helps focus the image on the retina.

3. Astigmatism: In this condition, the curvatures of either the cornea or the lens are different at different angles. A cylindrical lens helps to improve this condition.

4. Presbyopia: This condition is characterized by the inability to focus (especially objects which are closer). This condition, which is often seen in the elderly, is corrected by using a converging lens.

6.3 Endocrine Systems

The endocrine system is the set of glands, tissues and cells that secrete hormones directly into circulatory system (ductless). The hormones are transported by the blood system, sometimes bound to plasma proteins, en route to having an effect on the cells of a target organ. Thus hormones control many of the body's functions by acting - predominantly - in one of the following major ways:

1. By controlling transport of substances through cell membranes

2. By controlling the activity of some of the specific genes, which in turn determine the formation of specific enzymes

3. By controlling directly some metabolic systems of cells.

Steroid hormones can diffuse across the plasma membrane and bind to specific receptors in the cytosol or nucleus, thus forming a direct intracellular effect (i.e. on DNA; ORG 12.4.1). Non-steroid hormones do not diffuse across the membrane. They tend to bind plasma membrane receptors, which leads to the production of a second messenger.

Secondary messengers are a component of signal transduction cascades which amplify the strength of a signal (i.e. hormone, growth factors, neurotransmitter, etc.). Examples include cyclic AMP (cAMP), phosphoinositol, cyclic GMP and arachidonic acid systems.

In all four cases, a hormone (= the primary messenger or *agonist*) binds the receptor exposing a binding site for a G-protein (the *transducer*). The G-protein, named for its ability to exchange GDP on its alpha subunit for a GTP (BIO 4.4-4.10), is bound to the inner membrane. Once the exchange for GTP takes place, the alpha subunit of the G-protein transducer breaks free from the beta and gamma subunits, all parts remaining membrane-bound. The alpha subunit is now free to move along the inner membrane and eventually contacts another membrane-bound protein - the *primary effector*.

The primary effector has an action which creates a signal that can diffuse within the cell. This signal is the *secondary messenger*.

Calcium ions are important intracellular messengers which can regulate calmodulin and are responsible for many important physiological functions, such as in muscle contraction (BIO 5.2). The enzyme phospholipase C (primary effector) produces diacylglycerol and inositol trisphosphate (secondary messenger), which increases calcium ion (secondary effector) membrane permeability. Active G-protein can also open calcium channels. The other product of phospholipase C, diacylglycerol (secondary messenger), activates protein kinase C (secondary effector), which assists in the activation of cAMP (another second messenger).

The agonist epinephrine (hormone, BIO 6.1.3) can bind a receptor activating the transducer (G-protein) and using a primary effector (adenylyl cyclase) produces a secondary messenger (cAMP) which, in turn, brings about target cell responses that are recognized as the hormone's actions.

Of the following hormones, if there is no mention as to its chemical nature, then it is a non-steroidal hormone (i.e. protein, polypeptide, etc.).

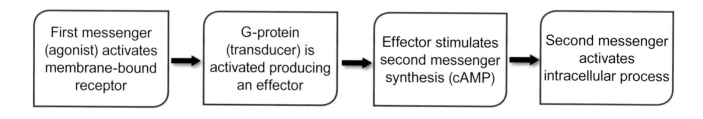

6.3.1 Pituitary Hormones

The **pituitary gland** secretes hormones that regulate a wide variety of functions in the body. This gland is divided into two major divisions: the anterior and the posterior pituitary gland. Six hormones are secreted by the anterior pituitary gland whereas two hormones are secreted by the posterior gland. The **hypothalamus** influences the secretion of hormones from both parts of the pituitary in different ways: i) it secretes specific *releas-* *ing factors* into special blood vessels (a *portal system* called hypothalamic-hypophysial portal system) which carries these factors (hormones) that affect the cells in the anterior pituitary by either stimulating or inhibiting the release of anterior pituitary hormones; ii) the hypothalamus contains neurosecretory cell bodies that synthesize, package and transport their products (esp. the two hormones oxytocin and ADH) down the axons directly into the posterior pituitary where they can be released into circulation.

The hormones secreted by the anterior pituitary gland are as follows:

1. Growth hormone (GH)
2. Thyroid Stimulating Hormone (TSH)
3. Adrenocorticotropic hormone (ACTH)
4. Prolactin
5. Follicle Stimulating Hormone (FSH) or Interstitial Cell Stimulating Hormone (ICSH)
6. Luteinizing Hormone (LH)

[N.B. these latter two hormones will be discussed in the section on Reproduction, see BIO 14.2, 14.3]

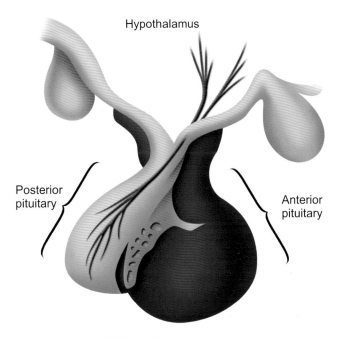

Figure IV.A.6.5: The pituitary gland.

Growth Hormone causes growth of the body. It causes enlargement and proliferation of cells in all parts of the body. Ultimately, the epiphyses of the long bones unite with the shaft of the bones (BIO 11.3.1). After adolescence, growth hormone continues to be secreted lower than the pre-adolescent rate. Though most of the growth in the body stops at this stage, the metabolic roles of the growth hormone continue such as the enhancement of protein synthesis and lean body mass, increasing blood glucose concentration, increasing lipolysis, etc.

Abnormal increase in the secretion of growth hormone at a young age results in a condition called gigantism, while a reduction in the production of growth hormone leads to dwarfism. Abnormal increase in the secretion of growth hormone in adults results

in a condition called acromegaly, a disorder characterized by a disproportionate bone enlargement, especially in the face, hands and feet.

Thyroid Stimulating Hormone stimulates the thyroid gland. The hormones produced by the thyroid gland (*thyroxine:* T_4, *triiodothyronine:* T_3) contain four and three iodine atoms, respectively. They increase the basal metabolic rate of the body (BMR). Therefore, indirectly, TSH increases the overall rate of metabolism of the body.

Adrenocorticotropic hormone strongly stimulates the production of cortisol by the adrenal cortex, and it also stimulates the production of the other adrenocortical hormones, but to a lesser extent.

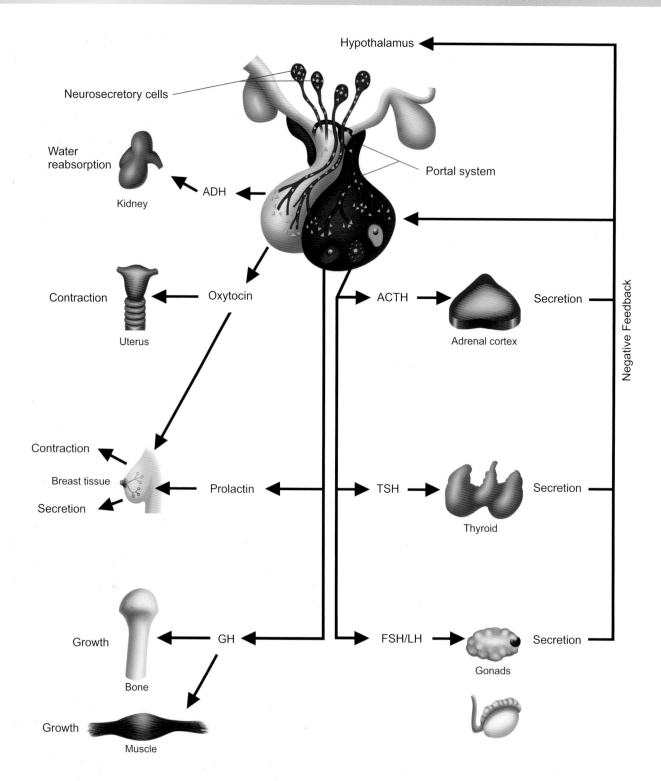

Figure IV.A.6.6: Pituitary hormones and their target organs.

Prolactin plays an important role in the development of the breast during pregnancy and promotes milk production in the breast. In addition, a high level of prolactin can inhibit ovulation.

Antidiuretic hormone (ADH) is synthesized by neurosecretory cells in the hypothalamus and then travels down the axons to the posterior pituitary for secretion. Antidiuretic hormone enhances the rate of water reabsorption from the renal tubules leading to the concentration of urine (BIO 10.3). ADH also constricts the arterioles and causes a rise in arterial pressure and hence it is also called *vasopressin*.

Similar to ADH, *oxytocin* originates in the hypothalamus and then travels down the axons to the posterior pituitary for secretion. Oxytocin causes contraction of the uterus and, to a lesser extent, the other smooth muscles of the body. It also stimulates the myoepithelial cells of the breast in a manner that makes the milk flow into the ducts. This is termed milk ejection or milk *let-down*.

6.3.2 Adrenocortical Hormones

On the top of each kidney lies an adrenal gland which contains an inner region (*medulla*) and an outer region (*cortex*). The adrenal cortex secretes three different types of steroid hormones that are similar chemically but vary widely in a physiological manner.

These are:

1. Mineralocorticoids - e.g., Aldosterone
2. Glucocorticoids - e.g., Cortisol, Cortisone
3. Sex Hormones e.g., Androgens, Estrogens

Mineralocorticoids - Aldosterone

The mineralocorticoids influence the electrolyte balance of the body. Aldosterone is a mineralocorticoid which is secreted and then enhances sodium transport from the renal tubules into the peritubular fluids, and at the same time enhances potassium transport from the peritubular fluids into the tubules. In other words, aldosterone causes conservation of sodium in the body and excretion of potassium in the urine. As a result of sodium retention, there is an increased passive reabsorption of chloride ions and water from the tubules. Overproduction of aldosterone will result in excessive retention of fluid, which leads to hypertension.

Glucocorticoids - Cortisol

Several different glucocorticoids are secreted by the adrenal cortex, but almost all of the glucocorticoid activity is caused by cortisol, also called hydrocortisone. Glucocorticoids affect the metabolism of carbohydrates, proteins and lipids. It causes an increase in the blood concentration of glucose by stimulation of gluconeogenesis (generation of glucose from non-carbohydrate carbon substrates). It causes degradation of proteins and causes increased use of fat for energy. Long term use of glucocorticoids suppresses the immune system. It also has an anti-inflammatory effect by inhibiting the release of inflammatory mediators.

Sex hormones

Androgens (i.e. testosterone) are the masculinizing hormones in the body. They are responsible for the development of the secondary sexual characteristics in a male (i.e. increased body hair). On the contrary estrogens have a feminizing effect in the body and they are responsible for the development of the secondary sexual characteristics in a female (i.e. breast development). The proceeding hormones supplement secretions from the gonads which will be discussed later (see "*Reproduction*"; BIO 14.2, 14.3).

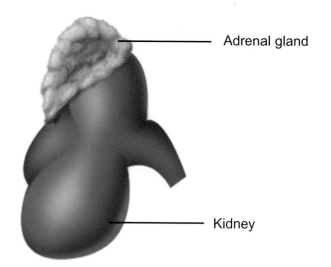

Figure IV.A.6.7: The adrenal gland sits on top of the kidney.

The Adrenal Medulla

The adrenal medulla synthesizes epinephrine (= *adrenaline*) and norepinephrine which: i) are non-steroidal stimulants of the sympathetic nervous system; ii) raise blood glucose concentrations; iii) increase heart rate and blood pressure; iv) increase blood supply to the brain, heart and skeletal muscle; and v) decrease blood supply to the skin, digestive system and renal system.

6.3.3 Thyroid Hormones

The thyroid gland is located anteriorly in the neck and is composed of follicles lined with thyroid glandular cells. These cells secrete a glycoprotein called thyroglobulin. The tyrosine residue of thyroglobulin then reacts with iodine forming mono-iodotyrosine (MIT) and di-iodotyrosine (DIT). When two molecules of DIT combine, thyroxine (T_4) is formed. When one molecule of DIT and one molecule of MIT combine, tri-iodothyronine (T_3) is formed. The rate of synthesis of thyroid hormone is influenced by TSH from the pituitary.

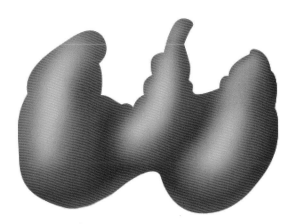

Figure IV.A.6.8: The thyroid gland.

Once thyroid hormones have been released into the blood stream they combine with several different plasma proteins. Then they are released into the cells from the blood stream. They play a vital role in maturation of CNS as thyroid hormone deficiency leads to irreversible mental retardation. They increase heart rate, ventilation rate and O_2 consumption. They also increase the size and numbers of mitochondria and these in turn increase the rate of production of ATP, which is a factor that promotes cellular metabolism; glycogenolysis and gluconeogenesis both increase; lipolysis increases; and protein synthesis also increases. The overall effect of thyroid hormone on metabolism is catabolic.

Hyperthyroidism is an excess of thyroid hormone secretion above that needed for normal function. Basically, an increased rate of metabolism throughout the body is observed. Other symptoms include fast heart rate and respiratory rate, weight loss, sweating, tremor, and protruding eyes.

Hypothyroidism is an inadequate amount of thyroid hormone secreted into the blood stream. Generally it slows down the metabolic rate and enhances the collection of mucinous fluid in the tissue spaces, creating an edematous (fluid filled) state called myxedema. Other symptoms include slowed heart rate and respiratory rate, weight gain, cold intolerance, fatigue, and mental slowness.

The thyroid and parathyroid glands affect blood calcium concentration in different ways. The thyroid produces *calcitonin* which inhibits osteoclast activity and stimulates osteoblasts to form bone tissue; thus blood $[Ca^{2+}]$ decreases. The parathyroid glands produce parathormone (= parathyroid hormone = PTH), which stimulates osteoclasts to break down bone, thus raising $[Ca^{2+}]$ and $[PO_4^{3-}]$ in the blood (BIO 5.4.4).

6.3.4 Pancreatic Hormones

The pancreas contains clusters of cells (= *islets of Langerhans*) closely associated with blood vessels. The islets of Langerhans, which perform the endocrine function of the pancreas, contain alpha cells that secrete *glucagon* and beta cells that secrete *insulin*. Glucagon increases blood glucose concentration by promoting the following events in the liver: the conversion of glycogen to glucose (*glycogenolysis*) and the production of glucose from amino acids (*gluconeogenesis*). Insulin decreases blood glucose by increasing cellular uptake of glucose, promoting glycogen formation and decreasing gluconeogenesis. A deficiency in insulin or insensitivity to insulin results in *diabetes mellitus*.

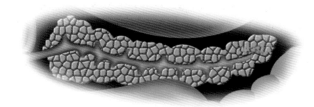

Figure IV.A.6.9: The pancreas.

6.3.5 Kidney Hormones

The kidney produces and secretes *renin*, *erythropoietin* and it helps in the activation of vitamin D. Renin is an enzyme that catalyzes the conversion of angiotensinogen to angiotensin I. Angiotensin I is then converted to angiotensin II by angiotensin-converting enzyme (ACE). Angiotensin II acts on the adrenal cortex to increase the synthesis and release of aldosterone, which increases Na^+ reabsorption, and causes vasoconstriction of arterioles leading to an increase in both blood volume and blood pressure. Erythropoietin increases the production of *erythrocytes* by acting on red bone marrow.

Vitamin D is a steroid which is critical for the proper absorption of calcium from the small intestine; thus it is essential for the normal growth and development of bone and teeth. Vitamin D can either be ingested or produced from a precursor by the activity of ultraviolet light on skin cells. It must be further activated in the liver and kidney by hydroxylation.

6.3.6 A Negative Feedback Loop

In order to maintain the internal environment of the body in equilibrium (= *homeostasis*), our hormones engage in various negative feedback loops. Negative feedback is self-limiting: a hormone produces biologic actions that, in turn, directly or indirectly inhibit further secretion of that hormone.

For example, if the body is exposed to extreme cold, the hypothalamus will activate systems to conserve heat (see *Skin as an Organ System*, BIO 13.1) and to produce heat. Heat production can be attained by increasing the basal metabolic rate. To achieve this, the hypothalamus secretes a releasing factor (thyrotropin releasing factor - TRF) which stimulates the anterior pituitary to secrete TSH. Thus the thyroid gland is stimulated to secrete the thyroid hormones.

Body temperature begins to return to normal. The high levels of circulating thyroid hormones begin to *inhibit* the production of TRF and TSH (= *negative feedback*) which in turn ensures the reduction in the levels of the thyroid hormones. Thus homeostasis is maintained.

6.3.7 A Positive Feedback Loop

As opposed to negative feedback, a positive feedback loop is where the body senses a change and activates mechanisms that accelerate or increase that change. Occasionally this may help homeostasis by working in conjunction with a larger negative feedback loop, but unfortunately it often produces the opposite effect and can be life-threatening.

An example of a beneficial positive feedback loop is seen in childbirth, where stretching of the uterus triggers the secretion of oxytocin (BIO 6.3.1), which stimulates uterine contractions and speeds up labor. Of course, once the baby is out of the mother's body, the loop is broken.

Often, however, positive feedback produces the very opposite of homeostasis: a rapid loss of internal stability with potentially fatal consequences. For example, most human deaths from SARS and the bird flu (H5N1) epidemic were caused by a "cytokine storm" which is a positive feedback loop between immune cells and cytokines (signalling molecules similar to hormones). Thus, in many cases, it is the body's exaggerated response to infection that is the cause of death rather than the direct action of the original infecting agent. Many diseases involve dangerous positive feedback loops.

GOLD STANDARD WARM-UP EXERCISES

CHAPTER 6: Nervous and Endocrine Systems

1) How many PAIRS of nerves leave the vertebrate brain?

   A. 3
   B. 6
   C. 8
   D. 12

2) The structure in the brain responsible for maintaining homeostasis (i.e. body temperature, heart rate, etc.) is the:

   A. pituitary.
   B. thalamus.
   C. hypothalamus.
   D. cerebellum.

3) Damage to which pair of nerves comprising the descending pathways, would likely cause persons with spinal-cord damage to have no control over the micturition process (i.e. urination)?

   A. Vagus
   B. Abducans
   C. Trigeminal
   D. Hypoglossal

4) Increased physical activity results in raising the heart rate and blood pressure. The nervous system specifically implicated is:

   A. somatic.
   B. peripheral.
   C. parasympathetic.
   D. sympathetic.

5) A collection of nerve cell bodies in the central nervous system is generally referred to as a:

   A. nerve.
   B. conus.
   C. ganglion.
   D. nucleus.

6) All of the following are correct concerning the autonomic nervous system EXCEPT:

   A. nicotinic receptors operate through a second messenger system involving the regulation of cAMP.
   B. both divisions of the ANS secrete acetylcholine from their preganglionic fibers.
   C. the parasympathetic postganglionic fibers are cholinergic.
   D. the sympathetic ganglia form chains which may extend longitudinally along each side of the vertebral column.

7) The vertebrate eyeball is bounded anteriorly by what convex, transparent tissue?

   A. Sclera
   B. Choroid
   C. Cornea
   D. Vitreous humor

8) What is the name given to the jelly-like substance filling the chamber behind the lens of the human eye?

   A. Vitreous humor
   B. Fovea centralis
   C. Ciliary body
   D. Choroid

9) All of the following are necessary for directing light onto the retina EXCEPT:

   A. cornea.
   B. iris.
   C. lens.
   D. aqueous humor.

10) The name of the ductless glands which secrete their products into the circulatory system are:

A. holocrine.
B. apocrine.
C. exocrine.
D. endocrine.

11) All of the following would be symptoms of hypothyroidism, EXCEPT:

A. hypothermia.
B. dry skin.
C. hyperactivity.
D. myxedema.

12) Which of the following endocrine glands would have the most direct antagonistic effect on the action of calcitonin?

A. Adrenal cortex
B. Thyroid
C. Pancreas
D. Parathyroid

13) Which of the following is the target organ of TRH?

A. Anterior pituitary
B. Posterior pituitary
C. Parathyroid
D. Thyroid

14) Increased levels of hormones in the adrenal gland would have which of the following effects?

A. Increased synthesis of proteins
B. Increased levels of sodium in the nephron
C. Increased metabolism of glycogen
D. Decreased blood volume

15) A certain compound has been found to strengthen bone by increasing calcium deposition in the bones. This compound would most likely stimulate which of the following?

A. Osteoclast activity
B. Calcitonin secretion

C. Parathyroid hormone secretion
D. Thyroxine secretion

16) The hypothalamus is best characterized as:

I. an endocrine gland.
II. a nexus of somatic receptor cells.
III. a producer of gonadotropin hormone.

A. I only
B. II only
C. II and III only
D. I, II, and III

17) This question refers to Fig. 1.

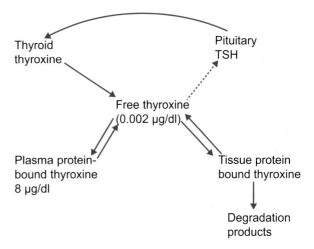

Figure 1

According to the equilibrium shown in Fig. 1, an elevation in the concentration of free thyroid hormone in the plasma is followed by:

A. an increase in tissue protein-bound thyroxine.
B. an increase in tissue protein-bound thyroxine and plasma protein-bound thyroxine.
C. an increase in the amount of TSH secreted from the pituitary gland.
D. an increase in both the amount of TSH secreted from the pituitary gland and the release of thyroxine from the thyroid gland.

18) Symptoms of hypothyroidism and hyperthyroidism, respectively, include:

A. a fine tremor and diminished concentration.
B. brittle nails and kidney stones.
C. rapid heart beat and increased irritability.
D. lethargy and nervous agitation.

19) Which of the following cell types would be expected to be maximally stimulated in a patient with hyperparathyroidism?

A. Osteoclasts
B. Osteoblasts
C. Fibroblasts
D. Chondrocytes

20) Parathormone influences calcium homeostasis by reducing tubular reabsorption of PO_4^{3-} in the kidneys. Which of the following, if true, would clarify the adaptive significance of this process?

A. PO_4^{3-} and Ca^{2+} feedback positively on each other.
B. Elevated levels of extracellular PO_4^{3-} result in calcification of bones and tissues.
C. Increased PO_4^{3-} levels cause an increase in parathormone secretion.
D. Decreased extracellular PO_4^{3-} levels cause a decrease in calcitonin production.

21) On a very hot day, the bladder would likely contain:

A. a large amount of urine hypertonic to blood plasma.
B. a large amount of urine hypotonic to blood plasma.
C. a small amount of urine hypertonic to blood plasma.
D. a small amount of urine hypotonic to blood plasma.

22) Which of the following best represents a possible series of physiological events following the detection by the hypothalamus of a cold environment?

A. heat promoting center → parasympathetic nerves → adrenal medulla → epinephrine production
B. heat promoting center → sympathetic nerves → sweat glands → stimulating local secretion
C. heat promoting center → sympathetic nerves → adrenal medulla → epinephrine production
D. heat promoting center → parasympathetic nerves → heart → dilated coronary vessels

23) Low blood pressure would normally result in which of the following?

A. Increased production of oxytocin in the hypothalamus.
B. Decreased levels of prolactin in the anterior pituitary.
C. Increased levels of parathyroid hormone.
D. Increased production of aldosterone in the adrenal cortex.

24) After radioactive iodine ^{131}I is injected into the vein of a patient, where would ^{131}I concentration be highest?

A. Liver
B. Parathyroid
C. Thyroid
D. Muscle cells

25) The hormone which exerts the most control on the concentration of the urine in the bladder is:

A. vasopressin.
B. oxytocin.
C. thyroxine.
D. prolactin.

26) Which of the following is an example of positive feedback?

A. An elevated body temperature of 101 °F causes a further increase.

B. Elevated TSH results in elevated thyroxine.

C. Calcitonin and parathromone regulate calcium levels.

D. Increased thyroid releasing factor (TRH) leads to increased TSH.

GS ANSWER KEY

CHAPTER 6

		Cross-Reference				Cross-Reference
1.	D	BIO 6.1		14.	C	BIO 6.3.1, 6.3.2
2.	C	BIO 6.1		15.	B	BIO 6.3.3
3.	A	BIO 6.1, 6.1.4		16.	A	BIO 6.3, 6.3.1
4.	D	BIO 6.1.4		17.	B	CHM 9.9, BIO 6.3.3, 6.3.6
5.	D	BIO 6.1		18.	D	BIO 6.3.3
6.	A	BIO 6.1.5		19.	A	BIO 5.4.4, 6.3.3
7.	C	BIO 6.2.4		20.	B	BIO 5.4.4, 6.3.3
8.	A	BIO 6.2.4		21.	C	BIO 1.1.1, 6.3.1 and F
9.	B	BIO 6.2.4		22.	C	BIO 6.1, 6.1.4, 6.3.2, 6.3.3
10.	D	BIO 6.3		23.	D	BIO 6.3.1, 6.3.2
11.	C	BIO 6.3.1, 6.3.3		24.	C	BIO 6.3.1
12.	D	BIO 6.3.3		25.	A	BIO 6.3, 6.3.1
13.	A	BIO 6.3.1, 6.3.3		26.	A	BIO 6.3.6, 6.3.7

* Explanations can be found at the back of the book.

Memorize	Understand	Importance
c. and lymphatic systems: basic uctures and functions mposition of blood, lymph, purpose ymph nodes C production and destruction; spleen, ne marrow sics: coagulation, clotting mechanisms uations for Q, EF, SV	* Circ: structure/function; 4 chambered heart: systolic/diastolic pressure * Oxygen transport; hemoglobin, oxygen content/affinity * Substances transported by blood, lymph * Source of lymph: diffusion from capillaries by differential pressure	**0 to 2 out of the 40 Biology** DAT questions are based on content in this chapter (in our estimation). * Note that between 25% and 50% of the questions in DAT Biology are from 5 chapters: 1, 2, 14, 15, and 16.

DAT-Prep.com

Introduction

The circulatory system is concerned with the movement of nutrients, gases and wastes to and from cells. The circulatory or cardiovascular system (closed) distributes blood while the lymphatic system (open) distributes lymph.

Additional Resources

| Free Online Q&A + Forum | Video: Online or DVD | Flashcards | Special Guest |

The circulatory system is composed of the heart, blood, and blood vessels. The heart (which acts like a pump) and its blood vessels (which act like a closed system of ducts) are called the *cardiovascular system* which moves the blood throughout the body.

The following represents some important functions of blood within the circulatory system.

* It transports:

- hormones from endocrine glands to target tissues
- molecules and cells which are components of the immune system
- nutrients from the digestive tract (usu. to the liver)
- oxygen from the respiratory system to body cells
- waste from the body cells to the respiratory and excretory systems.

* It aids in temperature control (*thermoregulation*) by:

- distributing heat from skeletal muscle and other active organs to the rest of the body
- being directed to or away from the skin depending on whether or not the body wants to release or conserve heat, respectively.

7.2 The Heart

The heart is a muscular, cone-shaped organ about the size of a fist. The heart is composed of connective tissue (BIO 5.4) and cardiac muscle (BIO 5.2) which includes a region that generates electrical signals (see BIO 11.2 for SA node). The heart contains four chambers: two thick muscular walled *ventricles* and two thinner walled *atria*. An inner wall or *septum* separates the heart (and therefore the preceding chambers) into left and right sides. The atria contract or *pump* blood more or less simultaneously and so do the ventricles.

Deoxygenated blood returning to the heart from all body tissues except the lungs (= *systemic circulation*) enters the right atrium through large veins (= *venae cavae*). The blood is then pumped into the right ventricle through the tricuspid valve (which is one of many one-way valves in the cardiovascular system). Next the blood is pumped to the lungs (= *pulmonary circulation*) through semilunar valves (pulmonary valves) and pulmonary arteries {remember: blood in arteries goes away from the heart}.

The blood loses CO_2 and is **oxygenated** in the lungs and returns through pulmonary veins to the left atrium. Now the blood is pumped through the mitral (= bicuspid) valve into the largest chamber of the heart: the left ventricle. This ventricle's task is to return

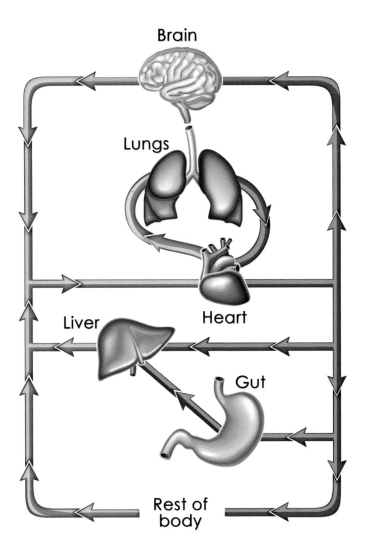

Figure IV.A.7.0: Overview of vascular anatomy.

The vascular anatomy of the human body or for an individual organ is comprised of both in-series and in-parallel vascular components. Blood leaves the heart through the aorta (high in oxygen, red in color) from which it is distributed to major organs by large arteries, each of which originates from the aorta. Therefore, these major distributing arteries are in parallel with each other. Thus the circulations of the head, arms, gastrointestinal systems, kidneys, and legs are all parallel circulations. There are some exceptions, notably the gastrointestinal (gut) and hepatic (liver) circulations, which are partly in series because the venous drainage from the intestines become the hepatic portal vein which supplies most of the blood flow to the liver. Vessels transporting from one capillary bed to another are called portal veins (besides the liver, note the portal system in the anterior pituitary, BIO 6.3.1).

blood into the systemic circulation by pumping into a huge artery: the *aorta* (its valve is the aortic valve).

The mitral (= bi̲cuspid = 2̲ leaflets) and tricuspid (tri̲ = 3̲ leaflets) valves are prevented from everting into the atria by strong fibrous cords (*chordae tendineae*) which are attached to small mounds of muscle (*papillary muscles*) in their respective ventricles. A major cause of heart murmurs is the inadequate functioning of these valves.

7.3 Blood Vessels

Blood vessels include arteries, arterioles, capillaries, venules and veins. Whereas arteries tend to have thick, smooth muscular walls and contain blood at high pressure, veins have thinner walls and low blood pressure. However, veins contain the highest proportion of blood in the cardiovascular system (about 2/3rds). The wall of a blood vessel is composed of an outer adventitia, an inner intima and a *mi*ddle *mu*scle layer, the me̲dia.

Oxygenated blood entering the systemic circulation must get to all the body's tissues. The aorta must divide into smaller and smaller arteries (small artery = **arteriole**) in order to get to the level of the capillary which i) is the smallest blood vessel; ii) often forms branching networks called *capillary beds*; and iii) is the level at which the exchange of wastes and gases (i.e. O_2 and CO_2) occurs by diffusion.

In the next step in circulation, the newly deoxygenated blood enters very small veins (= **venules**) and then into larger and larger veins until the blood enters the venae cavae and then the right atrium. There are two venae cavae: one drains blood from the upper body while the other drains blood from the lower body (*superior* and *inferior* venae cavae, respectively).

Since the walls of veins are thin and somewhat floppy, they are often located in muscles. Thus movement of the leg squeezes the veins, which pushes the blood through 1-way bicuspid valves toward the heart. This is referred to as the *muscle pump*.

Coronary arteries branch off the aorta to supply the heart muscle.

Systemic Circulation   **Pulmonary Circulation**

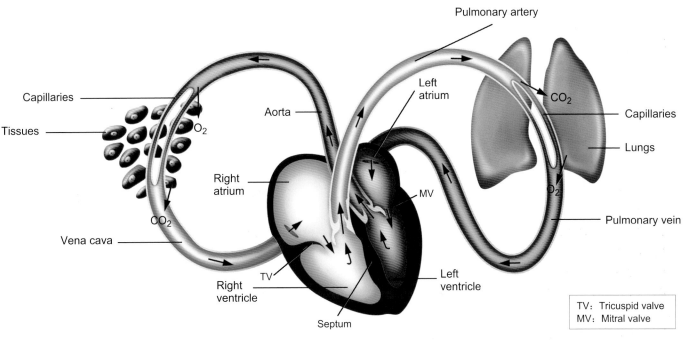

Figure IV.A.7.1: Schematic representation of the circulatory system.

Systemic circulation: transports blood from the left ventricle into the aorta then to all parts of the body and then returns to the right atrium from the superior and inferior venae cavae. *Pulmonary circulation:* transports blood from the right ventricle into pulmonary arteries to the lungs for exchange of oxygen and carbon dioxide and returns blood to the left atrium from pulmonary veins.

7.4 Blood Pressure

Blood pressure is the force exerted by the blood against the inner walls of blood vessels (esp. arteries). Maximum arterial pressure is measured when the ventricle contracts and blood is pumped into the arterial system (= *systolic pressure*). Minimal arterial pressure is measured when the ventricle is relaxed and blood is returned to the heart via veins (= *diastolic pressure*). Pulse pressure is the difference between the systolic pressure and the diastolic pressure. Blood pressure is usually measured in the brachial artery in the arm. A pressure of 120/80 signifies a systolic pressure of 120 mmHg and a diastolic pressure of 80 mmHg. The *pulse pressure* is the difference (i.e. 40 mmHg).

Peripheral resistance is essentially the result of arterioles and capillaries which resist the flow of blood from arteries to veins (the narrower the vessel, the higher the resistance). Arterioles are the site of the highest resistance in the cardiovascular system. An increase in peripheral resistance causes a rise in blood pressure. As blood travels down the systemic circulation, blood pressure decreases progressively due to the peripheral resistance to blood flow.

7.5 Blood Composition

Blood contains plasma (55%) and *formed elements* (45%). Plasma is a straw colored liquid which is mostly composed of water (92%), electrolytes, and the following plasma proteins:

* **Albumin** which is important in maintaining the osmotic pressure and helps to transport many substances in the blood

* **Globulins** which include both transport proteins and the proteins which form antibodies

* **Fibrinogen** which polymerizes to form the insoluble protein *fibrin* which is essential for normal blood clotting. If you take away fibrinogen and some other clotting factors from plasma you will be left with a fluid called *serum*.

The formed elements of the blood originate from precursors in the bone marrow which produce the following for the circulatory system: 99% red blood cells (= *erythrocytes*), then there are platelets (= *thrombocytes*), and white blood cells (= *leukocytes*). Red blood cells (RBCs) are biconcave cells without nuclei (*anucleate*) that circulate for 110-120 days before their components are recycled by macrophages. Interestingly, mature RBCs do not possess most organelles such as mitochondria, Golgi nor ER because RBCs are packed with hemoglobin. The primary function of hemoglobin is the transport of O_2 and CO_2 to and from tissue.

Platelets are cytoplasmic fragments of large bone marrow cells (*megakaryocytes*) which are involved in blood clotting by adhering to the collagen of injured vessels, releasing mediators which cause blood vessels to constrict (= *vasoconstriction*), etc.

Calcium ions (Ca^{2+}) are also important in blood clotting because they help in signaling platelets to aggregate.

White blood cells help in the defense against infection; they are divided into *granulocytes* and *agranulocytes* depending on whether or not the cell does or does not contain granules, respectively.

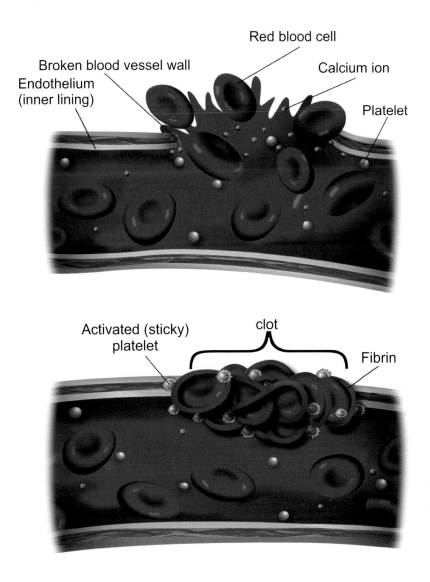

Figure IV.A.7.1.1: Schematic representation of blood clotting.

Granulocytes (= *polymorphonuclear leukocytes*) possess varying number of azurophilic (burgundy when stained) granules and are divided into: i) neutrophils which are the first white blood cells to respond to infection, they are important in controlling bacterial infection by phagocytosis - killing and digesting bacteria - and are the main cellular constituent of pus; ii) eosinophils which, like neutrophils, are phagocytic and also participate in allergic reactions and the destruction of parasites; iii) basophils which can release both anticoagulants (heparin) and substances important in hypersensitivity reactions (histamine).

Agranulocytes (= *mononuclear leuko-cytes*)) lack specific granules and are divided into: i) *lymphocytes* which are vital to the immune system (see *Immune System*, chapter 8); and monocytes (often called *phago-cytes* or *macrophages* when they are outside of the circulatory system) which can phagocytose large particles.

The hematocrit measures how much space (volume) in the blood is occupied by red blood cells and is expressed as a percentage. Normal hematocrit in adults is about 45%.

{*See BIO 15.2 for ABO Blood Types*}

7.5.1 Hemoglobin

Each red blood cell carries hundreds of molecules of a substance which is responsible for their red color: **hemoglobin**. Hemoglobin (Hb) is a complex of *heme*, which is an iron-containing porphyrin ring, and *globin*, which is a tetrameric (= has 4 subunits) protein consisting of two α-subunits and two β-subunits. The iron from the heme group is normally in its reduced state (Fe^{2+}); however, in the presence of O_2, it can be oxidized to Fe^{3+}.

In the lungs, oxygen concentration or *partial pressure* is high, thus O_2 dissolves in the blood; oxygen can then quickly and reversibly combine with the iron in Hb forming bright red *oxyhemoglobin*. The binding of oxygen to hemoglobin is cooperative. In other words, each oxygen that binds to Hb facilitates the binding of the next oxygen. Consequently, the dissociation curve for oxyhemoglobin is sigmoidal as a result of the change in affinity of hemoglobin as each O_2 successively binds to the globin subunit (see BIO 4.3).

Examine Figure IV.A.7.2 carefully. Notice that at a PO_2 of 100 mmHg (e.g. arterial blood), the percentage of saturation of hemoglobin is almost 100%, which means all four heme groups on the four hemoglobin subunits are bound with O_2. At a PO_2 of 40 mmHg (e.g. venous blood), the percentage of saturation of hemoglobin is about 75%, which means three of the four heme groups on the four hemoglobin subunits are bound with O_2. At a PO_2 of 27 mmHg, the percentage of saturation of hemoglobin is only 50%, which means half of the four heme groups on the four hemoglobin subunits are bound with O_2. The partial pressure of oxygen (PO_2) at 50% saturation is called P50.

The curve can: (i) shift to the left which means that for a given PO_2 in the tissue capillary there is decreased unloading (release) of oxygen and that the affinity of hemoglobin for O_2 is increased; or (ii) shift to the right which means that for a given PO_2 in the tissue capillary there is increased

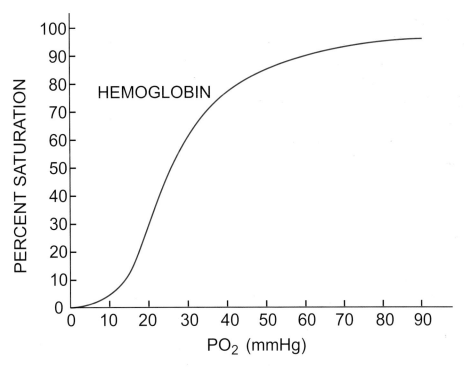

Figure IV.A.7.2: Oxygen dissociation curve: percent O_2 saturation versus O_2 partial pressure.

unloading of oxygen and that the affinity of hemoglobin for O_2 is decreased. The latter occurs when the tissue (i.e. muscle) is very active and thus requires more oxygen.

Thus a right shift occurs when the muscle is hot (↑ temperature during exercise), acid (↓ pH due to lactic acid produced in exercising muscle, see BIO 4.4. and 4.5), hypercarbic (↑CO_2 as during exercise, tissue produces more CO_2, see BIO 4.4. and 12.4.1), or contains high levels of organic phosphates (esp. increased synthesis of 2,3 DPG in red blood cells as a means to adapt to chronic hypoxemia).

In the body tissues where the partial pressure of O_2 is low and CO_2 is high, O_2 is released and CO_2 combines with the protein component of Hb forming the darker colored *carbaminohemoglobin* (also called: deoxyhemoglobin). The red color of muscle is due to a different heme-containing protein concentrated in muscle called myoglobin. Myoglobin is a monomeric protein containing one heme prosthetic group. The O_2 binding curve for myoglobin is hyperbolic, which means that it lacks cooperativity.

Capillary fluid movement can occur as a result of two processes: diffusion (dominant role) and filtration (secondary role but critical for the proper function of organs, especially the kidney; BIO 10.3). Osmotic pressure (BIO 1.1.1, CHM 5.1.3) due to proteins in blood plasma is sometimes called colloid osmotic pressure or oncotic pressure. The Starling equation is an equation that describes the role of hydrostatic and oncotic forces (= Starling forces) in the movement of fluid across capillary membranes as a result of filtration.

When blood enters the arteriole end of a capillary, it is still under pressure produced by the contraction of the ventricle. As a result of this pressure, a substantial amount of water (hydrostatic) and some plasma proteins filter through the walls of the capillaries into the tissue space. This fluid, called interstitial fluid (BIO 7.6), is simply blood plasma minus most of the proteins.

Interstitial fluid bathes the cells in the tissue space and substances in it can enter the cells by diffusion (mostly) or active transport. Substances, like carbon dioxide, can diffuse out of cells and into the interstitial fluid.

Near the venous end of a capillary, the blood pressure is greatly reduced. Here another force comes into play. Although the composition of interstitial fluid is similar to that of blood plasma, it contains a smaller concentration of proteins than plasma and thus a somewhat greater concentration of water.

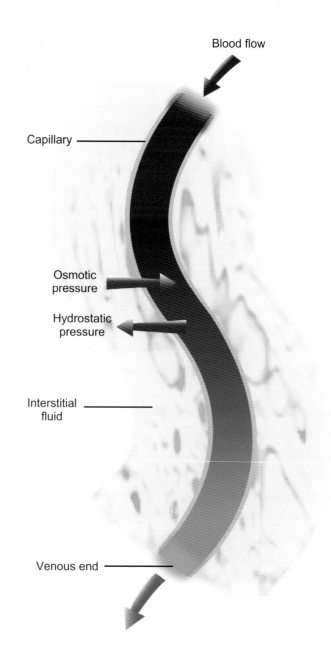

Figure IV.A.7.2b: Circulation at the level of the capillary. The exchange of water, oxygen, carbon dioxide, and many other nutrient and waste chemical substances between blood and surrounding tissues occurs at the level of the capillary.

This difference sets up an osmotic pressure. Although the osmotic pressure is small, it is greater than the blood pressure at the venous end of the capillary. Thus the fluid reenters the capillary here.

To summarize: when the blood pressure is greater than the osmotic pressure, filtration is favored and fluid tends to move out of the capillary; when the blood pressure is less than the osmotic pressure, reabsorption is favored and fluid tends to enter into the capillary.

7.6 The Lymphatic System

Body fluids can exist in blood vessels (intravascular), in cells (intracellular) or in a 3rd space which is intercellular (between cells) or extracellular (outside cells). Such fluids are called interstitial fluids. The **lymphatic system** is a network of vessels which can circulate fluid from the 3rd space to the cardiovascular system.

Aided by osmotic pressure, interstitial fluids enter the lymphatic system via small closed-ended tubes called *lymphatic capillaries* (in the small intestine they are called *lacteals*). Once the fluid enters it is called **lymph**. The lymph continues to flow into larger and larger vessels propelled by muscular contraction (esp. skeletal) and one-way valves. Then the lymph will usually pass through *lymph nodes* and then into a large vessel (esp. *the thoracic duct*) which drains into one of the large veins which eventually leads to the right atrium.

Lymph functions in important ways. Most protein molecules which leak out of blood capillaries are returned to the bloodstream by lymph. Also, microorganisms which invade tissue fluids are carried to lymph nodes by lymph. Lymph nodes contain *lymphocytes* and macrophages which are components of the immune system.

GOLD STANDARD WARM-UP EXERCISES

CHAPTER 7: The Circulatory System

1) In humans which of the following orders of blood circulation is correct?

   A. Vena cava → right atrium → right ventricle → pulmonary arteries → pulmonary veins → left atrium

   B. Vena cava → left atrium → left ventricle → pulmonary veins → pulmonary arteries → right ventricle

   C. Vena cava → right ventricle → left ventricle → pulmonary veins → pulmonary arteries → left atrium

   D. Vena cava → left atrium → left ventricle → pulmonary vein → pulmonary artery → right atrium

2) The rate of respiration is primarily dependent on the concentration of carbon dioxide in the blood. As carbon dioxide levels rise, chemoreceptors in blood vessels are stimulated to discharge neuronal impulses to the respiratory center in the medulla oblongata in the brain stem. These chemoreceptors are likely located in the:

   A. vena cava.
   B. pulmonary artery.
   C. femoral vein.
   D. aorta.

3) Veins tend to have ALL the following EXCEPT:

   A. very elastic walls.
   B. increasing size toward the heart.
   C. thin walls.
   D. valves for unidirectional flow.

4) Blood in the pulmonary veins is rich in:

   A. myoglobin.
   B. carbaminohemoglobin.
   C. oxyhemoglobin.
   D. lymph.

5) A biologically active agent, which completely diffuses through capillary beds, is injected into the brachiocephalic vein of the left arm. Which of the following would be most affected by the agent?

   A. Heart
   B. Lung
   C. Left arm
   D. Right arm

6) If the partial pressure of O_2 was increased to make up the total pressure of gas in blood which of the following would occur?

   A. There would be a decrease in HbO_2.
   B. There would be an increase in HbO_2.
   C. The concentrations of Hb would equal HbO_2.
   D. No answer can be determined from the information given.

7) Which of the following best explains why 97% of oxygen in blood is in the HbO_2 form?

   A. Oxygen binds irreversibly to the iron atoms in hemoglobin.
   B. Oxygen does not dissolve well in blood plasma.
   C. There are allosteric interactions between hemoglobin subunits
   D. Hemoglobin consists of four proteinacious subunits.

8) Which of the following graphs best represents the relationship between percent saturation of hemoglobin and pO_2 (mmHg) at different temperatures?

A.

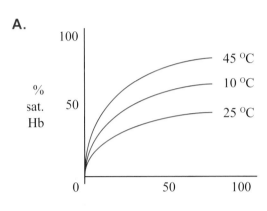

B.

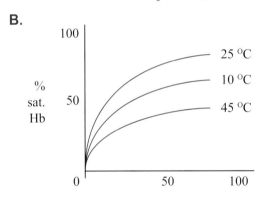

C.

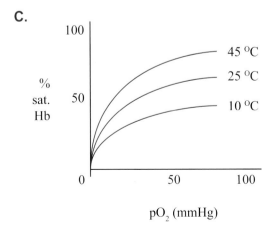

D.

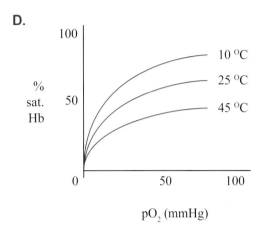

9) Which of the following body systems in humans is implicated in thermoregulation and transportation of components of the immune and endocrine systems?

A. The lymphatic system
B. Skin
C. The excretory system
D. The circulatory system

10) Once the erythrocytes enter the blood in humans, it is estimated that they have an average lifetime of how many days?

A. 75 days
B. 120 days
C. 220 days
D. 365 days

11) The net effect of the glycerate 2,3-biphosphate (GBP) is to shift the hemoglobin oxygen binding curve to higher oxygen tensions. Which of the following graphs represents the oxygen-binding curve in the presence of GBP?

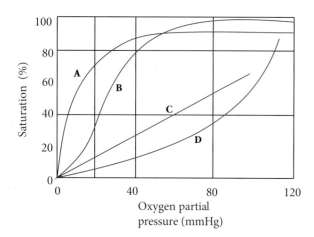

12) Glycerate 2,3-biphosphate functions to shift the oxygen binding curve by:

A. increasing the carbon carbon-dioxide concentration in the red blood cells.

B. altering the pH of the tissue fluid surrounding the red blood cells.

C. reducing the affinity between oxygen and hemoglobin at low oxygen concentrations.

D. forming a complex with oxygen at low oxygen concentrations.

13) Which of the following tissues most benefits from the shifts in the oxygen-binding curves caused by GBP and myoglobin?

A. Cardiac muscle tissue

B. Skeletal muscle tissue

C. Loose connective tissue

D. Intestinal wall tissue

14) In regions with an increased partial pressure of carbon dioxide, the oxygen dissociation curve is shifted to the right. This is known as the Bohr effect or shift. What is the physiological significance of this shift?

A. It counteracts the shift in the oxygen-binding curve caused by the presence of GBP.

B. It counteracts the shift in the oxygen-binding curve caused by the presence of myoglobin.

C. It increases the pH of actively respiring tissue.

D. It facilitates the delivery of increased quantities of oxygen from the blood to cells which produce energy.

15) Protons, like GBP, bind preferentially to deoxyhemoglobin. Thus, which of the following equations best explains the Bohr shift?

A. $CO_2 + H_2O \leftrightarrow H_2CO_3 \leftrightarrow H^+ + HCO_3^-$
(tissues)

B. $H^+ + HbO_2 \leftrightarrow HHb^+ + O_2$ (tissues)

C. $HCO_3^- + H^+ \leftrightarrow H_2CO_3 \leftrightarrow CO_2 + H_2O$ (lungs)

D. $HHb^+ + O_2 + HCO_3^- \leftrightarrow HbO_2 + CO_2 + H_2O$
(lungs)

16) Would the walls of the atria or ventricles expected to be thicker?

A. Atria, because blood ejection due to atrial contraction is high.

B. Atria, because blood ejection due to atrial contraction is low.

C. Ventricles, because ventricular stroke volume is high.

D. Ventricles, because ventricular stroke volume is low.

GS ANSWER KEY

CHAPTER 7

		Cross-Reference
1.	A	BIO 7.2, 7.3
2.	D	BIO 7.3
3.	A	BIO 7.3
4.	C	BIO 7.2, 7.3, 7.5.1
5.	B	BIO 7.3
6.	B	BIO 7.5.1
7.	C	BIO 3.0, 4.3, 7.5.1
8.	D	BIO 7.5.1

		Cross-Reference
9.	D	BIO 7.1
10.	B	BIO 7.5
11.	B	BIO 7.5.1
12.	C	BIO 7.5.1
13.	B	BIO 4.2, 11.2
14.	D	BIO 4.4-4.5, 7.5.1, 12.4.1
15.	B	BIO 7.5.1
16.	C	BIO 7.2

⋆ Explanations can be found at the back of the book.

Go online to DAT-prep.com for additional chapter review Q&A and forum.

APPENDIX

CHAPTER 7: The Circulatory System

Advanced DAT-30 Passage: The Cardiac Cycle

The cardiac cycle is the series of events comprising a complete contraction and relaxation of the heart's four chambers. The process of depolarization in the SA node (BIO 11.2) triggers the cardiac cycle which normally lasts about 0.22 seconds. The electronics of the cycle can be monitored by an electrocardiogram (EKG). The cycle is divided into two major phases, both named for events in the ventricle: the period of ventricular contraction and blood ejection, *systole*, followed by the period of ventricular relaxation and blood filling, *diastole*.

During the very first part of systole, the ventricles are contracting but all valves in the heart are closed thus no blood can be ejected. Once the rising pressure in the ventricles becomes great enough to open the aortic and pulmonary valves, the ventricular ejection or systole occurs. Blood is forced into the aorta and pulmonary trunk as the contracting ventricular muscle fibers shorten. The volume of blood ejected from a ventricle during systole is termed *stroke volume*. The total volume of blood pumped by the heart in one minute is the *cardiac output* (Q) and can be calculated as follows (the equations in this section should be memorized):

$$Q = \text{Stroke Volume} \times \text{Heart rate}$$

An average resting cardiac output would be 4.9 L/min for a human female and 5.6 L/min for a male.

During the very first part of diastole, the ventricles begin to relax, and the aortic and pulmonary valves close. No blood is entering or leaving the ventricles since once again all the valves are closed. Once ventricular pressure falls below atrial pressure, the atrioventricular (AV) valves open (i.e. mitral and tricuspid valves). Atrial contraction occurs towards the end of diastole, after most of the ventricular filling has taken place. The ventricle receives blood throughout most of diastole, not just when the atrium contracts. When the left ventricle is filled to capacity, it is known as End Diastolic Volume (EDV). Ejection fraction (EF) is the fraction of blood ejected by the left ventricle during systole and is usually given as a percentage:

$$EF = (\text{Stroke Volume})/(\text{EDV}) \times 100\%$$

17) Position P on the EKG of Fig. 1 probably correspond to:

A. atrial contraction.

B. ventricular contraction.

C. the beginning of ventricular systole.

D. the beginning of ventricular diastole.

C. during ventricular diastole, blood in the ventricle is forced against the closed atrio-ventricular valve.

D. during ventricular systole, blood in the arteries is forced against the aortic and pulmonary artery pocket valves.

19) The graph below shows the effects on stroke volume of stimulating the sympathetic nerves to the heart.

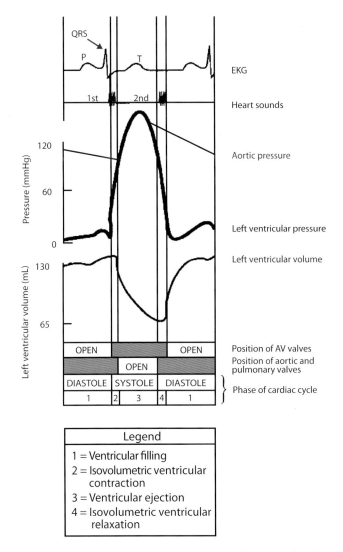

Figure 1: Electronic and pressure changes in the heart and aorta during the cardiac cycle.

Legend
1 = Ventricular filling
2 = Isovolumetric ventricular contraction
3 = Ventricular ejection
4 = Isovolumetric ventricular relaxation

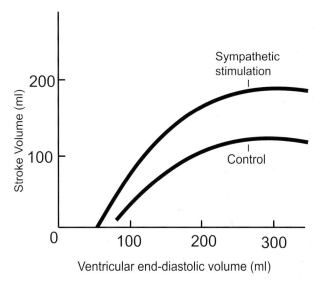

According to the graph, the net result of sympathetic stimulation on ejection fraction is to:

A. approximately double ejection fraction at any given end diastolic volume.

B. decrease ejection fraction at any given end diastolic volume.

C. increase ejection fraction at any given end diastolic volume.

D. leave ejection fraction relatively unchanged.

18) The first heart sound represented in Fig. 1 is probably made when:

A. during ventricular systole, blood in the ventricle is forced against the closed atrio-ventricular valve.

B. during ventricular diastole, blood in the arteries is forced against the aortic and pulmonary artery pocket valves.

20) According to Fig. 1, the opening of the aortic and pulmonary valves is associated with all of the following EXCEPT one. Which one is the EXCEPTION?

A. Ventricular systole
B. A rise and fall in aortic pressure
C. A drop and rise in left ventricular volume
D. The third phase of the cardiac cycle

21) Stroke Volume / End Diastolic Volume is equal to which of the following?

A. Cardiac output
B. Ejection fraction
C. Stroke volume
D. End systolic volume

22) Which of the following correctly defines stroke volume (SV)?

A. SV = cardiac output - end systolic volume
B. SV = end diastolic volume - ejection fraction
C. SV = end systolic volume - end diastolic volume
D. SV = end diastolic volume - end systolic volume

Go online to DAT-prep.com for additional chapter review Q&A and forum.

GOLD NOTES

Memorize	Understand	Importance
es in immunity: T-lymphocytes; _mphocytes _ues in the immune system including _e marrow _en, thymus, lymph nodes	* Concepts of antigen, antibody, interaction * Structure of antibody molecule * Mechanism of stimulation by antigen	**0 to 2 out of the 40 Biology** DAT questions are based on content in this chapter (in our estimation). * Note that between 25% and 50% of the questions in DAT Biology are from 5 chapters: 1, 2, 14, 15, and 16.

DAT-Prep.com

Introduction

The immune system protects against disease. Many processes are used in order to identify and kill various microbes (see Microbiology, Chapter 2, for examples) as well as tumor cells. There are 2 acquired responses of the immune system: cell-mediated and humoral.

Additional Resources

Free Online Q&A + Forum   Video: Online or DVD   Flashcards   Special Guest

The immune system is composed of various cells and organs which defend the body against pathogens, toxins or any other foreign agents. Substances (usu. proteins) on the foreign agent causing an immune response are called **antigens**. There are two acquired responses to an antigen: (1) the **cell mediated response** where T-lymphocytes are the dominant force and act against microorganisms, tumors, and virus infected cells; and (2) the **humoral response** where B-lymphocytes are the dominant force and act against specific proteins present on foreign molecules.

8.2 Cells of the Immune System

B-lymphocytes originate in the bone marrow. Though T-lymphocytes also originate in the bone marrow, they go on to mature in the thymus gland. T-lymphocytes learn with the help of macrophages to recognize and attack only foreign substances (i.e. antigens) in a direct cell to cell manner (= *cell-mediated* or *cellular immunity*). T-lymphocytes have two major subtypes: T-helper cells and T-cytotoxic cells. Some T-cells (T_8, T_C, or T cytotoxic) mediate the apoptosis of foreign cells and virus-infected cells. Some T-cells (T_4, T_H or T *helper*) mediate the cellular response by secreting substances to activate macrophages, other T-cells and even B-cells. {T_H-cells are specifically targeted and killed by the HIV virus in AIDS patients}

B-lymphocytes act indirectly against the foreign agent by producing and secreting antigen-specific proteins called **antibodies**, which are sometimes called immunoglobulins = *humoral immunity*). Antibodies are "designer" proteins which can specifically attack the antigen for which it was designed. The antibodies along with other proteins (i.e. complement proteins) can attack the antigen-bearing particle in many ways:

• **Lysis** by digesting the plasma membrane of the foreign cell

• **Opsonization** which is the altering of cell membranes so the foreign particle is more susceptible to phagocytosis by neutrophils and macrophages

• **Agglutination** which is the clumping of antigen-bearing cells

• **Chemotaxis** which is the attracting of other cells (i.e. phagocytes) to the area

• **Inflammation** which includes migration of cells, release of fluids and dilatation of blood vessels.

The activated antibody secreting B-lymphocyte is called a *plasma cell*. After the first or *primary* response to an antigen, both T- and B-cells produce *memory cells* which are formed during the initial response to an anti-

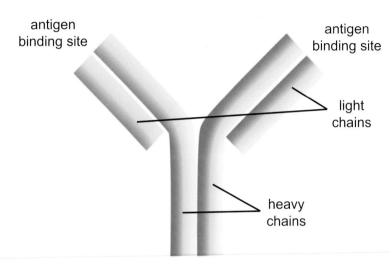

antigen binding site

antigen binding site

light chains

heavy chains

Figure IV.A.8.1: Schematic representation of an antibody. Antibodies are composed of disulfide bond-linked heavy and light chains. The unique part of the antigen recognized by an antibody is called the epitope. The antigen binding site on the antibody is extremely variable (= hypervariable).

Antibody (= Immunoglobulin = Ig)	Description
IgA	Found in saliva, tears and breast milk. Found in mucosal areas, such as the GI, respiratory and urogenital tracts thus prevents colonization by pathogens.
IgD	Functions mainly as an antigen receptor on B-cells that have not been exposed to antigens. Activates mast cells and basophils (BIO 7.5) to produce antimicrobial factors.
IgE	Binds to particles that induce allergic reactions (= allergens) and triggers histamine release from mast cells and basophils. Also protects against parasitic worms.
IgG	In its four forms, provides the majority of antibody-based immunity against invading germs or pathogens. The only antibody capable of crossing the placenta (BIO 14.6) to give passive immunity to the fetus.
IgM	Expressed on the surface of B-cells (monomer) and in a secreted form (pentamer = complex of 5 monomers). Eliminates pathogens in the early stages of B-cell mediated (humoral) immunity before there is sufficient IgG.

Table IV.A.8.1: Antibody isotypes of mammals. Antibodies are grouped into different "isotypes" based on which heavy chain they possess. The five different antibody isotypes known in mammals are displayed in the table.

genic challenge. These memory cells remain in the circulation and will make the next or secondary response much faster and much greater. {Note: though lymphocytes are vital to the immune system, it is the neutrophil which responds to injury first; BIO 7.5}

T-cells cannot recognise, and there-fore react to, 'free' floating antigen. T-cells can only recognize an antigen that has been processed and presented by cells in associa-tion will a special cell surface molecule called the major histocompatibility complex (MHC). In fact, "antigen presenting cells", through the use of MHC, can teach both B-cells and T-cells which antigens are safe (*self*) and which are dangerous and should be attacked (*nonself*). MHC Class I molecules present to T_C cells while MHC Class II molecules pres-ent to T_H cells.

8.3 Tissues of the Immune System

The important tissues of the immune sys-tem are the bone marrow, and the lymphatic organs which include the thymus, the lymph nodes and the spleen. The roles of the bone marrow and the thymus have already been discussed. It is of value to add that the thymus secretes a hormone (= *thymosin*) which appears to help stimulate the activity of T-lymphocytes.

Lymph nodes are often the size of a pea and are found in groups or chains along the paths of the larger lymphatic vessels. Their functions can be broken down into three general categories: i) a non-specific filtration of bacteria and other particles from the lymph using the phagocytic activity of macrophages; ii) the storage and prolifera-tion of T-cells, B-cells and antibody produc-tion; (iii) initiate immune response on the recognition of antigen.

The **spleen** is the largest lymphatic organ and is situated in the upper left part of the abdominal cavity. Within its lobules it has tissue called red and white pulp. The white pulp of the spleen contains all of the organ's lymphoid tissue (T-cells, B-cells, macro-phages, and other antigen presenting cells) and is the site of active immune responses via the proliferation of T- and B-lymphocytes and the production of antibodies by plasma cells. The red pulp is composed of several types of blood cells including red blood cells, platelets and granulocytes. Its main function is to filter the blood of antigen and phagocy-tose damaged or aged red blood cells (the latter has a lifespan of approximately 110-120 days). In addition, the red pulp of the spleen is a site for red blood cell storage (i.e. a blood storage organ).

Autoimmunity!

Figure IV.A.8.2: Actually, "autoimmunity" refers to a disease process where the immune system attacks one's own cells and tissues as opposed to one's own car.

8.4 Advanced Topic: ELISA

ELISA, enzyme-linked-immunosorbent serologic assay, is a rapid test used to determine if a particular protein is in a sample and, if so, to quantify it (= assay). ELISA relies on an enzymatic conversion reaction and an antibody-antigen interaction which would lead to a detectable signal – usually a color change. Consequently, ELISA has no need of any radioisotope nor any radiation-counting apparatus.

There are 2 forms of ELISA: (1) direct ELISA uses monoclonal antibodies to detect antigen in a sample; (2) indirect ELISA is used to find a specific antibody in a sample (i.e. HIV antibodies in serum). {Notice the similarity with the concept of "direct" and "indirect" immunofluorescence, BIO 1.5.1}

GOLD STANDARD WARM-UP EXERCISES

CHAPTER 8: The Immune System

1) Helper T-cells are required to activate:

   A. hemoglobin and T lymphocytes.
   B. thrombocytes and B lymphocytes.
   C. B lymphocytes and T lymphocytes.
   D. erythrocytes and thrombocytes.

2) The retrovirus HIV infects primarily the helper T cells by making specific interactions with the cell's receptors. What must first occur in order for the retrovirus to infect the cell?

   A. The protein coat of the virus fuse with the helper T cell plasma membrane.
   B. The viral envelope must make contact and be recognized by helper T cell receptors.
   C. The viral RNA must be translated.
   D. The helper T cell must engulf the virus via phagocytosis.

3) Before being injected into humans as a vaccine, the hepatitis B virus (HBV) would first have to:

   A. be cloned in yeast cells to ensure that enough of the virus had been injected to elicit an immune response.
   B. have its protein coat removed.
   C. be purified.
   D. be inactivated.

4) The following graph shows the immune response for an initial injection of Hepatitis B Surface Antigen (HBsAg) and a subsequent injection of the HBV virus. Which of the following best explains the differences in the two responses?

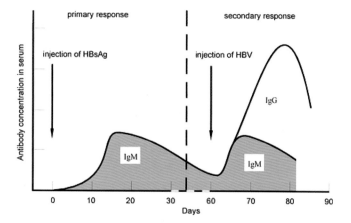

   A. During the initial response, the immune response was carried out primarily by macrophages and B-lymphocytes.
   B. During the secondary response, T-cells possessing membrane receptors, recognized and attacked the viral antigens.
   C. Memory cells produced by T- and B-cells during the first exposure made the second response faster and more intense.
   D. Memory cells produced by macrophages during the first infection recognized the viral antigens more quickly during the second infection, causing antibody production to be increased.

5) In terms of immunity, what is the major disadvantage of injecting monoclonal antibodies directly into the circulatory system instead of an inactivated form of the antigen?

A. Activated antigens can cause infection.
B. The immune response is faster when the inactivated antigen is injected.
C. The antibodies injected are often recognized as antigens by the immune system, thereby eliciting an immune response.
D. No memory cells are produced when the monoclonal antibody is directly injected into the circulatory system.

6) Which of the following biological processes would be inhibited by the removal of an adult human spleen?

A. The production of erythrocytes
B. The production of macrophages
C. The production of T-lymphocytes
D. The destruction of erythrocytes

7) Tissue transplantation is a technique which also can stimulate an immune response in recipients. Several methods are used to prevent rejection. These might include all but which of the following?

A. Exposure of the tissue to be transplanted to X-irradiation to prevent infection from occurring
B. Exposure of bone marrow and lymph tissues to X-irradiation
C. Immunosuppression
D. Tissue matching

8) Each antibody molecule is made up of how many PAIR of polypeptide chains joined together by disulfide bonds?

A. 1
B. 2
C. 3
D. 4

9) The immune system normally discriminates between which types of antigens?

A. Primary and secondary
B. Humoral and cell-mediated
C. B and T cells
D. Self and non-self

10) Surplus red blood cells, needed to meet an emergency, are MAINLY stored in what organ of the human body?

A. Spleen
B. Liver
C. Yellow marrow
D. Pancreas

GS ANSWER KEY

CHAPTER 8

		Cross-Reference				Cross-Reference
1.	C	BIO 8.2	6.	D	BIO 8.3
2.	B	BIO 2.1, 2.1.1, 8.2	7.	A	BIO 8.2, deduce
3.	D	BIO 2.1, 8.2	8.	B	BIO 8.2
4.	C	BIO 8.1, 8.2	9.	D	BIO 8.1, 8.2
5.	D	BIO 8.1, 8.2	10.	A	BIO 8.3

* Explanations can be found at the back of the book.

Go online to DAT-prep.com for additional chapter review Q&A and forum.

Go online to DAT-prep.com for additional chapter review Q&A and forum.

Memorize	Understand	Importance
c anatomy of the upper GI and lower racts va as lubrication and enzyme source nach low pH, gastric juice, mucal ection against self-destruction for production of digestive enzymes, of digestion : nutrient metabolism, vitamin storage; d glucose regulation, detoxification	* Basic function of the upper GI and lower GI tracts * Bile: storage in gallbladder, function * Pancreas: production of enzymes; transport of enzymes to small intestine * Small intestine: production of enzymes, site of digestion, neutralize stomach acid * Peristalsis; structure and function of villi, microvilli	**0 to 2 out of the 40 Biology** DAT questions are based on content in this chapter (in our estimation). * Note that between 25% and 50% of the questions in DAT Biology are from 5 chapters: 1, 2, 14, 15, and 16.

DAT-Prep.com

Introduction

The digestive system is involved in the mechanical and chemical break down of food into smaller components with the aim of absorption into, for example, blood or lymph. Thus digestion is a form of catabolism.

Additional Resources

Free Online Q&A + Forum

Video: Online or DVD

Flashcards

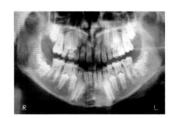

Special Guest

9.1 Overview

The digestive or *gastrointestinal* (= GI) system is principally concerned with the intake and reduction of food into subunits for absorption. These events occur in five main phases which are located in specific parts of the GI system: i) **ingestion** which is the taking of food or liquid into the mouth; ii) **fragmentation** which is when larger pieces of food are *mechanically* broken down; iii) **digestion** where macromolecules are *chemically* broken down into subunits which can be absorbed; iv) **absorption** through cell membranes; and v) **elimination** of the waste products. The GI system secretes enzymes and hormones that facilitate in the process of ingestion, digestion, absorption as well as elimination.

The GI tract (gut or *alimentary canal*) is a muscular tract about 9 meters long covered by a layer of mucosa which has definable characteristics in each area along the tract. The GI tract includes the oral cavity (mouth), pharynx, esophagus, stomach, small intestine, large intestine, and anus. The GI system includes the accessory organs which release secretions into the tract: the salivary glands, gallbladder, liver, and pancreas (*see Figure IV.A.9.1*).

9.2 The Oral Cavity and Esophagus

Ingestion, fragmentation and digestion begin in the oral cavity. Teeth are calcified, hard structures in the oral cavity used to fragment food (= *mastication*). Children have twenty teeth (= *deciduous*) and adults have thirty-two (= *permanent*). From front to back, each quadrant (= *quarter)* of the mouth contains: two incisors for cutting, one cuspid (= *canine*) for tearing, two bicuspids (= *premolars*) for crushing, and three molars for grinding.

Digestion of food begins in the oral cavity when the 3 pairs of salivary glands (*parotid, sublingual*, and *submandibular*) synthesize and secrete saliva. Saliva lubricates the oral cavity, assists in the process of deglutition, controls bacterial flora and initiates the process of digestion. Its production is unique in that it is increased by both sympathetic and parasympathetic innervation. Major components of saliva include salivary amylase, lysozyme, lingual lipase and mucus. Amylase is an enzyme which starts the initial digestion of carbohydrates by splitting starch and glycogen into disaccharide subunits. Lipase is an enzyme which starts the initial digestion of triglyceride (fats). The mucous helps to bind food particles together and lubricate it as it is swallowed.

Swallowing (= *deglutition*) occurs in a coordinated manner in which the tongue and pharyngeal muscles propel the bolus of food into the esophagus while at the same time the upper esophageal sphincter relaxes to permit food to enter. The epiglottis is a small flap of

Basic Dental Anatomy and Pathology

32 Adult Teeth
8 Teeth per Quadrant

| 3 molars | 2 premolars | 1 canine | 2 incisors |

Pathology
• Cavity (C): hole left by infection, tooth decay.
• Filling (F): fills the cavity with metal or composite.
• Bridge (B): false tooth supported by metal.
• Wisdom Tooth (WT; 3rd molar): blocked from erupting (*impaction* likely).

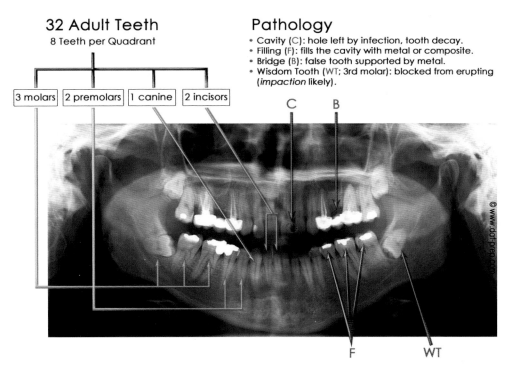

Figure IV.A.9.0a: Dental X-ray of an adult. The pathology of teeth is not prerequisite knowledge for the DAT and is only presented for your interest (and as a minor contribution to your future studies!).

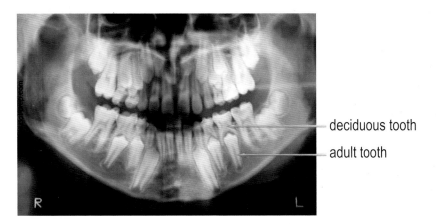

deciduous tooth
adult tooth

Figure IV.A.9.0b: Dental X-ray of a child showing deciduous (AKA: baby, primary, milk, temporary) teeth and emerging adult (permanent) teeth. Note the "R" on the X-ray indicates the right side of the patient who is facing the observer.

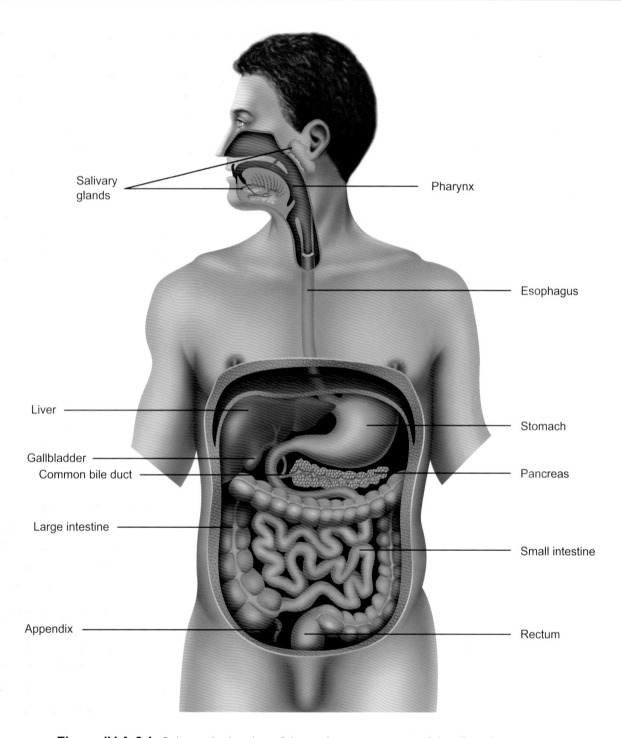

Figure IV.A.9.1: Schematic drawing of the major components of the digestive system.

tissue which covers the opening to the airway (= *glottis*) while swallowing. Gravity and peristalsis help bring the food through the esophagus to the stomach.

The GI system is supplied by both extrinsic innervation and intrinsic innervation. The extrinsic innervation includes the sympathetic and parasympathetic nervous system. The parasympathetic nervous system, mediated by the vagus and pelvic nerves, usually stimulates the functions of the GI tract while the sympathetic nervous system usually inhibits the functions of the GI tract. The intrinsic innervation located in the gut wall includes the *myenteric nerve plexus* and *submucosal nerve plexus* which control GI tract motility including peristalsis.

Peristalsis, which is largely the result of two muscle layers in the GI tract (i.e. the inner circular and outer longitudinal layers), is the sequential wave-like muscular contractions which propell food along the tract. The rate, strength and velocity of muscular contractions are modulated by the ANS.

9.3 The Stomach

The stomach continues in fragmenting and digesting the food with its strong muscular activity, its acidic gastric juice and various digestive enzymes present in the gastric juice. The walls of the stomach are lined by thick mucosa which contains goblet cells. These goblet cells of the GI tract protect the lumen from the acidic environment by secreting mucous.

The important components of gastric juice are: i) HCl which keeps the pH low (approximately = 2) to kill microorganisms, to aid in partial hydrolysis of proteins, and to provide the environment for ii) *pepsinogen*, an inactive form of enzyme (= *zymogen*) secreted by gastric chief cells, which is later converted to its active form *pepsin* in the presence of a low pH. Pepsin is involved in the breakdown of proteins. Both the hormone gastrin, which is produced in the stomach; and parasympathetic impulses can increase the production of gastric juice.

The preceding events turns food into a semi-digested fluid called chyme. Chyme is squirted through a muscular sphincter in the stomach, the *pyloric sphincter*, into the first part of the small intestine, the *duodenum*. Many secretions are produced by exocrine glands in the liver and pancreas and enter the duodenum via the *common bile duct*. Exocrine secretions eventually exit the body through ducts. For example, *goblet cells*, which are found in the stomach and throughout the intestine, are exocrine secretory cells which produce mucus which lines the epithelium of the gastrointestinal tract.

9.4.1 The Liver

The liver occupies the upper right part of the abdominal cavity. It has many roles including: the conversion of glucose to glycogen; the synthesis of glucose from non-carbohydrates; the production of plasma proteins; the destruction of red blood cells; the deamination of amino acids and the formation of urea; the conversion of toxic ammonia to much less toxic urea (the urea cycle); the storage of iron and certain vitamins; the alteration of toxic substances and most medicinal products (*detoxification*); and its exocrine role - the production of **bile** by liver cells (= *hepatocytes*).

Bile is a yellowish - green fluid mainly composed of water, cholesterol, pigments (from the destruction of red blood cells)

and salts. It is the **bile salts** which have a digestive function by the emulsification of fats. Emulsification is the dissolving of fat globules into tiny droplets called *micelles* which have hydrophobic interiors and hydrophilic exteriors (cf. Plasma Membrane, BIO 1.1). Bile salts orient themselves around those lipid droplets with their hydrophilic portions towards the aqueous environment and their hydrophobic portions towards the micelle interior and keep them dispersed. Emulsification also helps in the absorption of the fat soluble vitamins A, D, E, and K.

Thus bile is produced by the liver, stored and concentrated in a small muscular sac, the **gallbladder**, and then secreted into the duodenum via the common bile duct.

9.4.2 The Pancreas

The pancreas is close to the duodenum and extends behind the stomach. The pancreas has both endocrine (*see Endocrine Systems; BIO 6.3.4*) and exocrine functions. It secretes pancreatic juice, which consists of alkaline fluid and digestive enzymes, into the pancreatic duct that joins the common bile duct. Pancreatic juice is secreted both due to parasympathetic and hormonal stimuli. The hormones *secretin* and *CCK* are produced and released by the duodenum in response

to the presence of chyme. Secretin acts on the pancreatic ductal cells to stimulate HCO_3^- secretion, whose purpose is to neutralize the acidic chyme. CCK acts on pancreatic acinar cells to stimulate the exocrine pancreatic secretion of digestive enzymes. These enzymes are secreted as enzymes or proenzymes (= *zymogens*; BIO 4.3) that must be activated in the intestinal lumen. The enzymes include pancreatic amylase, which can break down carbohydrates into monosaccharides; pancreatic lipase, which can break down fats into fatty acids and monoglycerides; and nuclease, which can break down nucleic acids. The protein enzymes

(proteases) include trypsin, chymotrypsin, carboxypeptidase, which can break down proteins into amino acids, dipeptides or tripeptides.

9.5 The Intestines

The **small intestine** is divided into the duodenum, the jejunum, and the ileum, in that order. It is this part of the GI system that completes the digestion of chyme, absorbs the nutrients (i.e. monosaccharides, amino acids, nucleic acids, etc.), and passes the rest onto the large intestine. Peristalsis is the primary mode of transport. Contraction behind the bolus and simultaneous relaxation in front of the bolus propel chyme forward. Segmentation also aids in small intestine movement - it helps to mix the intestinal contents without any forward movement of chyme. Of course, parasympathetic impulses increase intestinal smooth muscle contraction while sympathetic impulses decrease intestinal smooth muscle contraction.

Absorption is aided by the great surface area involved including the finger-like projections **villi** and **microvilli** (*see the Generalized Eukaryotic Cell*, BIO 1.1F and 1.2). Intestinal villi, which increase the surface area ten-fold, are evaginations into the lumen of the small intestine and contain blood capillaries and a single lacteal (lymphatic capillary). Microvilli, which increase the surface area twenty-fold, contain a dense

bundle of actin microfilaments cross-linked by proteins fimbrin and villin.

Absorption of carbohydrates, proteins and lipids is completed in the small intestine. Carbohydrates must be broken down into glucose, galactose and fructose for absorption to occur. In contrast, proteins can be absorbed as amino acids, dipeptides and tripeptides. Specific transporters are required for amino acids and peptides to facilitate the absorption across the luminal membrane. Lipids are absorbed in the form of fatty acids, monoglycerides and cholesterol. In the intestinal cells, they are re-esterified to triglycerides, cholesterol ester and phospholipids.

The lacteals absorb most fat products into the lymphatic system while the blood capillaries absorb the rest taking these nutrients to the liver for processing via a special vein - the *hepatic portal vein* [A portal vein carries blood from one capillary bed to another; BIO 7.3]. Goblet cells secrete a copious amount of mucus in order to lubricate the passage of material through the intestine and to protect the epithelium from abrasive chemicals (i.e. acids, enzymes, etc.).

Intestinal folds (plicae circulares)

Cross-section of the small intestine.

Blood vessels

Lacteal

4 intestinal villi.

Microvilli

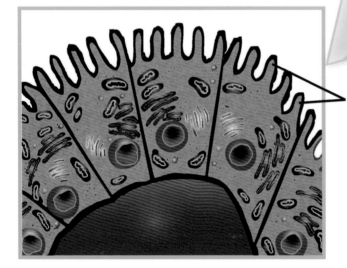

Columnar cells (i.e. intestinal cells arranged in columns) with microvilli facing the lumen (brush border).

Figure IV.A.9.2: Levels of organization of the small intestine.

9.5.1 The Large Intestines

The large intestine is divided into: the cecum which connects to the ileum and projects a closed-ended tube - the appendix; the <u>colon</u> which is subdivided into ascending, transverse, descending, and sigmoid portions; <u>the rectum</u> which can store feces; and <u>the anal canal</u> which can expel feces (*defecation*) through the anus with the relaxation of the anal sphincter and the increase in abdominal pressure. The large intestine has little or no digestive functions. It absorbs water and electrolytes from the residual chyme and it forms feces. Feces is mostly water, undigested material, mucous, bile pigments (responsible for the characteristic color) and bacteria (= gut flora = 60% of the dry weight of feces).

Essentially, the relationship between the gut and bacteria is mutualistic and symbiotic (BIO 2.2). Though people can survive with no bacterial flora, these microorganisms perform a host of useful functions, such as fermenting unused energy substrates, training the immune system, preventing growth of harmful species, producing vitamins for the host (i.e. vitamin K), and bile pigments.

GOLD STANDARD WARM-UP EXERCISES

CHAPTER 9: The Digestive System

1) Cellulose is likely not broken down in the small intestine because:

   A. it is actively transported from the lumen of the intestine, across the epithelial lining, in the polysaccharide form.

   B. mastication, salivary amylase and enzymes in the upper part of the stomach completely break it down before it reaches the small intestine.

   C. humans do not possess the enzymes that break down cellulose.

   D. it is needed to propagate the necessary bacterial population in the large intestine.

2) In addition to starch, which of the following substances is also broken down by enzymes in the stomach?

   A. Glucose

   B. Fatty acids

   C. Protein

   D. Glycerol

3) After a meal rich in carbohydrates, monosaccharides are likely transported across the epithelium primarily by:

   A. diffusion.

   B. exocytosis.

   C. endocytosis.

   D. carrier mediated transport.

4) From the lumen of the small intestine, fat products are absorbed by and transported to:

   A. bile salts and the liver, respectively.

   B. bile salts and the lymphatic system, respectively.

   C. lacteals directly to the liver.

   D. lacteals and the lymphatic system, respectively.

5) Along with gastric acid, a zymogen exists in the stomach. The enzyme exists in this form in order to:

   A. prevent the enzyme's degradation while the stomach is empty.

   B. prevent the enzyme from neutralizing the gastric acid in the stomach.

   C. enhance the enzyme's activity.

   D. prevent the enzyme from digesting the cells which produce it.

6) A clogging of the bile duct interferes with the digestion of what category of food?

   A. Fats

   B. Fat soluble vitamins

   C. Triacyl glycerols

   D. All of the above

7) Extracts of the intestinal parasite Ascaris were found to contain irreversible non-competitive inhibitors of human enzymes. The enzymes were likely:

   A. HMG CoA synthetase and lyase.

   B. kinase and carboxypeptidase.

   C. trypsin and pepsin.

   D. hexokinase and vitamin D.

GS ANSWER KEY

CHAPTER 9

Cross-Reference

1.	C	BIO 9.5; ORG 12.3.3; deduce
2.	C	BIO 9.3
3.	D	BIO 1.1.2
4.	D	BIO 9.5
5.	D	BIO 4.3, 9.3, 9.4
6.	D	BIO 9.4.1; ORG 12.4
7.	C	9.3, 9.4.2; cf BIO 4.1, 4.2

* Explanations can be found at the back of the book.

Go online to DAT-prep.com for additional chapter review Q&A and forum.

Go online to DAT-prep.com for additional chapter review Q&A and forum.

GOLD NOTES

Memorize	Understand	Importance
...ney structure: cortex, medulla ...hron structure: glomerulus, ...man's capsule, proximal tubule, etc. ... of Henle, distal tubule, ...cting duct ...age and elimination: ureter, ...der, urethra	* Roles of the excretory system in homeostasis * Blood pressure, osmoregulation, acid-base balance, N waste removal * Formation of urine: glomerular filtration, secretion and reabsorption of solutes * Concentration of urine; counter-current multiplier mechanism	**0 to 2 out of the 40 Biology** DAT questions are based on content in this chapter (in our estimation). * Note that between 25% and 50% of the questions in DAT Biology are from 5 chapters: 1, 2, 14, 15, and 16.

DAT-Prep.com

Introduction

The excretory system excretes waste. The focus of this chapter is to examine the kidney's role in excretion. This includes eliminating nitrogen waste products of metabolism such as urea.

Additional Resources

Free Online Q&A + Forum   Video: Online or DVD   Flashcards   Special Guest

Excretion is the elimination of substances (usu. wastes) from the body. It begins at the level of the cell. Broken down red blood cells are excreted as bile pigments into the GI tract; CO_2, an end product of cellular aerobic respiration, is blown away in the lungs; urea and ammonia (NH_3), breakdown products of amino acid metabolism, creatinine, a product of muscle metabolism, and H_2O, a breakdown product of aerobic metabolism, are eliminated by the urinary system. In fact, the urinary system eliminates such a great quantity of waste it is often called the excretory system. It is composed of a pair of kidneys, a pair of ureters and one bladder and urethra.

The composition of body fluids remains within a fairly narrow range. The urinary system is the dominant organ system involved in electrolyte and water homeostasis (*osmoregulation*). It is also responsible for the excretion of toxic nitrogenous compounds (i.e. urea, uric acid, creatinine) and many drugs into the urine. The urine is produced in the kidneys (mostly by the filtration of blood) and is transported, with the help of peristaltic waves, down the tubular ureters to the muscular sack which can store urine, the bladder. Through the process of urination (= *micturition*), urine is expelled from the bladder to the outside via a tubular urethra.

The amount of volume within blood vessels (= *intravascular* or blood volume) and blood pressure are proportional to the rate the kidneys filter blood. Hormones act on the kidney to affect urine formation (*see Endocrine Systems*, BIO 6.3).

10.2 Kidney Structure

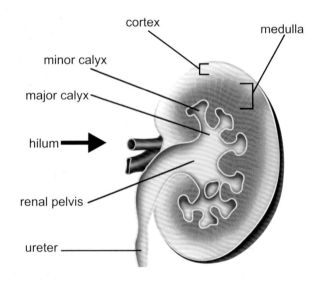

cortex

medulla

minor calyx

major calyx

hilum

renal pelvis

ureter

Figure IV.A.10.1: Kidney structure.

The kidney regulates the electrolyte levels in the extracellular fluid and maintains water homeostasis through the production and excretion of urine. The kidney resembles a bean with a concave border (= *the hilum*) where the ureter, nerves, and vessels (blood and lymph) attach. The kidney can be grossly divided into an outer granular-looking **cortex** and an inner dark striated **medulla**. The upper end of the ureter expands into the *renal pelvis* which can be divided into two or three *major calyces*. Each major calyx can be divided into several small branched *minor calyces*. The renal medulla lies deep to the cortex. It is composed of 10-18 medullary pyramids which consist mainly of loop of Henle and collecting tubules. The renal cortex is the superficial layer of the kidney right underneath the capsule. It is composed mainly of renal corpuscles and convoluted tubules.

The kidney is a *filtration-reabsorption-secretion* (excretion) organ. These events are clearly demonstrated at the level of the nephron.

10.3 The Nephron

The nephron is the functional unit of the kidney and consists of the **renal corpuscle** and the **renal tubule**. A renal corpuscle is responsible for the filtration of blood and is composed of a tangled ball of blood capillaries (= *the glomerulus*) and a sac-like structure which surrounds the glomerulus (= *Bowman's capsule*). *Afferent* and *efferent* arterioles lead towards and away from the glomerulus, respectively. The renal tubule is divided into *proximal* and *distal convoluted tubules* with a *loop of Henle* in between. The tube ends in a *collecting duct*.

Blood plasma is **filtered** by the glomerulus through three layers before entering Bowman's capsule. The first layer is formed by the *endothelial cells* of the capillary that possess small holes (= *fenestrae*); the second layer is the *glomerular basement membrane* (BIO 5.3); and the third layer is formed by the negatively charged cells (= *podocytes*) in Bowman's capsule which help repel proteins (most proteins are negatively charged).

The filtration barrier permits passage of water, ions, and small particles from the capillary into Bowman's capsule but prevents pas-

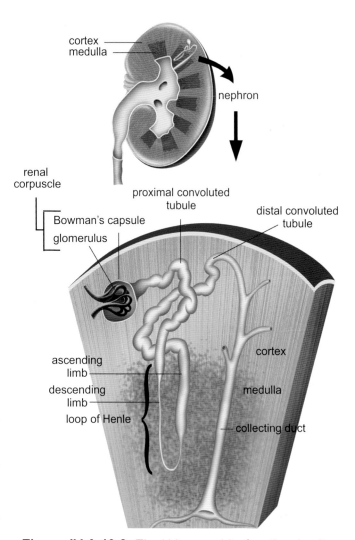

Figure IV.A.10.2: The kidney and its functional unit, the nephron.

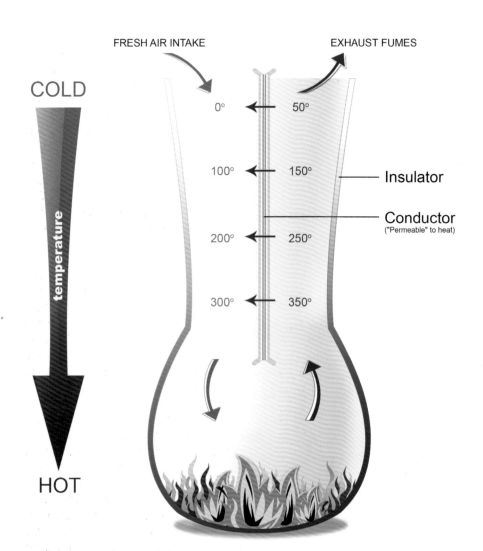

COLD

temperature

HOT

FRESH AIR INTAKE

EXHAUST FUMES

0° ← 50°

100° ← 150° ── Insulator

── Conductor
("Permeable" to heat)

200° ← 250°

300° ← 350°

The countercurrent principle depends on a parallel flow arrangement moving in 2 different directions (countercurrent) in close proximity to each other. Our example is that of the air intake and exhaust pipe in this simplified schematic of a furnace.

Heat is transferred from the exhaust fumes to the incoming air.

The small horizontal temperature gradient of only 50° is multiplied longitudinally to a gradient of 300°. This conserves heath that would otherwise be lost.

Furnace

Figure IV.A.10.3: The countercurrent principle (= counter-current mechanism) using a simplified furnace as an example.

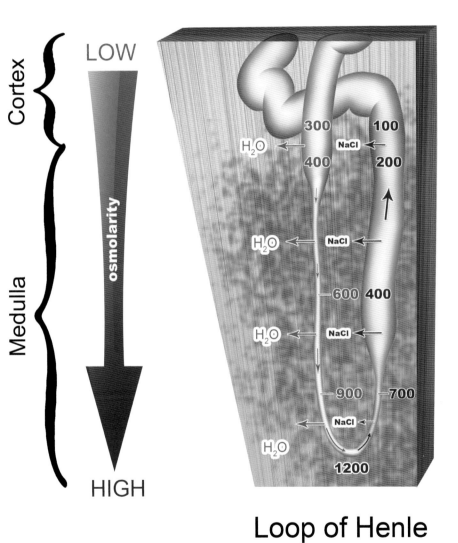

The countercurrent system involving the loop of Henle results in an osmotic gradient increasing from cortex to inner medulla (*juxtamedullary* nephrons). Solutes enter and exit at different segments of the nephron. The descending limb of the loop of Henle is highly permeable to water and relatively impermeable to NaCl (thus the filtrate becomes increasingly hypertonic). The ascending limb is impermeable to water but relatively (through active transport) permeable to NaCl.

Due to the increased osmolarity of the interstitial fluid, water moves out of the descending limb into the interstitial fluid by osmosis. Volume of the filtrate decreases as water leaves. Osmotic concentration of the filtrate increases (1200) as it rounds the hairpin turn of the loop of Henle.

Some of the NaCl leaving the ascending limb moves by diffusion into the descending limb from the interstitial fluid thus increasing the solute concentration in the descending limb. Also, new NaCl in the filtrate continuously enters the tubule inflow to be transported out of the ascending limb into the interstitial fluid. Thus this recycling multiplies NaCl concentration.

Figure IV.A.10.4: The countercurrent principle (= counter-current mechanism) in the loop of Henle.

sage of large/negatively charged particles (= *ultrafiltration*) and forms a filtrate in the Bowman's space. The rate of filtration is proportional to the net ultrafiltration pressure across the glomerular capillaries. This net pressure, which is usually positive and favors fluid filtration out of the capillary, can be derived from the difference between glomerular capillary hydrostatic pressure, which favors fluid out of the capillary, and the combined effect of glomerular capillary oncotic pressure and Bowman's space *hydrostatic* pressure, which favor fluid back into the capillary. {The oncotic pressure of Bowman's space is typically zero, so it is ignored here; keep in mind that 'oncotic pressure' is simply the osmotic pressure caused by proteins; see BIO 7.5.2}

The <u>filtrate</u>, which is similar to plasma but with minimal proteins, now passes into the proximal convoluted tubule (PCT). It is here that the body actively **reabsorbs** compounds that it needs (i.e. proteins, amino acids, and especially glucose); and over 75% of all ions and water are reabsorbed by *obligate* (= required) reabsorption from the PCT. To increase the surface area for absorption, the cells of the PCT have a lot of microvilli (= *brush border*, cf. BIO 1.2). Some substances like H^+, urea and penicillin are **secreted** into the PCT.

From the PCT the filtrate goes through the descending and ascending limbs of the loop of Henle which extend into the renal medulla. The purpose of the loop of Henle is to concentrate the filtrate by the transport of ions (Na^+ and Cl^-) into the medulla which produces an osmotic gradient (= *a countercurrent mechanism*). As a consequence of this system, the medulla of the kidney becomes concentrated with ions and tends to "pull" water out of the renal tubule by osmosis.

The filtrate now passes on to the distal convoluted tubule (DCT) which reabsorbs ions actively and water passively and secretes various ions (i.e. H^+). Hormones can modulate the reabsorption of substances from the DCT (= *facultative* reabsorption). Aldosterone acts at the DCT to absorb Na^+ which is coupled to the secretion of K^+ and the passive retention of H_2O.

Finally the filtrate, now called urine, passes into the collecting duct which drains into larger and larger ducts which lead to renal papillae, calyces, the renal pelvis, and then the ureter. ADH concentrates urine by increasing the permeability of the DCT and the collecting ducts allowing the medulla to draw water out by osmosis. Water returns to the circulation via a system of vessels called the *vasa recta*.

Renin is a hormone (BIO 6.3.5) which is secreted by cells that are "near the glomerulus" (= *juxtaglomerular cells*). At the beginning of the DCT is a region of modified tubular cells which can influence the secretion of renin (= *macula densa*). The juxtaglomerular cells and the macula densa are collectively known as the juxtaglomerular apparatus.

10.4 The Bladder

Urine flow through the ureters to the bladder is propelled by muscular contractions of the ureter wall - peristalsis. The urine is stored in the bladder and intermittently ejected during urination, termed micturition.

The bladder is a balloon-like chamber with walls of muscle collectively termed the detrusor muscle. The contraction of this muscle squeezes the urine into the lumen (= *space inside*) of the bladder to produce urination. That part of the detrusor muscle at the base of the bladder, where the urethra begins, functions as a sphincter - the internal urethral sphincter. Beyond the outlet of the urethra is the external urethral sphincter, the contraction of which can prevent urination even when the detrusor muscle contracts strongly.

The basic micturition reflex is a spinal reflex (BIO 6.1.3), which can be influenced by descending pathways from the brain. The bladder wall contains stretch receptors whose afferent fibers enter the spinal cord and stimulate the parasympathetic nerves that supply and stimulate the detrusor muscle. As the bladder fills with urine, the pressure within it increases and the stretch receptors are stim-ulated, thereby reflexively eliciting stimulation of the parasympathetic neurons and contractions of the detrusor muscle. When the bladder reaches a certain volume, the induced contraction of the detrusor muscle becomes strong enough to open the internal urethral sphincter. Simultaneously, the afferent input from the stretch receptors inhibits, within the spinal cord, the motor neurons that tonically stimulate the external urethral sphincter to contract. Both sphincters are now open and the contraction of the detrusor muscle is able to produce urination.

In summary:

- The internal sphincter is a continuation of the detrusor muscle and is thus composed of smooth muscle under involuntary or autonomic control. This is the primary muscle for preventing the release of urine.

- The external sphincter is made of skeletal muscle is thus under voluntary control of the somatic nervous system (BIO 6.1.4, 6.1.5, 11.2).

GOLD STANDARD WARM-UP EXERCISES

CHAPTER 10: The Excretory System

1) The functional unit of the kidney is the:
   A. renal corpuscle.
   B. Bowman's capsule.
   C. major calyx.
   D. nephron.

2) Through the process of micturition, urine is expelled from the bladder into the:
   A. urethra.
   B. ureter.
   C. major calyx.
   D. minor calyx.

3) In studies of the human body, which of the following terms is used to describe the first step in the production of urine?
   A. Minor calyces
   B. Glomerular filtration
   C. Tubular reabsorption
   D. Tubular secretion

4) In mammals, the primary function of the loop of Henle is:
   A. bicarbonate reabsorption.
   B. reabsorption of water.
   C. ammonia secretion.
   D. water secretion.

5) The internal urethral sphincter is:
   A. closed when the detrusor muscle is relaxed.
   B. open when the detrusor muscle is relaxed.
   C. not under the direct control of the detrusor muscle.
   D. innervated directly by motor neurons extending from the descending pathways.

6) Which of the following is the countercurrent multiplier in the kidney?
   A. Bowman's capsule around the glomerulus
   B. The proximal convoluted tubules
   C. The loop of Henle of a juxtamedullary nephron
   D. The vasa recta

7) Relative to the capillaries, the fluid in the descending limb of the loop of Henle is which of the following?
   A. Strongly hypotonic
   B. Weakly hypotonic
   C. Hypertonic
   D. Isotonic

8) Most tubular reabsorption occurs at the level of the:
   A. glomerulus.
   B. proximal convoluted tubule.
   C. loop of Henle.
   D. distal convoluted tubule.

9) The internal and external urethral sphincters consist of:
   A. skeletal and smooth muscle, respectively.
   B. skeletal muscle and connective tissue, respectively.
   C. smooth muscle and skeletal muscle, respectively.
   D. smooth muscle and connective tissue, respectively.

GS ANSWER KEY

CHAPTER 10

		Cross-Reference
1.	D	BIO 10.3
2.	A	BIO 10.1
3.	B	BIO 10.3
4.	B	BIO 10.3
5.	A	BIO 10.4

		Cross-Reference
6.	C	BIO 10.3
7.	C	BIO 10.3
8.	B	BIO 10.3, 1.1.1, 7.5.2
9.	C	BIO 10.4, 11.2

⋆ Explanations can be found at the back of the book.

Go online to DAT-prep.com for additional chapter review Q&A and forum.

<table>
<tr><th>Memorize</th><th>Understand</th><th>Importance</th></tr>
</table>

Memorize	Understand	Importance
icture of three basic muscle types: ated, smooth, cardiac intary/involuntary muscles; sympa- tic/parasympathetic innervation ics: cartilage, ligaments, tendons ie basics: structure, calcium/protein rix, growth	* Muscle system, important functions * Support, mobility, peripheral circulatory assistance, thermoregulation (shivering reflex) * Control: motor neurons, neuromuscular junctions, motor end plates * Skeletal system: structural rigidity/support, calcium storage, physical protection * Skeletal structure: specialization of bone types, basic joint, endo/exoskeleton	**0 to 2 out of the 40 Biology** DAT questions are based on content in this chapter (in our estimation). * Note that between 25% and 50% of the questions in DAT Biology are from 5 chapters: 1, 2, 14, 15, and 16.

DAT-Prep.com

Introduction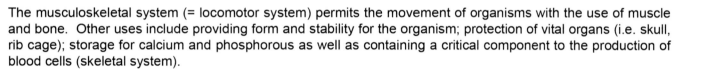

The musculoskeletal system (= locomotor system) permits the movement of organisms with the use of muscle and bone. Other uses include providing form and stability for the organism; protection of vital organs (i.e. skull, rib cage); storage for calcium and phosphorous as well as containing a critical component to the production of blood cells (skeletal system).

Additional Resources

Free Online Q&A + Forum

Flashcards

Special Guest

The musculoskeletal system supports, protects and enables body parts to move. Muscles convert chemical energy (i.e. ATP, creatine phosphate) into mechanical energy (→ contraction). Thus body heat is produced, body fluids are moved (i.e. lymph), and body parts can move in accordance with lever systems of muscle and bone.

11.2 Muscle

There are many general features of muscle. A latent period is the lag between the stimulation of a muscle and its response. A twitch is a single contraction in response to a brief stimulus which lasts for a fraction of a second. Muscles can either *contract* or *relax* but they cannot actively expand. When muscles are stimulated frequently, they cannot fully relax - this is known as *summation.* Tetany is a sustained contraction (a summation of multiple contractions) that lacks even partial relaxation. If tetany is maintained, the muscle will eventually fatigue or tire. Muscle tone (*tonus*) occurs because even when a muscle appears to be at rest, some degree of sustained contraction is occurring.

The cellular characteristics of muscle have already been described (see *Contractile Cells and Tissues,* BIO 5.2). We will now examine the gross features of the three basic muscle types.

Cardiac muscle forms the walls of the heart and is responsible for the pumping action. Its contractions are continuous and are initiated by inherent mechanisms (i.e., they are myogenic) and modulated by the autonomic nervous system. Its activity is decreased by the parasympathetic nervous system and increased by the sympathetic nervous system. The sinoatrial node (SA node) or *pacemaker* contains specialized cardiac muscle cells in the right atrium which initiate the contraction of the heart (BIO 7.2). The electrical signal then progresses to the atrioventricular node (AV node) in the cardiac muscle (myocardium) - between the atria and ventricles - then through the bundle of His which splits and branches out to Purkinje fibers which can then stimulate the contraction of the ventricles (systole; BIO 7.2).

Smooth Muscle has two forms. One type occurs as separate fibers and can contract in response to motor nerve stimuli. These are found in the iris (*pupillary dilation or constriction*) and the walls of blood vessels (*vasodilation or constriction).* The second and more dominant form occurs as sheets of muscle fibers and is sometimes called *visceral muscle*. It forms the walls of many hollow visceral organs like the stomach, intestines, uterus, and the urinary bladder. Like cardiac muscle, its contractions are inherent, involuntary, and rhythmic. Visceral muscle is responsible for peristalsis. Its contractility is usually slow and can be modulated by the autonomic nervous system, hormones, and local metabolites. The activity of visceral muscle is increased by the parasympathetic nervous system and decreased by the sympathetic nervous system.

Skeletal muscle is responsible for voluntary movements. This includes the skeleton and organs such as the tongue and the globe of the eye. Its cells can form a syncytium which is a mass of cells which merge and can function together. Thus skeletal muscle can contract and relax relatively rapidly (*see the Reflex Arc,* BIO 6.1.3).

It should be noted that there are 2 meanings of the word "syncytium" when describing muscle cells. A classic example is the formation of large multinucleated skeletal muscle cells produced from the fusion of thousands of individual muscle cells (= *myocytes*) as alluded to in the previous paragraph ("true syncytium"). However, "syncytium" can also refer to cells that are interconnected by gap junctions (BIO 1.4), as seen in cardiac muscle cells and certain smooth muscle cells, and are thus synchronized electrically during an action potential ("functional syncytium").

Most skeletal muscles act across joints. Each muscle has a movable end (= *the insertion*) and an immovable end (= *the origin*). When a muscle contracts its insertion is moved towards its origin. When the angle of the joint decreases it is called flexion, when it increases it is called extension. Abduction is movement away from the midline of the body and adduction is movement toward the midline. {Adduction is addicted to the middle (= midline)}

Muscles which assist each other are synergistic (for example: while the deltoid muscle abducts the arm, other muscles hold the shoulder steady). Muscles that can move a joint in opposite directions are antagonistic (for example: at the elbow the biceps can flex while the triceps can extend).

Control of skeletal muscle originates in the cerebral cortex. Skeletal muscle is innervated by the somatic nervous system. Motor (*efferent*) neurons carry nerve impulses from the CNS to synapse with muscle fibers at the *neuro-muscular junction*. The terminal end of the motor neuron (motor end plate) can secrete

Skeletal muscle

acetylcholine which can depolarize the muscle fiber (BIO 5.1, 5.2). One motor neuron can depolarize many muscle fibers (= *a motor unit*).

The autonomic nervous system can supply skeletal muscle with more oxygenated blood in emergencies (sympathetic response) or redirect the blood to the viscera during relaxed states (parasympathetic response).

Skeletal muscle can be categorized as Type I or Type II. Type I fibers (= *cells*) appear red because of the oxygen-binding protein myoglobin (BIO 7.5.1). These fibers are suited for endurance and are slow to fatigue since they use oxidative metabolism to generate ATP (BIO 4.7-4.10). Type II fibers are white due to the absence of myoglobin and a reliance on glycolytic enzymes (BIO 4.5, 4.6). These fibers are efficient for short bursts of speed and power and use both oxidative metabolism and anaerobic metabolism depending on the particular sub-type. Type II myocytes are quicker to fatigue.

11.3 The Skeletal System

The microscopic features of bone and cartilage have already been described (*see Connective Cells and Tissues*, BIO 5.4.3/4). We will now examine the relevant gross features of the skeletal system.

The bones of the skeleton have many functions: i) acting like levers that aid in **body movement**; ii) the **storage** of inorganic salts like calcium and phosphorus (and to a lesser extent sodium and magnesium); iii) the production of blood cells (= **hematopoiesis**) in the metabolically active red marrow of the spongy parts of many bones. Bone also has a yellow marrow which contains fat storage cells.

11.3.1 Bone Structure and Development

Bone structure can be classified as follows: i) long bones which have a long shaft, the diaphysis, that is made up mostly of compact bone and expanded ends, like arm and leg bones; ii) short bones which are shaped like long bones but are smaller and have only a thin layer of compact bone surrounding a spongy bone interior; iii) flat bones which have broad surfaces like the skull, ribs, and the scapula and have two layers of compact bones with a layer of spongy bone in the middle; iv) irregular bones like the vertebrae and many facial bones and consist of a thin layer of compact bone covering a spongy bone

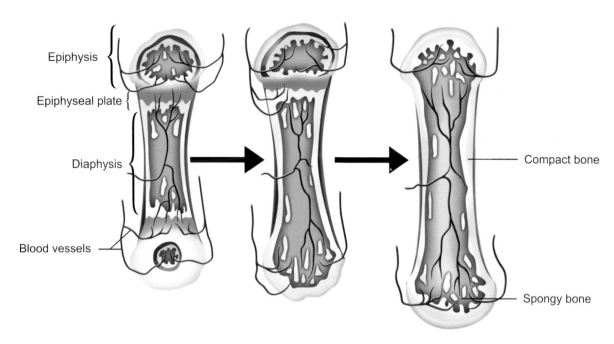

Epiphysis

Epiphyseal plate

Diaphysis

Blood vessels

Compact bone

Spongy bone

Figure IV.A.11.1: Bone structure and development.

interior. Bone structure can also be classified as: i) <u>primary bone</u>, also known as immature or woven bone, which contains many cells and has a low mineral content; ii) <u>secondary bone</u>, also known as mature or lamellar bone, which has a calcified matrix arranged in regular layers, or lamella.

The rounded expanded end of a long bone is called the *epiphysis* which contains <u>spongy bone</u>. The epiphysis is covered by fibrous tissue (*the periosteum*) and it forms a joint with another bone. Spongy bone contains bony plates called *trabeculae (= spicules)*. The shaft of the bone which connects the expanded ends is called the *diaphysis.* It is predominately composed of <u>compact bone</u>. This kind of bone is very strong and resistant to bending and has no trabeculae or bone marrow cavities.

Animals that fly have less dense, more light bones (spongy bone) in order to facilitate flying. Animals that swim do not need to have as strong bones as land animals as the buoyant force of the water takes away from the everyday stress on the bones. In the adult, yellow marrow is likely to be found in the diaphysis while red marrow is likely to be found in the epiphysis.

Bone growth occurs in two ways, intramembranous and endochondral bone formation. Both formations produce bones that are histologically identical. Intramembranous bone formation begins as layers of membranous connective tissue, which are later calcified by osteoblasts. Most of the flat bones are formed by this process. Endochondral bone formation is the process by which most of long bones are formed. It begins with hyaline cartilage that functions as a template for the bone to grow on.

Vascularizaton of the cartilage causes the transformation of cartilage cells to bone cells (osteoblasts), which later form a cartilage-calcified bone matrix. The osteoblasts continue to replace cartilage with bone and the osteoclasts create perforations to form bone marrow cavities. In children one can detect an **epiphyseal growth plate** on X-ray. This plate is a disk of cartilage between the epiphysis and diaphysis where bone is being actively deposited (= *ossification*).

11.3.2 Joint Structure

Articulations or joints are junctions between bones. They can be **immovable** like the dense connective tissue sutures which hold the flat bones of the skull together; **partly movable** like the hyaline and fibrocartilage joints on disks of the vertebrae; or **freely movable** like the synovial joints which are the most prominent joints in the skeletal system. Synovial joints contain a joint capsule composed of outer ligaments and an inner layer (= *the synovial membrane*) which secretes a lubricant (= *synovial fluid*).

Freely movable joints can be of many types. For example, ball and socket joints have a wide range of motion, like the shoulder and hip joints. On the other hand, hinge joints allow motion in only one plane like a hinged door (i.e. the knee, elbow, and interphalangeal joints).

11.3.3 Cartilage

The microscopic aspects of cartilage have already been discussed (*see Dense Connective Tissue*, BIO 5.4.2/3). Opposing and mobile surfaces of bone are covered by various forms of cartilage. As already mentioned, joints with hyaline or fibrocartilage allow little movement.

Ligaments attach bone to bone. They are formed by dense bands of fibrous connective tissue which reinforce the joint capsule and help to maintain bones in the proper anatomical arrangement.

Tendons connect muscle to bone. They are formed by the densest kind of fibrous connective tissue. Tendons allow muscular forces to be exerted even when the body (*or belly*) of the muscle is at some distance from the action.

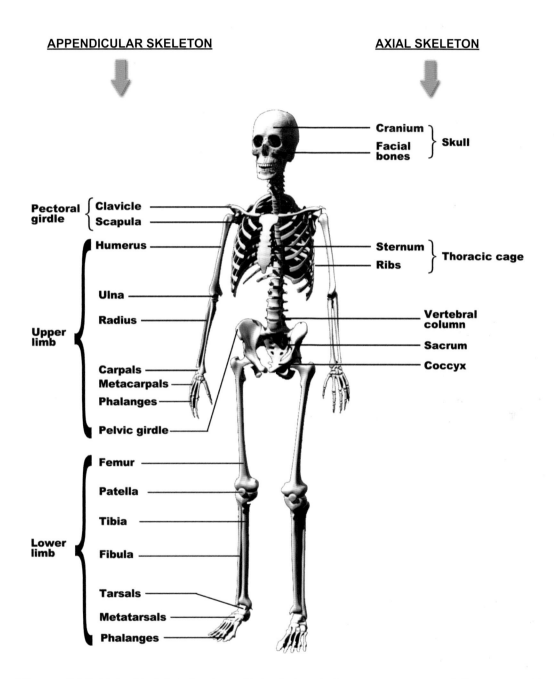

APPENDICULAR SKELETON

AXIAL SKELETON

Figure IV.A.11.2: Skeletal structure. Note: in brackets some common relations - scapula (shoulder blade), clavicle (collarbone), carpals (wrist), metacarpals (palm), phalanges (fingers), tibia (shin), patella (kneecap), tarsals (ankle), metatarsals (foot), phalanges (toes), vertebral column (backbone). Note that the appendicular skeleton includes the bones of the appendages and the pectoral and pelvic girdles. The axial skeleton consists of the skull, vertebral column, and the rib cage.

GOLD STANDARD WARM-UP EXERCISES

CHAPTER 11: The Musculoskeletal System

1) As red muscle fibers go from a resting state to a rapidly contracting state, which of the following occurs?

A. Increased rate of consumption of oxygen
B. Decreased rate of production of carbon dioxide
C. Decreased rate of hydrolysis of ATP
D. Decreased rate of degradation of glucose

2) Suppose that the oxygen supply to continuously contracting red muscles fibers is abruptly cut off. Which of the following processes would occur in the muscles?

A. Increased rate of synthesis of muscle glycogen
B. Increased rate of production of ATP
C. Increased rate of production of carbon dioxide
D. Increased rate of production of lactic acid

3) Which of the following metabolic processes predominates in rapidly contracting white muscle fibers?

A. Oxidative phosphorylation
B. Alcoholic fermentation
C. Glycolysis
D. Krebs Citric Acid Cycle reaction

4) Cartilage is likely to be found in all the following adult tissues EXCEPT:

A. bronchus.
B. tendons and sternum.
C. pinna of the ear.
D. between the epiphysis and diaphysis of long bones.

5) Which of the following refers to a continuous partial contraction of a muscle?

A. Tetany
B. Tonus
C. Twitch
D. Pacemaker

6) Skeletal muscle is connected to bones by:

A. joints.
B. ligaments.
C. tendons.
D. loose connective tissue.

7) A joint that allows motion in only one plane (i.e. the knee, elbow) is called a:

A. ball and socket joint.
B. synovial joint.
C. hinged joint.
D. prominent joint.

8) Which of the following joints is formed by the articulation of the tibia, the malleolus of the fibula, and the tarsals?

   A. Ankle
   B. Knee
   C. Hip
   D. Wrist

9) Which of the following is NOT a component of the human axial skeleton?

   A. Tarsals
   B. Sternum
   C. Vertebral column
   D. Skull

10) Phalanges are found in the:

   A. skull.
   B. hip.
   C. feet.
   D. chest.

GS ANSWER KEY

CHAPTER 11

		Cross-Reference				Cross-Reference
1.	A	BIO 11.2, 4.5, 5.2	6.	C	BIO 11.3.3
2.	D	BIO 11.2, 4.5, 5.2	7.	C	BIO 11.3.2
3.	C	BIO 11.2, 4.5, 5.2	8.	A	BIO 11.3.2, 11.3.3
4.	D	BIO 5.4.3, 11.3.1	9.	A	BIO 11.3.3
5.	B	BIO 11.2	10.	C	BIO 11.3.3

* Explanations can be found at the back of the book.

Go online to DAT-prep.com for additional chapter review Q&A and forum.

GOLD NOTES

Memorize	Understand	Importance
c anatomy and order	* Basic functions: gas exchange, thermoregulation, . . . * Protection against disease, particulate matter * Breathing mechanisms: diaphragm, rib cage, differential pressure * Resiliency and surface tension effects * The carbonic-acid-bicarbonate buffer	**0 to 2 out of the 40 Biology** DAT questions are based on content in this chapter (in our estimation). * Note that between 25% and 50% of the questions in DAT Biology are from 5 chapters: 1, 2, 14, 15, and 16.

DAT-Prep.com

Introduction

The respiratory system permits the exchange of gases with the organism's environment. This critical process occurs in the microscopic space between alveoli and capillaries. It is here where molecules of oxygen and carbon dioxide passively diffuse between the gaseous external environment and the blood.

Additional Resources

Free Online Q&A + Forum

Flashcards

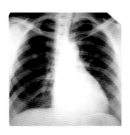

Special Guest

12.1 Overview

There are two forms of respiration: cellular respiration which refers to the oxidation of organic molecules (*see* BIO 4.4 - 4.10) and mechanical respiration where the gases related to cellular respiration are exchanged between the atmosphere and the circulatory system (O_2 in and CO_2 out).

The respiratory system, which is concerned with mechanical respiration, has the following principal functions:

- providing a conducting system for the exchange of gases

- the filtration of incoming particles

- to help control the water content and temperature (= *thermoregulation*) of the incoming air

- to assist in speech production, the sense of smell, and the regulation of pH.

The respiratory system is composed of the lungs and a series of airways that connect the lungs to the external environment, deliver air to the lungs and perform gas exchange.

12.2 The Upper Respiratory Tract

The respiratory system can be divided into an *upper* and *lower respiratory tract* which are separated by the pharynx. The **upper respiratory tract** is composed of the nose, the nasal cavity, the sinuses, and the nasopharynx. This portion of the respiratory system warms, moistens and filters the air before it reaches the lower respiratory system. The nose (*nares*) has receptors for the sense of smell. It is guarded by hair to entrap coarse particles. The nasal cavity, the hollow space behind the nose, contains a ciliated mucous membrane (= a form of *respiratory epithelium*) to entrap smaller particles and prevent infection (this arrangement is common throughout the respiratory tract; for cilia *see the Generalized Eukaryotic Cell*, BIO 1.2). The nasal cavity adjusts the humidity and temperature of incoming air. The nasopharynx helps to equilibrate pressure between the environment and the middle ear via the eustachian tube (BIO 6.2.3).

12.3 The Lower Respiratory Tract

The **lower respiratory tract** is composed of the larynx which contains the vocal cords, the trachea which divides into left and right main bronchi which continue to divide into smaller airways ($\rightarrow$ 2° bronchi $\rightarrow$ 3° bronchi $\rightarrow$ bronchioles $\rightarrow$ terminal bronchioles). The terminal bronchioles are the most distal part of the conducting portion of the respira-

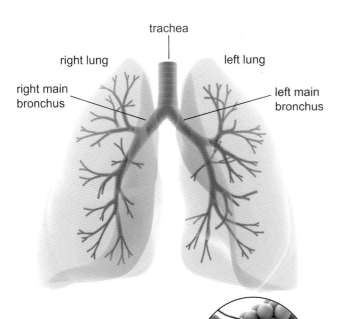

Figure IV.A.12.1: Illustration representing the lower respiratory tract including the dividing bronchial tree and grape-shaped alveoli with blood supply. Note that "right" refers to the patient's perspective which means the left side from your perspective.

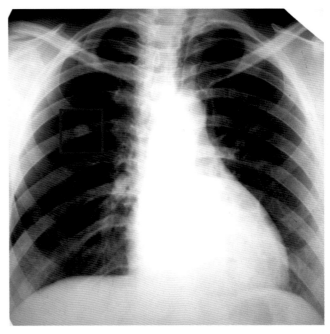

Figure IV.A.12.2: Chest x-ray of an adult male smoker. Notice the coin-shaped shadow in the right lung which presented with coughing blood. Further tests confirmed the presence of a right lung cancer. Cancer-causing chemicals (carcinogens) can irritate any of the cells lining the lower respiratory tract.

tory system. Starting from respiratory bronchioles → alveolar ducts → alveolar sacs until the level of the alveolus, these are considered the respiratory portion of respiratory system, where gas exchange takes place.

It is in these microscopic air sacs called *alveoli* that O_2 diffuses through the alveolar walls and enters the blood in nearby capillaries (where the concentration or *partial pressure* of O_2 is lowest and CO_2 is highest) and CO_2 diffuses from the blood through the walls to enter the alveoli (where the partial pressure of CO_2 is lowest and O_2 is highest). Gas exchange occurs by diffusion across the blood-gas barrier

between the alveolar airspace and the capillary lumen. The blood-gas barrier is composed of three layers: type I pneumocyte cells, fused basal laminae and the endothelium of capillaries. *Alveolar macrophages* are phagocytes which help to engulf particles which reach the alveolus. A *surfactant* is secreted into alveoli by special lung cells (*pneumocytes type II*). The surfactant reduces surface tension and prevents the fragile alveoli from collapsing.

Sneezing and coughing, which are reflexes mediated by the medulla, can expel particles from the upper and lower respiratory tract, respectively.

The **lungs** are separated into left and right and are enclosed by the diaphragm and the thoracic cage. It is covered by a membrane (= *pleura*) which secretes a lubricant to reduce friction while breathing. The lungs contain the air passages, nerves, alveoli, blood and lymphatic vessels of the lower respiratory tract.

12.4 Breathing: Structures and Mechanisms

Inspiration is <u>active</u> and occurs according to the following main events: i) nerve impulses from the <u>phrenic nerve</u> cause the muscular <u>diaphragm</u> to contract; as the dome shaped diaphragm moves downward, the thoracic cavity increases; ii) simultaneously, the intercostal (= *between ribs*) muscles and/or certain neck muscles may contract further increasing the thoracic cavity (the muscles mentioned here are called *accessory respiratory muscles* and under normal circumstances the action of the diaphragm is much more important); iii) as the size of the thoracic cavity increases, its <u>internal pressure</u> decreases leaving it relatively negative; iv) the relatively positive <u>atmospheric pressure</u> forces air into the respiratory tract thus inflating the lungs.

Expiration is <u>passive</u> and occurs according to the following main events: i) the diaphragm and the accessory respiratory muscles relax and the chest wall pushed inward; ii) the elastic tissues of the lung, thoracic cage, and the abdominal organs recoil to their original position; iii) this recoil increases the pressure within the lungs (making the pressure relatively positive) thus forcing air out of the lungs and passageways.

12.4.1 Control of Breathing

Though voluntary breathing is possible (!), normally breathing is involuntary, rhythmic, and controlled by the *respiratory center* in the medulla of the brain stem. The respiratory center is sensitive to pH of the cerebrospinal fluid (CSF). An increase in blood CO_2 or consequently, decrease in pH of the CSF, acts on the respiratory center and stimulates breathing, returning the arterial PCO_2 back to normal. The increase in blood CO_2 and the decrease in pH are two interrelated events since CO_2 can be picked up by hemoglobin forming carbamino-hemoglobin (about 20%, BIO 7.5.1), but it can also be <u>converted into carbonic acid</u> by dissolving in blood plasma (about 5%) or by conversion in red blood cells by the enzyme *carbonic anhydrase* (about 75%). The reaction is summarized as follows:

$$CO_2 + H_2O \leftrightarrow \underset{\substack{\text{carbonic} \\ \text{acid}}}{H_2CO_3} \leftrightarrow \underset{\text{bicarbonate}}{HCO_3^- + H^+}$$

According to Henry's Law, the concentration of a gas dissolved in solution is directly proportional to its partial pressure. From the preceding you can see why the respiratory system, through the regulation of the partial pressure of CO_2 in blood, also helps in maintaining pH homeostasis (= a buffer). More generally, the carbonic-acid-bicarbonate buffer is the most important buffer for maintaining acid-base balance in the blood and helps to maintain pH around 7.4.

GOLD STANDARD WARM-UP EXERCISES

CHAPTER 12: The Respiratory System

1) All of the following are in the correct anatomic order EXCEPT:

   A. trachea --> larynx --> bronchus.

   B. bronchus --> bronchioles --> alveolar ducts.

   C. alveolar ducts --> alveolar sacs --> alveolus.

   D. nose --> nasal cavity --> nasopharynx.

2) The vocal cords form part of which of the following?

   A. Pharynx
   B. Larynx
   C. Trachea
   D. Bronchus

3) Which of the following can NOT engage in gas exchange?

   A. Alveolus
   B. Respiratory bronchiole
   C. Alveolar duct
   D. Terminal bronchiole

4) Which of the following secretes surfactant?

   A. Pneumocytes type I
   B. Pneumocytes type II
   C. Alveolar macrophage
   D. Alveolar adipocyte

5) Which of the following factors favors an increase in breathing rate?

   A. Increased blood carbon dioxide
   B. Decreased CSF acidity
   C. Increased CSF pH
   D. Increased blood oxygen

6) One of the the possible injuries during a high speed motor vehicle accident includes a traumatic hemothorax in which blood accumulates in the pleural cavity. With regards to a traumatic hemothorax, which of the following would be of greatest concern?

   A. High oxygenation due to spasms of the diaphragm
   B. Low oxygenation due to blood in the right bronchus
   C. High oxygenation due to hyperventilation
   D. Low oxygenation due to compression of the lung

7) The following are physiological systems which depend on stretch receptors EXCEPT:

   A. the circulatory system.
   B. the respiratory system.
   C. the endocrine system.
   D. the digestive system.

8) Active transport assumes particular importance in all but which of the following structures?

   A. Cells of the large intestine
   B. Alveoli
   C. Nerve and muscle cells
   D. Loop of Henle

GS ANSWER KEY

CHAPTER 12

Cross-Reference

1.	A	BIO 12.2, 12.3
2.	B	BIO 12.3
3.	D	BIO 12.3
4.	B	BIO 12.3
5.	A	BIO 12.4.1
6.	D	BIO 12.3
7.	C	BIO 7.2-7.3, 9.1-9.3, 9.5, 12.3-12.4
8.	B	BIO 1.1.2, 12.3

* Explanations can be found at the back of the book.

Go online to DAT-prep.com for additional chapter review Q&A and forum.

APPENDIX

CHAPTER 12: The Respiratory System

Advanced DAT-30 Passage: Lung Function and Transpulmonary Pressure

The volume of air that flows into or out of an alveolus per unit time is directly proportional to the pressure difference between the atmosphere and alveolus and inversely proportional to the resistance to flow caused by the airways. During normal relaxed breathing, about 500 ml of air flows in and out of the lungs. This is the tidal volume. After expiration, approximately 2.5 liters of air remains in the lungs which is referred to as the functional residual capacity. A spirometer is an instrument for measuring air inhaled and exhaled; it provides a simple way of determining most of the lung volumes and capacities that are measured in pulmonary function tests. The

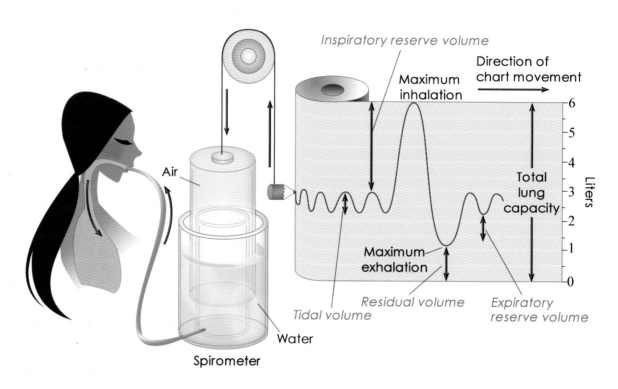

Figure IV.A.12.3: The four lung volumes measured by spirometer. Note that there are 4 key lung capacities: (1) the functional residual capacity which is the sum of the residual volume and the expiratory reserve volume (= ERV which is the maximum volume that can be exhaled following a normal quiet exhalation); (2) the vital capacity (VC) is the maximum volume that can be exhaled following a maximal inhalation; VC = inspiratory reserve volume (IRV) + tidal volume (VT) + ERV; (3) the inspiratory capacity (IC) is the maximum volume that can be inhaled following a normal quiet exhalation; IC = IRV + VT; (4) total lung capacity is the amount of air in the lung after maximal inhalation.

minute ventilation can be calculated as follows:

> Minute ventilation =
> Tidal volume x Respiratory rate

Airway resistance is: i) directly proportional to the magnitude of the viscosity between the flowing gas molecules; ii) directly proportional to the length of the airway; and iii) inversely proportional to the fourth power of the radius of the airway.

Resistance to air flow in the lung is normally small thus small pressure differences allow large volumes of air to flow. Physical, neural and chemical factors affect airway radii and therefore resistance. Transpulmonary pressure is a physical factor which exerts a distending force on the airways and alveoli. Such a force is critical to prevent small airways from collapsing.

The rate of respiration is primarily dependent on the concentration of carbon dioxide in the blood. As carbon dioxide levels rise, chemoreceptors in blood vessels are stimulated to discharge neuronal impulses to the respiratory center in the medulla oblongata in the brain stem. The respiratory center would then send impulses to the diaphragm causing an increase in the rate of contraction thus increasing the respiratory rate.

9) Given a resting respiratory rate of 12 breaths per minute, give an approximation of the minute ventilation.

A. 2.5 L/min
B. 5.0 L/min
C. 6.0 L/min
D. 3 0 L/min

10) Which of the following is consistent with the total lung capacity?

A. The amount of air inhaled and exhaled normally at rest
B. The sum of the residual volume and the expiratory reserve volume
C. The maximum volume that can be exhaled following a maximal inhalation
D. The maximum volume of air present in the lungs

11) During inspiration, transpulmonary pressure should:

A. increase, increasing airway radius and decreasing airway resistance.
B. increase, increasing airway radius and increasing airway resistance.
C. decrease, decreasing airway radius and decreasing airway resistance.
D. decrease, decreasing airway radius and increasing airway resistance.

12) Lateral traction refers to the process by which connective tissue fibers maintain airway patency by continuously pulling outward on the sides of the airways. As the lungs expand these fibers become stretched. Thus during inspiration lateral traction acts:

A. in the same direction as transpulmonary pressure, by increasing the viscosity of air.
B. in the opposite direction to transpulmonary pressure, by decreasing the viscosity of air.
C. in the same direction as transpulmonary pressure, by increasing the airway radius.
D. in the opposite direction to transpulmonary pressure, by increasing the airway radius.

13) The Heimlich Maneuver is used to aid individuals who are choking on matter caught in the upper respiratory tract through the application of a sudden abdominal pressure with an upward thrust. The procedure includes:

A. forcing the diaphragm downward, increasing thoracic size and causing a passive expiration.

B. forcing the diaphragm upward, increasing thoracic size and causing a forced expiration.

C. forcing the diaphragm upward, reducing thoracic size and causing a forced expiration.

D. forcing the diaphragm upward, increasing thoracic size and causing a passive expiration.

Go online to DAT-prep.com for additional chapter review Q&A and forum.

GOLD NOTES

Memorize

...cture and function of skin,
... differentiation
...t glands, location in dermis

Understand

* Skin system: homeostasis and osmoregulation
* Functions in thermoregulation: hair, erectile musculature, fat layer for insulation
* Vasoconstriction and vasodilation in surface capillaries
* Physical protection: nails, calluses, hair; protection against abrasion, disease organisms
* Relative impermeability to water

Importance

0 to 1 out of the 40 Biology
DAT questions are based on content in this chapter (in our estimation).
* Note that between 25% and 50% of the questions in DAT Biology are from 5 chapters: 1, 2, 14, 15, and 16.

DAT-Prep.com

Introduction

Skin is composed of layers of epithelial tissues which protect underlying muscle, bone, ligaments and internal organs. Thus skin has many roles including protecting the body from microbes, insulation, temperature regulation, sensation and synthesis of vitamin D.

Additional Resources

Free Online Q&A + Forum

Flashcards

Special Guest

The skin, or *integument*, is the body's largest organ. The following represents its major functions:

* **Physical protection:** The skin protects against the onslaught of the environment including uv light, chemical, thermal or even mechanical agents. It also serves as a barrier to the invasion of microorganisms.

* **Sensation:** The skin, being the body's largest sensory organ, contains a wide range of sensory receptors including those for pain, temperature, light touch, and pressure.

* **Metabolism:** Vitamin D synthesis can occur in the epidermis of skin (*see Endocrine Systems*, BIO 6.3). Also, energy is stored as fat in subcutaneous adipose tissue.

* **Thermoregulation and osmoregulation:** Skin is vital for the homeostatic mechanism of thermoregulation and to a lesser degree osmoregulation. Hair (*piloerection*, which can trap a layer of warm air against the skin's surface) and especially subcutaneous fat (*adipose tissue*) insulate the body against heat loss. Shivering, which allows muscle to generate heat, and decreasing blood flow to the skin (= *vasoconstriction*) are important in emergencies.

On the other hand, heat and water loss can be increased by increasing blood flow to the multitude of blood vessels (= *vasodilation*) in the dermis (cooling by radiation), the production of sweat, and the evaporation of sweat due to the heat at the surface of the skin; thus the skin cools. {Remember: the **hypothalamus** also regulates body temperature (*see The Nervous System*, BIO 6.1); it is like a thermostat which uses other organs as tools to maintain our body temperatures at about 37 °C (98.6 °F)}.

13.2 The Structure of Skin

Skin is divided into three layers: i) the outer **epidermis** which contains a stratified squamous keratinized epithelium; ii) the inner **dermis** which contains vessels, nerves, muscle, and connective tissues; iii) the innermost **subcutaneous layer**, known as hypodermis, which contains adipose and a loose connective tissue; this layer binds to any underlying organs.

The epidermis is divided into several different layers or *strata*. The deepest layer, *stratum basale*, contains actively dividing cells (keratinocytes) which are nourished by the vessels in the dermis. The mitotic activity of keratinocytes can keep regenerating epidermis approximately every 30 days. As these cells continue to divide, older epidermal cells are pushed towards the surface of the skin - *away from the nutrient providing dermal layer*; thus in time they die. Simultaneously, these cells are actively producing strands of a tough, fibrous, waterproof protein called keratin. This process is called *keratinization*. The two preceding events lead to the formation of an outermost layer (= *stratum corneum*) of keratin-filled dead cells which are devoid of organelles and are continuously shed by a process called *desquamation*.

Melanin is a dark pigment produced by cells (= *melanocytes*) whose cell bodies are usually found in the stratum basale. Melanin absorbs light thus protects against uv light induced cell damage (i.e. sunburns, skin cancer). Individuals have about the same number of melanocytes - regardless of race. Melanin production depends on genetic factors (i.e. race) and it can be stimulated by exposure to sunlight (i.e. tanning).

Langerhans cells have long processes and contain characteristic tennis-racket-shaped Birbeck granules. They function as antigen presenting cells in the immune response (BIO 8.2, 8.3).

Merkel cells are present in the richly innervated areas of stratum basale. They are responsible for receiving afferent nerve impulses and function as sensory mechano-receptors (BIO 6.1.1).

The dermis is composed of dense irregular connective tissue including type I collagen fibers and a network of elastic fibers. It contains the blood vessels which nourish the various cells in the skin. It also contains motor fibers and many types of sensory nerve fibers such as fine touch receptors, pressure receptors and cold receptors.

13.3 Skin Appendages

The **appendages** of the skin include hair, sebaceous glands and sweat glands. Hair is a modified keratinized structure produced by a cylindrical downgrowth of epithelium (= *hair follicle*). The follicle extends into the dermis (sometimes the subcutaneous tissue as well). The arrector pili muscle attaches to the connective tissue surrounding a hair follicle. When this bundle of smooth muscle contracts (= *piloerection*), it elevates the hair and "goose bumps" are produced.

The sebaceous glands are lobular acinar glands that empty their ducts into the hair follicles. They are most abundant on the face, forehead and scalp. They release an oily/ waxy secretion called sebum to lubricate and waterproof the skin.

Sweat glands can be classified as either eccrine sweat glands, which are simple tubular glands present in the skin throughout the body or apocrine sweat glands, which are large specialized glands located only in certain areas of the body (i.e. areola of the nipple, perianal area, axilla which is the "armpit") and will not function until puberty.

We have previously explored endocrine glands and saw how they secrete their products - without the use of a duct - directly into the bloodstream (BIO 6.3). Alternatively, endo-

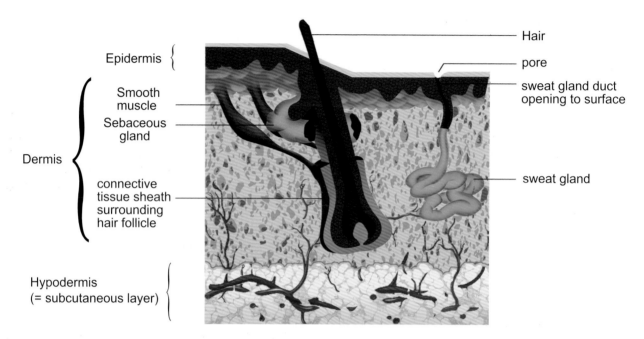

Figure IV.A.13.1: Skin structure with appendages.

crine products may diffuse into surrounding tissue (*paracrine signaling*) where they often affect only target cells near the release site.

An exocrine gland is distinguished by the fact that it excretes its product via a duct to some environment external to itself, either inside the body (BIO 9.3, 9.4) or on a surface of the body. Examples of exocrine glands include the sebaceous glands, sweat glands, salivary glands, mammary glands, pancreas and liver.

Holocrine (= *wholly secretory*) is a type of glandular secretion in which the entire secreting cell, along with its accumulated secretion, forms the secreted matter of the gland; for example, the sebaceous glands. Apocrine concentrates products at the free end of the secreting cell and are thrown off along with a portion of the cytoplasm (i.e. mammary gland, axilla). Eccrine, apocrine and holocrine are subdivisions of exocrine.

13.3.1 Nails, Calluses

Nails are flat, translucent, keratinized coverings near the tip of fingers and toes. They are useful for scratching and fine manipulation (including picking up dimes!).

A callus is a toughened, thickened area of skin. It is usually created in response to repeated friction or pressure thus they are normally found on the hands or feet.

GOLD STANDARD WARM-UP EXERCISES

CHAPTER 13: The Skin As An Organ

1) The skin, the body's largest organ, is divided into 3 layers including the epidermis. The latter contains a waterproof, tough protein called *keratin*. How then is it possible that humans can sweat freely in hot temperatures?

   A. Specialized sweat glands can secrete their products into channels which pass through the epidermis.
   B. Active and passive transport systems carry sweat across the epidermis.
   C. Specialized sebaceous glands can secrete their products into channels which pass through the epidermis.
   D. Osmotic pressure releases sweat across the epidermis.

2) Which of the following best describe why perspiring causes a reduction in body temperature?

   A. Perspiration carries heated water to the surface.
   B. Perspiration removes excess Na$^+$ and Cl$^-$ ions from cells.
   C. Perspiration evaporates and cools skin.
   D. Perspiration causes vasoconstriction.

3) Which of the following is the best way to reduce body temperature?

   A. Increase kidney function.
   B. Constrict skeletal muscle.
   C. Reduce insulin levels.
   D. Relax smooth muscle of blood vessels.

4) Experiments have now confirmed that sweating only occurs as a result of a rise in core body temperature. Drinking iced water results in a lowering of core body temperature. Thus, exposing the skin to heat while drinking iced water would result in which of the following?

   A. An increase in sweating
   B. A decrease in sweating
   C. An increase in sweating followed by a decrease in sweating
   D. No change in sweat production

5) The name of the process by which oil glands in mammalian skins secrete oils is called:

   A. osmosis.
   B. active transport.
   C. apocrine secretion.
   D. holocrine secretion.

GS ANSWER KEY

CHAPTER 13

Cross-Reference

1.	A	BIO 13.3
2.	C	BIO 13.1
3.	D	BIO 13.1, 7.3
4.	B	BIO 7.1, 13.1
5.	D	BIO 13.3

* Explanations can be found at the back of the book.

Go online to DAT-prep.com for additional chapter review Q&A and forum.

Memorize	Understand	Importance
e and female reproductive structures, ctions m, sperm: differences in formation, ive contribution to next generation roductive sequence: fertilization; antation; development or structures arising out of primary n layers	* Gametogenesis by meiosis * Formation of primary germ layers: endoderm, mesoderm, ectoderm * Embryogenesis: stages of early development: order and general features of each * Cell specialization, communication in development, gene regulation in development * Programmed cell death; basic: the menstrual cycle	1 to 3 out of the 40 Biology DAT questions are based on content in this chapter (in our estimation). * Note that between 25% and 50% of the questions in DAT Biology are from 5 chapters: 1, 2, 14, 15, and 16.

DAT-Prep.com

Introduction

Reproduction refers to the process by which new organisms are produced. The process of development follows as the single celled zygote grows into a fully formed adult. These two processes are fundamental to life as we know it.

Additional Resources

Free Online Q&A + Forum

Video: Online or DVD

Flashcards

Special Guests

Gonads are the organs which produce gametes (= germ cells = reproductive cells). The female gonads are the two ovaries which lie in the pelvic cavity. Opening around the ovaries and connecting to the uterus are the Fallopian tubes (= *oviducts*) which conduct the egg (= *ovum*) from the ovary to the uterus. The uterus is a muscular organ. Part of the uterus (= the cervix) protrudes into the vagina or *birth canal*. The vagina leads to the external genitalia. The vulva includes the openings of the vagina, various glands, and folds of skin which are large (= labia majora) and small (= labia minora). The clitoris is found between the labia minora at the anterior end of the vulva. Like the glans penis, it is very sensitive as it is richly innervated. However, the clitoris is unique in being the only organ in the human body devoted solely to sensory pleasure.

The male gonads are the two testicles (= *testes*) which are suspended by spermatic cords in a sac-like scrotum outside the body cavity (this is because the optimal temperature for spermatogenesis is less than body temperature). Sperm (= *spermatozoa*) are produced in the seminiferous tubules in the testes and then continue along a system of ducts including: the epididymis where sperm complete their maturation and are collected and stored; the vas deferens which leads to the ejaculatory duct which in turn leads to the penile urethra which conducts to the exterior. The accessory organs include the seminal vesicles, the bulbourethral and prostate glands. They are exocrine glands whose secretions contribute greatly to the volume of the *ejaculate* (= semen = seminal fluid). The penis is composed of a body or shaft, which contains an erectile tissue which can be engorged by blood; a penile urethra which can conduct either urine or sperm; and a very sensitive head or glans penis which may be covered by foreskin (= *prepuce*, which is removed by circumcision).

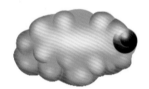 

Figure IV.A.14.0: An ovulating ovary and a testicle with spermatic cord.

Gametogenesis refers to the production of gametes (eggs and sperm) which occurs by meiosis (*see Mitosis*, BIO 1.3, *for comparison*). Meiosis involves two successive divisions which can produce four cells from one parent cell. The first division, the reduction division, reduces the number of chromosomes from 2N (= *diploid*) to N (= *haploid*) where N = 23 for humans. This reduction division occurs as follows: i) in **prophase I** the chromosomes appear (= *condensed chromatin*), the nuclear membrane and nucleoli disappear and the spindle fibers become organized. Homologous paternal and maternal chromosomes pair[1] (= *synapsis*) forming a tetrad as each pair of homologous chromosomes consists of four chromatids. The exchange of genetic information (DNA) may occur by crossing over between homologous chromosomes at sites called *chiasmata*, therefore redistributing maternal and paternal genetic information ensuring variability; ii) **in metaphase I** the synaptic pairs of chromosomes line up midway between the poles of the developing spindle (= *the equatorial plate*). Thus each pair consists of 2 chromosomes (= 4 chromatids), each attached to a spindle fiber; iii) in **anaphase I** the homologous chromosomes migrate to opposite poles of the spindle, separating its paternal chromosomes from maternal ones. Thus, each daughter cell will have a unique mixture of paternal and maternal origin of chromosomes. In contrast to anaphase in mitosis, the two chromatids remain held together. Consequently, the centromeres do *not* divide; iv) in **telophase I** the parent cell divides into two daughter cells (= *cytokinesis*), the nuclear membranes and nucleoli reappear, and the spindle fibers are no longer visible. Each daughter cell now contains 23 chromosomes (1N).

The first meiotic division is followed by a short interphase I and then the second meiotic division which proceeds essentially the same as mitosis. Thus prophase II, metaphase II, anaphase II, and telophase II proceed like the corresponding mitotic phases.

Gametogenesis in males (= *spermatogenesis*) proceeds as follows: before the age of sexual maturity only a small number of primordial germ cells (= *spermatogonia*) are present in the testes. There are two types of spermatogonia, type A and type B. Type A spermatogonia (2N) are mitotically active and continuously provide a supply of type A or type B spermatogonia. Type B spermatogonia (2N) undergo meiosis and will give rise to primary spermatocytes. After sexual maturation these cells prolifically multiply throughout a male's life.

In the seminiferous tubules, the type B spermatogonia (2N) enter meiosis I and undergo chromosome replication forming primary spermatocytes with 2N chromosomes. Primary spermatocytes complete meiosis I producing two secondary spermatocytes with 1N chromosomes. Secondary spermatocytes quickly enter meiosis II without an intervening S phase to form four spermatids. Spermatids are haploid (1N) cells.

In summary, each primary spermatocyte results in the production of four spermatids. Spermatids undergo a post-meiotic cytodifferentiation whereby spermatids are transformed into **four** motile sperm (1N) through a process called *spermiogenesis*.

Sperm can be divided into: i) a *head* which is oval and contains the nucleus with its 23 chromosomes {since the nucleus carries either an X or Y sex chromosome, sperm determine the sex of the offspring}. The head is partly surrounded by the acrosome which contains enzymes (esp. hyaluronidase) which help the sperm penetrate the egg. The

---

[1]synapsing homologous chromosomes are often called *tetrads* or *bivalents*.

Spermatogenesis

Oogenesis

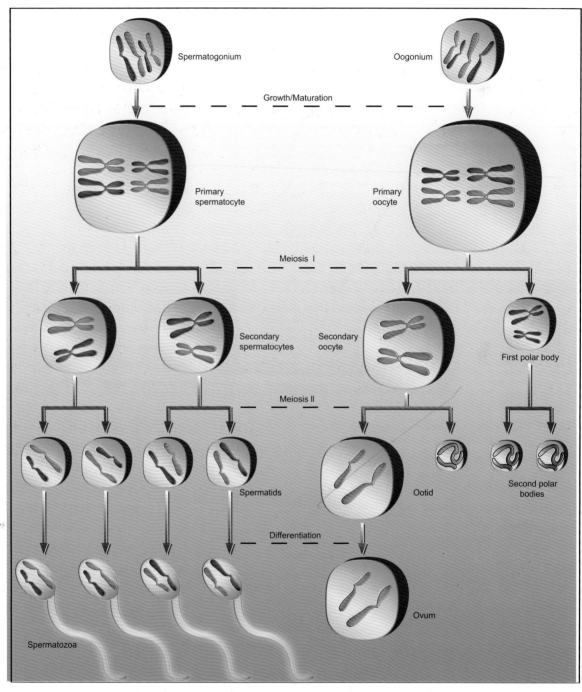

Figure IV.A.14.0a: Gametogenesis.

release of these enzymes is known as the acrosomal reaction; ii) the *body* of the sperm contains a central core surrounded by a large number of mitochondria for power; and iii) the *tail* constitutes a flagellum which is critical for the cell's locomotion. Newly formed sperm are incapable of fertilization until they undergo a process called capacitation, which happens in the female reproductive duct. After removal of its protein coating, the sperm becomes capable of fertilization. Also in the seminiferous tubules are Sertoli cells which support and nourish developing sperm and Leydig cells which produce and secrete testosterone. While LH stimulates the latter, FSH stimulates primary spermatocytes to undergo meiosis. {Remember: LH = Leydig, FSH = spermatogenesis}

Gametogenesis in females (= *oogenesis*) proceeds as follows: in fetal development, groups of cells (= *ovarian or primordial follicles*) develop from the germinal epithelium of the ovary) and differentiate into oogonia (2N). Oogonia (2N) enter meiosis I and undergo DNA replication producing primary oocytes (2N) which are surrounded by epithelia (= *follicular cells*) in the primordial follicle. The oocytes remain arrested in prophase I of meiosis until ovulation which occurs between the ages of about 13 (sexual maturity) and 50 (menopause). Thus, unlike males, all female germ cells are present at birth. Some follicles degenerate and are called *atretic*. During puberty, when the ovarian cycle begins, up to 20 primordial follicles may begin to differentiate to *Graafian follicles*. During this development,

meiosis continues. In response to an LH surge from the pituitary gland, the primary oocyte (2N) completes meiosis I just prior to ovulation to form the secondary oocyte (1N) and the first polar body, which will probably degenerate. The secondary oocyte is surrounded by (from the inside out): a thick, tough membrane (= *the zona pellucida*), follicular cells (= *the corona radiata*), and estrogen-secreting thecal cells. It then enters meiosis II and remains arrested in metaphase of meiosis II until fertilization occurs.

Of the twenty or so maturing follicles, all the remaining secondary follicles will degenerate (= *atresia*) except for one which becomes the Graafian (mature) follicle. In response to the LH surge, the secondary oocyte leaves the ruptured Graafian follicle in the process called ovulation. This ovum, along with its zona pellucida and corona radiata, migrate to and through the Fallopian tube (oviduct) where a sperm may penetrate the secondary oocyte (= *fertilization*). If fertilization occurs then the second meiotic division proceeds, forming a mature oocyte, known as ovum, (1N) and a second polar body; if fertilization does not occur, then the ovum degenerates. Unlike in males, each primary germ cell (oocyte) produces one gamete and not four. This is a consequence of the production of *polar bodies* which are degenerated nuclear material. Up to three polar bodies can be formed: one from the division of the primary oocyte, one from the division of the secondary oocyte, and sometimes the first polar body divides.

The "period" or menstrual cycle occurs in about 28 days and can be divided as follows: i) **Menses:** the first four days (days 1-4) of the cycle are notable for the menstrual blood flow. This occurs as a result of an estrogen and progesterone withdrawal which leads to vasoconstriction in the uterus causing the uterine lining (= *endometrium*) to disintegrate and slough away; ii) **Follicular** (ovary) or **Proliferative Phase** (days 5-14): FSH stimulates follicles to mature, and all but one of these follicles will stop growing, and the one dominant follicle in the ovary will continue to mature into a Graafian follicle, which in turn produces and secretes estrogen. Estrogen causes the uterine lining to thicken (= proliferate); iii) **Ovulation**: a very high concentration of estrogen is followed by an LH surge (estrogen-induced LH surge) at about day 15 (midcycle) which stimulates ovulation; iv) **Luteal** or **Secretory Phase** (days 15-28): the follicular cells degenerate into the corpus luteum which secretes estrogen *and* progesterone. Progesterone is responsible for a transient body temperature rise immediately after ovulation and it stimulates the uterine lining to become more vascular and glandular. Estrogen continues to stimulate uterine wall development and, along with progesterone, inhibits the secretion of LH and FSH (= negative feedback).

If the ovum is fertilized, the implanted embryo would produce the hormone *human chorionic gonadotropin* (= hCG) which would stimulate the corpus luteum to continue the secretion of estrogen and progesterone {hCG is the basis for most pregnancy tests}. If there is no fertilization, the corpus luteum degenerates causing a withdrawal of estrogen and progesterone thus the cycle continues [*see* i) *above*].

14.4 The Reproductive Sequence

During sexual stimulation parasympathetic impulses in the male lead to the dilatation of penile arteries combined with restricted flow in the veins resulting in the engorgement of the penis with blood (= *an erection*). In the female, the preceding occurs in a similar manner to the clitoris, along with the expansion and increase in secretions in the vagina. Intercourse or copulation may lead to orgasm which includes many responses from the sympathetic nervous system. In the male, the ejaculation of semen accompanies orgasm. In the female, orgasm is accompanied by many reflexes including an increase in muscular activity of the uterus and the Fallopian tubes. The latter may help in the transport of the already motile sperm to reach the tubes where the egg might be.

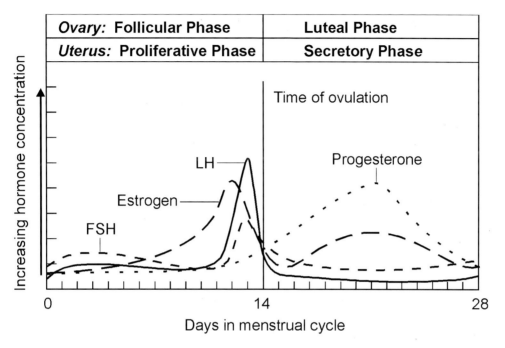

Figure IV.A.14.1: Changing hormone concentration during the menstrual cycle.

14.5 Embryogenesis

The formation of the embryo or *embryogenesis* occurs in a number of steps within two weeks of fertilization. Many parts of the developing embryo take shape during this period (= *morphogenesis*).

Penetration of the zona pellucida leads to the *cortical reaction*, in which the secondary oocyte is no longer permeable to other sperm.

Fertilization is a sequence of events which include: the sperm penetrating the corona radiata and the zona pellucidum due to the release of lytic enzymes from the acrosome known as the <u>acrosome reaction</u>; the fusion of the plasma membranes of the sperm and egg; the egg, which is really a secondary oocyte, becomes a mature ovum by completing the second meiotic division; the nuclei of the ovum and sperm are now called *pronuclei*; the male and female pronuclei fuse forming a <u>zygote</u> (2N). Fertilization, which normally occurs in the Fallopian tubes, is completed within 24 hours of ovulation.

Cleavage consists of rapid, repeated mitotic divisions beginning with the zygote.

Because the resultant daughter cells or blas-tomeres are still contained within the zona pellucidum, the cytoplasmic mass remains constant. Thus the increasing number of cells requires that each daughter cell be smaller than its parent cell. A morula is a solid ball of about 16 blastomeres which enters the uterus.

Blastulation is the process by which the morula develops a fluid filled cavity (= blastocoel) thus converting it to a blastocyst. Since the zona pellucidum degenerates at this point, the blastocyst is free to implant in the uterine lining or endometrium. The blas-tocyst contains some centrally located cells (= the inner cell mass) called the embryoblast which develops into the embryo. The outer cell mass called the trophoblast becomes part of the placenta.

Implantation. The zona pellucida must degenerate before the blastocyst can implant into the endometrium of the uterus. Once implantation is completed, the blastocyst becomes surrounded by layers of cells that further invade the endometrium.

Gastrulation is the process by which the blastula invaginates, and the inner cell mass is converted into a three layered (= trilaminar) disk. The trilaminar disk includes the **three primary germ layers**: an outer ectoderm, a middle mesoderm, and an inner endoderm. The ectoderm will develop into the epidermis and the nervous system; the mesoderm will become muscle, connective tissue (incl. blood, bone), and circulatory, reproductive and excretory organs; the endo-derm will become the epithelial linings of the respiratory tract, and digestive tract, includ-ing the glands of the accessory organs (i.e. the liver and pancreas). During this stage the embryo may be called a gastrula.

Neurulation is the process by which the neural plate and neural folds form and close to produce the neural tube. The neural plate is formed by the thickening of ectoderm which is induced by the developing noto-chord. The notochord is a cellular rod that defines the axis of the embryo and provides some rigidity. Days later, the neural plate invaginates along its central axis producing a central neural groove with neural folds on each side. The neural folds come together and fuse thus converting the neural plate into a neural tube which separates from the sur-face ectoderm. Special cells on the crest of the neural folds (= neural crest cells) migrate to either side of the developing neural tube to a region called the neural crest.

As a consequence, we are left with **three** regions: the surface ectoderm which will become the epidermis; the neural tube which will become the central nervous system (CNS); and the neural crest which will become cranial and spinal ganglia and nerves and the medulla of the adrenal gland. During this stage the embryo may be called a neurula.

14.5.1 Mechanisms of Development

Though this is a subject which is still poorly understood, it seems clear that morphogenesis relies on the <u>coordinated interaction of genetic and environmental factors</u>. When the zygote passes through its first few divisions, the blastomeres remain <u>indeterminate</u> or uncommitted to a specific fate. As development proceeds the cells become increasingly committed to a specific outcome (i.e. neural tube cells → CNS). This is called **determination**.

In order for a cell to specialize it must <u>differentiate</u> into a committed or <u>determined</u> cell. Since essentially all cells in a person's body have the same amount of genetic information, differentiation relies on the *difference* in the way these genes are *activated*. For example, though brain cells (neurons) have the same genes as osteoblasts, neurons do not activate such genes (otherwise we would have bone forming in our brains!). The general mechanism by which cells differentiate is called **induction**.

<u>Induction</u> can occur by many means. If two cells <u>divide unevenly</u>, the cell with more cytoplasm might have the necessary amount of a substance which could *induce* its chromosomes to activate cell-specific genes. Fur-

thermore, sometimes a cell, through contact (i.e. *contact inhibition*) or the <u>release of a chemical mediator</u>, can influence the development of nearby cells (*recall that the notochord induces the development of the neural plate*). The <u>physical environment</u> (pH, temperature, etc.) may also influence the development of certain cells. Irrespective of what form of induction is used, the signal must be translated into an intracellular message which influences the genetic activity of the responding cells.

Programmed cell-death (PCD = apoptosis) is death of a cell in any form, which is controlled by an intracellular program. PCD is carried out in a regulated process directed by DNA which normally confers advantage during an organism's life-cycle. PCD serves fundamental functions during tissue development. For example, the development of the spaces between your fingers requires cells to undergo PCD.

Thus cells specialize and develop into organ systems (morphogenesis). The embryo develops from the second to the ninth week, followed by the fetus which develops from the ninth week to birth (*parturition*).

14.6 The Placenta

The **placenta** is a complex vascular structure formed by part of the maternal endometrium (= *the decidua basalis*) and cells of embryonic origin (= *the chorion*). The placenta begins to form when the blastocyst implants in the endometrium. A cell layer from the embryo invades the endometrium with fingerlike bumps (= *chorionic villi*) which project into intervillous spaces which contain maternal blood. Maternal spiral arteries enter the intervillous spaces allowing blood to circulate.

The placenta has three main functions: i) the **transfer** of substances necessary for the development of the embryo or fetus from the mother (O_2, H_2O, carbohydrates, amino acids, IgG antibodies - BIO 8.2, vitamins, etc.) and the **transfer** of wastes from the embryo or fetus to the mother (CO_2, urea, uric acid, etc.); ii) the placenta can synthesize substances (i.e. glycogen, fatty acids) to use as an energy source for itself and the embryo or fetus; iii) the placenta produces and secretes a number of hormones including human chorionic gonadotropin (hCG), estrogen and progesterone. The hCG rescues the corpus luteum from regression and stimulates its production of progesterone.

14.7 Fetal Circulation

Consider the following: the fetus has lungs but does not breathe O_2. In fact, the placenta is, metaphorically, the "fetal lung." Oxygenated and nutrient-rich blood returns to the fetus from the placenta via the left umbilical vein. Most of the blood is directed to the inferior vena cava through the ductus venosus. From there, blood joins the deoxygenated and nutrient-poor blood from the superior vena cava and empties into the right atrium. However, most of the blood is diverted from the pulmonary circulation (bypassing the right ventricle) to the left atrium via a hole in the atrial septum: the patent foramen ovale (for adult circulation and anatomy, see chapter 7). Blood then enters the left ventricle and is distributed through the body (systemic circulation) via the aorta.

Some blood in the right atrium enters into the right ventricle and then proceeds into the pulmonary trunk. However, resistance in the collapsed lung is high and the pulmonary artery pressure is higher than it is in the aorta. Consequently, most of the blood bypasses the lung via the ductus arteriosus back to the aorta.

Blood circulates through the body and is sent back to the placenta via right and left umbilical arteries. The placenta re-oxygenates this deoxygenated and nutrient-poor blood and returns it to the fetus through the umbilical vein and the cardiovascular cycle repeats. Notice that in the fetus, oxygenated and nutrient-rich blood can be carried by veins to the right chambers of the heart which cannot occur in normal adult circulation.

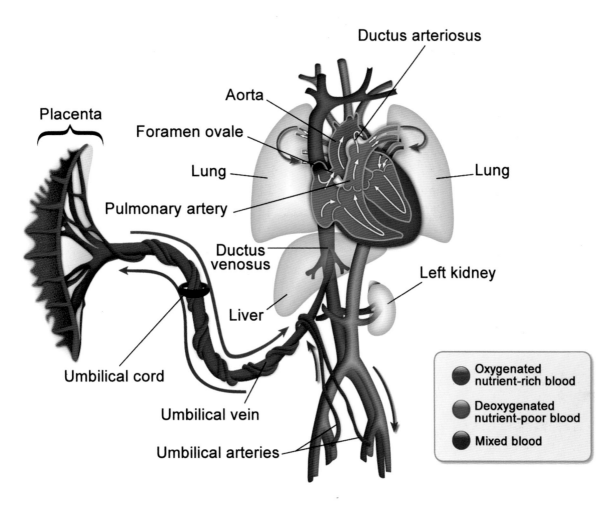

Fig.IV.A.14.2: Fetal circulation.

14.8 Fetal Sexual Development

The normal sexual development of the fetus depends on the genotype (XX female, XY male), the morphology of the internal organs and gonads, and the phenotype or external genitalia. Later, these many factors combine to influence the individual's self-perception along with the development of secondary sexual characteristics (i.e. breast development in females, hair growth and lower pitched voice in males).

Every fetus, regardless of genotype, has the capacity to become a normally formed individual of either sex. Development naturally proceeds towards "female" unless there is a Y chromosome factor present. Thus the XX genotype leads to the maturation of the Müllerian ducts into the uterus, fallopian tubes, and part of the vagina. The primitive gonad will develop into a testis only if the Y chromosome is present and encodes the appropriate factor and eventually the secretion of testosterone. Thus the XY genotype leads to the involution of the Müllerian ducts and the maturation of the Wolffian ducts into the vas deferens, seminiferous tubules and prostate.

Reproductive biology is the only science where multiplication and division mean the same thing.   :)

GOLD STANDARD WARM-UP EXERCISES

CHAPTER 14: Reproduction and Development

1) Fertilization of the ovum by the sperm usually occurs in the:

   A. vagina.
   B. uterus.
   C. oviduct.
   D. ovary.

2) Sperm can travel through each of the following EXCEPT one. Which one is the EXCEPTION?

   A. Ureter
   B. Urethra
   C. Vas deferens
   D. Epididymis

3) Which of the following does NOT follow the normal anatomic sequence?

   I.   gametogenesis → seminal vesicles → seminiferous tubules
   II. seminiferous tubules → epididymis → vas deferens
   III. vas deferens → ejaculatory duct → urethra

   A. I only
   B. II only
   C. I and II only
   D. II and III only

4) Which of the following can initiate a second meiotic division?

   A. FSH
   B. LH
   C. Estrogen and progesterone
   D. Fertilization

5) The corpus luteum secretes:

   A. FSH.
   B. LH.
   C. progesterone.
   D. HCG.

6) The hormone causing growth of the endometrium is:

   A. oxytocin.
   B. estrogen.
   C. luteinizing hormone.
   D. prolactin.

7) In the human menstrual cycle, which hormone is preferentially secreted in the follicular phase by the ovary?

   A. Estrogen
   B. FSH
   C. LH
   D. Progesterone

8) Which of the following hormones leads to the expulsion of the egg from the ovaries?

   A. LH
   B. FSH
   C. Estrogen
   D. Progesterone

9) In vitro fertilization begins by injecting a woman with medications which stimulate multiple egg production in the ovary. Drugs that stimulate multiple egg production probably contain, or increase the production of, which of the following hormones?

I. LH
II. FSH
III. ACTH
IV. Estrogen

A. I only
B. IV only
C. I, II and IV only
D. I, II, III and IV

10) After fertilization, the zygote will develop into a female if:

A. the zygote possesses an X chromosome.
B. the primary oocyte possesses an X chromosome.
C. the egg possesses an X chromosome.
D. the sperm possesses an X chromosome.

11) Damage to the ectoderm during gastrulation will result in an embryo with an underdeveloped:

A. reproductive system.
B. nervous system.
C. excretory system.
D. digestive system.

12) The blastula develops into which of the following?

A. The morula
B. The blastula
C. The gastrula
D. The neurula

13) The developing fetus has a blood vessel called the ductus arteriosus which connects the pulmonary artery to the aorta. When a baby is born, the ductus arteriosus closes permanently. Which is the dominant feature found in a newborn whose ductus arteriosus failed to obliterate?

A. Increased O_2 partial pressure in pulmonary arteries
B. Decreased CO_2 partial pressure in pulmonary arteries
C. Increased O_2 partial pressure in systemic arteries
D. Decreased O_2 partial pressure in systemic arteries

14) The placenta in humans is derived from the:

A. embryo only.
B. uterus only.
C. endometrium and embryo.
D. uterus and fallopian tube.

15) Synapsis and crossing over of chromosomes occurs is which phase of meiosis?

A. Prophase I
B. Prophase II
C. Metaphase I
D. Metaphase II

GS ANSWER KEY

CHAPTER 14

		Cross-Reference				Cross-Reference
1.	C	BIO 14.1, 14.5	9.	C		BIO 14.3
2.	A	BIO 14.1, 10.1, 10.2	10.	D		BIO 14.2, 14.8
3.	A	BIO 14.1	11.	B		BIO 14.5
4.	D	BIO 14.2	12.	C		BIO 14.5
5.	C	BIO 3.0	13.	D		BIO 7.2, 7.3, 14.7
6.	B	BIO 14.3	14.	C		BIO 14.6
7.	A	BIO 6.3.1F, 14.3	15.	C		BIO 14.2
8.	A	BIO 14.3				

* Explanations can be found at the back of the book.

Go online to DAT-prep.com for additional chapter review Q&A and forum.

Go online to DAT-prep.com for additional chapter review Q&A and forum.

GOLD NOTES

Memorize	Understand	Importance
...e: phenotype, genotype, gene, locus, : single and multiple ...o/heterozygosity, wild type, recessiveness, ...lete/co-dominance ...nplete dominance, gene pool ...inked characteristics, sex determination s of mutations: random, translation error, ...cription error, base subs., etc.	* Importance of meiosis; compare/contrast with mitosis; segregation of genes, assortment, linkage, recombination * Single/double crossovers; relationship of mutagens to carcinogens * Hardy-Weinberg Principle, inborn errors of metabolism * Test cross: back cross, concepts of parental, F1 and F2 generations * DNA recombination and genetic technology	**3 to 7 out of the 40 Biology** DAT questions are based on content in this chapter (in our estimation). * Note that between 25% and 50% of the questions in DAT Biology are from 5 chapters: 1, 2, 14, 15, and 16.

DAT-Prep.com

Introduction

Genetics is the study of heredity and variation in organisms. The observations of Gregor Mendel in the mid-nineteenth century gave birth to the science which would reveal the physical basis for his conclusions, DNA, about 100 years later.

Additional Resources

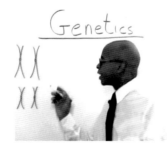

Free Online Q&A + Forum   Video: Online or DVD   Flashcards   Special Guest

Genetics is a branch of biology which deals with the principles and mechanics of heredity; in other words, the *means* by which *traits* are passed from parents to offspring. To begin, we will first examine some relevant definitions - a few of which we have already discussed.

Chromosomes are a complex of DNA and proteins (incl. histones; BIO 1.2.2). A gene is that sequence of DNA that codes for a protein or polypeptide. A locus is the *position* of the gene on the DNA molecule. Recall that humans inherit 46 chromosomes - 23 from maternal origin and 23 from paternal origin (BIO 14.2). A given chromosome from maternal origin has a counterpart from paternal origin which codes for the same products. This is called a **homologous pair** of chromosomes.

Any homologous pair of chromosomes have a pair of genes which codes for the same product (i.e. hair color). Such pairs of genes are called **alleles**. Thus for one gene product, a nucleus contains one allele from maternal origin and one allele from paternal origin. If both alleles are identical (i.e. they code for the same hair color), then the individual is called **homozygous** for that trait. If the two alleles differ (i.e. one codes for dark hair while the other codes for light hair), then the individual is called **heterozygous** for that trait.

The set of genes possessed by a particular organism is its genotype. The appearance or phenotype of an individual is expressed as a consequence of the genotype and the environment. Consider a heterozygote that expressed one gene (dark hair) but not the other (light hair). The expressed gene would be called dominant while the other unexpressed allele would be called recessive. The individual would have dark hair as their phenotype, yet their genotype would be heterozygous for that trait. The dominant allele is expressed in the phenotype. This is known as Mendel's Law of Dominance.

It is common to symbolize dominant genes with capital letters (A) and recessive genes with small letters (a). From the preceding paragraphs, we can conclude that with two alleles, three genotypes are possible: homozygous dominant (AA), heterozygous (Aa), and homozygous recessive (aa). Note that this only results in two phenotypes since both AA and Aa express the dominant gene, while only aa expresses the recessive gene.

Each individual carries **two** alleles while populations may have many or **multiple alleles**. Sometimes these genes are not strictly dominant or recessive. There may be degrees of blending (= *incomplete dominance*) or sometimes two alleles may be equally dominant (= *codominance*). ABO blood types are an important example of multiple alleles with codominance.

Incomplete dominance occurs when the phenotype of the heterozygote is an intermediate of the phenotypes of the homozygotes. A classic example is flower color in snapdragon: the snapdragon flower color is red for homozygous dominant and white for homozygous recessive. When the red homozygous flower is crossed with the white homozygous flower, the result yields a 100% pink snapdragon flower. The pink snapdragon is the result of the combined effect of both dominant and recessive genes.

15.2 ABO Blood Types

Codominance occurs when multiple alleles exist for a particular gene and more than one is dominant. When a dominant allele is combined with a recessive allele, the phenotype of the recessive allele is completely masked. But when two dominant alleles are present, the contributions of both alleles do not overpower each other and the phenotype is the result of the expression of both alleles. A classic example of codominance is the ABO blood type in humans.

Red blood cells can have various antigens or *agglutinogens* on their plasma membranes which aid in blood typing. The important two are antigens A and B. If the red blood cells have only antigen A, the blood type is A; if they have only antigen B, then the blood type is B; if they have both antigens, the blood type is AB; if neither antigen is present, the blood type is O. There are three allelic genes in the population (I^A, I^B, i^O). Two are codominant (I^A, I^B) and one is recessive (i^O). Thus in a given population, there are six possible genotypes which result in four possible phenotypes:

Genotype	Phenotype
$I^A I^A$, $I^A i^O$	blood type A
$I^B I^B$, $I^B i^O$	blood type B
$I^A I^B$	blood type AB
$i^O i^O$	blood type O

Blood typing is critical before doing a blood transfusion. This is because people with blood type A have anti-B antibodies, those with type B have anti-A, those with type AB have neither antibody, while type O has both anti-A and anti-B antibodies. If a person with type O blood is given types A, B, or AB, the clumping of the red blood cells will occur (= *agglutination*). Though type O can only receive from type O, it can give to the other blood types since its red blood cells have no antigens {type O = universal donor}. Type AB has neither antibody to react against A or B antigens so it can receive blood from all blood types {type AB = universal recipient}.

The only other antigens which have some importance are the Rh factors which are coded by different genes at different loci from the A and B antigens. Rh factors are either there (Rh⁺) or they are not there (Rh⁻). 85% of the population are Rh⁺. The problem occurs when a woman is Rh⁻ and has been exposed to Rh⁺ blood and then forms anti-Rh⁺ antibod-ies (note: unlike the previous case, exposure is necessary to produce these antibodies). If this woman is pregnant with an Rh⁺ fetus her antibodies may cross the placenta and cause the fetus' red blood cells to agglutinate (*eryth-roblastosis fetalis*). This condition is fatal if left untreated.

15.3 Mendelian Genetics

Recall that in gametogenesis homolo-gous chromosomes separate during the first meiotic division. Thus alleles that code for the same trait are segregated: this is **Mendel's First Law of Segregation. Mendel's Sec-ond Law of Independent Assortment** states that different chromosomes (*or factors which carry different traits*) separate independently of each other. For example, consider a pri-mary spermatocyte (2N) undergoing its first meiotic division. It is not the case that all 23 chromosomes of paternal origin will end up in one secondary spermatocyte while the other 23 chromosomes of maternal origin ends up in the other. Rather, each chromosome in a homologous pair separates *independently* of any other chromosome in other homologous pairs.

However, it has been noted experi-mentally that sometimes traits on the same chromosome assort independently! This non-Mendelian concept is a result of *cross-ing over* (recall that this is when homologous chromosomes exchange parts, BIO 14.2). In fact, it has been shown that two traits located far apart on a chromosome are more likely to cross over and thus assort independently, as compared to two traits that are close. The pro-pensity for some traits to refrain from assort-ing independently is called linkage. Double crossovers occur when two crossovers hap-pen in a chromosomal region being studied.

Another exception to Mendel's laws involves **sex linkage**. Mendel's laws would predict that the results of a genetic cross should be the same regardless of which parent introduces the allele. However, it can be shown that some traits follow the inheri-tance of the sex chromosomes. Humans have one pair of sex chromosomes (XX = female, XY = male), and the remaining 22 pairs of homologous chromosomes are called **autosomes**.

Since females have two X chromo-somes and males have only one, a single recessive allele carried on an X chromosome could be expressed in a male since there is no second allele present to mask it. When males inherit one copy of the recessive allele from an X chromosome, they will express the trait. In contrast, females must inherit two copies to express the trait. Therefore, an X-linked recessive phenotype is much more frequently found in males than females. In fact, a typical pattern of sex linkage is when a mother passes her phenotype to all her sons but **none** of her daughters. Her daughters become *carriers* for the recessive allele. Certain forms of hemophilia, colorblindness, and one kind of muscular dystrophy are well-known recessive sex-linked traits. {In what was once known as Lyon's Hypothesis, it has been shown that every female has a condensed, inactivated X chromosome in her body or somatic cells called a Barr body.}

Let us examine the predictions of Mendel's First Law. Consider two parents, one homozygous dominant (AA) and the other homozygous recessive (aa). Each parent can only form one type of gamete with respect to that trait (*either* A *or* a, *respectively*). The next generation (*called* first filial *or* **F₁**) must then be uniformly heterozygotes or *hybrids* (Aa). Now the F₁ hybrids can produce gametes that can be either A *half the time* or a *half the time*. When the F₁ generation is self-crossed, i.e. Aa X Aa, the F₂ generation will be more genotypically and phenotypically diverse and we can predict the outcome in the next generation (F₂) using a Punnett square:

	1/2 A	1/2 a
1/2 A	1/4 AA	1/4 Aa
1/2 a	1/4 Aa	1/4 aa

Here is an example as to how you derive the information within the square: when you cross A with A you get AA (i.e. $1/2$ A × $1/2$ A = 1/4 AA). Thus by doing a simple *monohybrid* cross (Aa × Aa) with random mating, the Punnett square indicates that in the F₂ generation, 1/4 of the population would be AA, 1/2 would be Aa (1/4 + 1/4), and 1/4 would be aa. In other words the *genotypic* ratio of homozygous dominant to heterozygous to homozygous recessive is 1:2:1. However, since AA and Aa demonstrate the same *phenotype* (i.e. dominant) the ratio of dominant phenotype to recessive phenotype is 3:1.

Now we will consider the predictions of Mendel's Second Law. To examine independent assortment, we will have to consider a case with two traits (usu. on different chromosomes) or a *di*hybrid cross. Imagine a parent which is homozygous dominant for two traits (AABB) while the other is homozygous recessive (aabb). Each parent can only form one type of gamete with respect to those traits (*either* AB *or* ab, *respectively*). The F₁ generation will be uniform for the dominant trait (i.e. *the* genotypes *would all be* AaBb). In the gametes of the F₁ generation, the alleles will assort independently.

Consequently, an equal amount of all the possible gametes will form: 1/4 AB, 1/4 Ab, 1/4 aB, and 1/4 ab. When the F_1 generation is self-crossed, i.e. AaBb X AaBb, we can predict the outcome in the F_2 generation using the Punnett square:

	1/4 AB	1/4 Ab	1/4 aB	1/4 ab
1/4 AB	1/16 AABB	1/16 AABb	1/16 AaBB	1/16 AaBb
1/4 Ab	1/16 AABb	1/16 AAbb	1/16 AaBb	1/16 Aabb
1/4 aB	1/16 AaBB	1/16 AaBb	1/16 aaBB	1/16 aaBb
1/4 ab	1/16 AaBb	1/16 Aabb	1/16 aaBb	1/16 aabb

Thus by doing a dihybrid cross with random mating, the Punnett square indicates that there are nine possible genotypes (*the frequency is given in brackets*): AABB (1), AABb (2), AaBb (4), AaBB (2), Aabb (2), aaBb (2), AAbb (1), aaBB (1), and aabb (1). Since A and B are dominant, there are only four phenotypic classes in the ratio 9:3:3:1 which are: the expression of <u>both</u> traits (AABB + AABb + AaBb + AaBB = 9), the expression of only the <u>first</u> trait (AAbb + Aabb = 3), the expression of only the <u>second</u> trait (aaBB + aaBb = 3), and the expression of <u>neither</u> trait (aabb = 1). Now we know, for example, that 9/16 represents that fraction of the population which will have the phenotype of both dominant traits.

15.3.1 A Word about Probability

If you were to flip a quarter, the probability of getting "heads" is 50% (p = 0.5). If you flipped the quarter ten times and each time it came up heads, the probability of getting heads on the next trial is still 50%. After all, previous trials have no effect on the next trial.

Since chance events, such as fertilization of a particular kind of egg by a particular kind of sperm, occur independently, the genotype of one child has no effect on the genotypes of other children produced by a set of parents. Thus in the previous example of the dihybrid cross, the chance of producing the genotype AaBb is 4/16 (25%) irrespective of the genotypes which have already been produced.

15.4 The Hardy-Weinberg Law

The Hardy-Weinberg Law deals with population genetics. A **population** includes all the members of a species which occupy a more or less well defined geographical area and have demonstrated the ability to reproduce from generation to generation. A **gene pool** is the sum of all the unique alleles for a given population. A central component to evolution is the changing of alleles in a gene pool from one generation to the next.

Evolution can be viewed as a changing of gene frequencies within a population over successive generations. The Hardy-Weinberg Law or *equilibrium* predicts the outcome of a randomly mating population of sexually reproducing diploid organisms who are <u>not</u> undergoing evolution.

For the Hardy-Weinberg Law to be applied, the idealized population must meet the following conditions: i) **random mating**: the members of the population must have no mating preferences; ii) **no mutations**: there must be no errors in replication nor similar event resulting in a change in the genome; iii) **isolation**: there must be no exchange of genes between the population being considered and any other population; iv) **large population**: since the law is based on statistical probabilities, to avoid sampling errors, the population cannot be small; v) **no selection pressures**: there must be no reproductive advantage of one allele over the other.

To illustrate a use of the law, consider an idealized population that abides by the preceding conditions and have a gene locus occupied by either A or a. Let p = the frequency of allele A in the population and let q = the frequency of allele a. Since they are the only alleles, $p + q = 1$. Squaring both sides we get:

$$(p + q)^2 = (1)^2$$

OR

$$p^2 + 2pq + q^2 = 1$$

The preceding equation (= *the Hardy-Weinberg equation*) can be used to calculate genotype frequencies once the allelic frequencies are given. This can be summarized by the following:

	pA	qa
pA	p^2AA	pqAa
qa	pqAa	q^2aa

The Punnett square illustrates the expected frequencies of the three genotypes in the next generation: AA = p^2, Aa = 2pq, and aa= q^2.

For example, let us calculate the percentage of heterozygous individuals in a population where the recessive allele q has a frequency of 0.2. Since p + q = 1, then p = 0.8. Using the Hardy-Weinberg equation and squaring p and q we get:

$$0.64 + 2pq + 0.04 = 1$$

$$2pq = 1 - 0.68 = 0.32$$

Thus the percentage of heterozygous (2pq) individuals is 32%.

A practical application of the Hardy-Weinberg equation is the prediction of how many people in a generation are carriers for a particular recessive allele. The values would have to be recalculated for every generation since humans do not abide by all the conditions of the Hardy-Weinberg Law (i.e. *humans continually evolve*).

15.4.1 Back Cross, Test Cross

A back cross is the cross of an individual (F_1) with one of its parents (P) or an organism with the same genotype as a parent. Back crosses can be used to help identify the genotypes of the individual in a specific type of back cross called a test cross. A test cross is a cross between an organism whose genotype for a certain trait is unknown and an organism that is homozygous recessive for that trait so the unknown genotype can be determined from that of the offspring. For example, for P: AA x aa and F_1: Aa, we get:

Backcross #1: Aa x AA
Progeny #1: 1/2 Aa and 1/2 AA

Backcross #2: Aa x aa
Progeny #2: 1/2 Aa and 1/2 aa

15.5 Genetic Variability

Meiosis and mutations are sources of genetic variability. During meiosis I, crossing over occurs between the parental and maternal genes which leads to a recombination of parental genes yielding unique haploid gametes. Thus recombination can result in alleles of linked traits separating into different gametes. However, the closer two traits are on a chromosome, the more likely they will be linked and thus remain together, and vice versa.

Further recombination occurs during the random fusion of gametes during fertilization.

Consequently, taking Mendel's two laws and recombination together, we can predict that parents can give their offspring combinations of alleles which the parents never had. This leads to **genetic variability**.

Mutations are rare, inheritable, random changes in the genetic material (DNA) of a cell. Mutations are much more likely to be either neutral (esp. *silent mutations*) or negative (i.e. cancer) than positive for an organism's survival. Nonetheless, such a change in the genome increases genetic variability. Only mutations of gametes, and not somatic cells, are passed on to offspring.

The following are some forms of mutations:

• **Point mutation** is a change affecting a single base pair in a gene

• **Deletion** is the removal of a sequence of DNA, the regions on either side being joined together

• **Inversion** is the reversal of a segment of DNA

• **Translocation** is when one chromosome breaks and attaches to another

• **Duplication** is when a sequence of DNA is repeated.

• **Frame shift mutations** occur when bases are added or deleted in numbers other than multiples of three. Such deletions or additions cause the rest of the sequence to be shifted such that each triplet reading frame is altered.

A mutagen is any substance or agent that can cause a mutation. A mutagen is not the same as a carcinogen. Carcinogens are agents that cause cancer. While many mutagens are carcinogens as well, many others are not. The Ames test is a widely used test to screen chemicals used in foods or medications for mutagenic potential.

Mutations can produce many types of genetic diseases including inborn errors of metabolism. These disorders in normal metabolism are usually due to defects of a single gene that codes for one enzyme.

15.6 Genetics and Heredity: A Closer Look

The rest of this chapter begins to push into more advanced topics in genetics. However, these topics continue to represent legitimate exam material.

Epistasis occurs when one gene masks the phenotype of a second gene. This is often the case in pigmentation where one gene turns on (or off) the production of pigment, while a second gene controls the amount of pigment produced. Such is the case in mice fur where one gene codes for the presence or absence of pigmentation and the other codes for the color. If C and c represent the alleles for the presence or absence of color and B and b represent black and brown then a phenotype of CCbb and Ccbb would both correspond to a brown phenotype. Whenever cc is inherited the fur will be white.

Pleiotropy occurs when a single gene has more than one phenotypic expression. This is often seen in pea plants where the gene that expresses round or wrinkled texture of seeds also influences the expression of starch metabolism. For example, in wrinkled seeds there is more unconverted glucose which leads to an increase of the osmotic gradient. These seeds will subsequently contain more water than round seeds. When they mature they will dehydrate and produce the wrinkled appearance.

Polygenic inheritance refers to traits that cannot be expressed in just a few types but rather as a range of varieties. The most popular example would be human height which ranges from very short to very tall. This phenomenon (many genes shaping one phenotype) is the opposite of pleiotropy.

Penetrance refers to the proportion of individuals carrying a particular variant of a gene (allele or genotype) that also express the associated phenotype. Alleles which are highly penetrant are more likely to be noticed. Penetrance only considers whether individuals express the trait or not. *Expressivity* refers to the variation in the degree of expression of a given trait.

Nondisjunction occurs when the chromosomes do not separate properly and do not migrate to opposite poles as in normal anaphase of meiosis (BIO 14.2). This could arise from a failure of homologous chromosomes to separate in meiosis I, or the failure of sister chromatids to separate during meiosis II or mitosis. Most of the time, gametes produced after nondisjunction are sterile; however, certain imbalances can be fertile and lead to genetic defects. Down Syndrome (Trisomy 21 = 3 copies of chromosome 21 due to its nondisjunction, thus the person has an extra chromosome making a total of 47 chromosomes); Turner and Klinefelter Syndrome (nondisjunction of sex chromosomes); and Cri du Chat (deletion in chromosome 5) are well known genetic disorders. Hemophilia and red-green color blindness are common sex-linked disorders and are recessive.

Phenylketonuria, sickle-cell anemia and Tay-Sachs disease are common autosomal recessive disorders.

Gene linkage refers to genes that reside on the same chromosome and are unable to display independent assortment because they are physically connected (BIO 15.3). The further away the two genes are on the chromosome the higher probability there is that they will crossover during synapsis. In these cases recombination frequencies are used to provide a linkage map where the arrangement of the genes can be ascertained. For example, say you have a fly with genotype BBTTYY and the crossover frequency between B and T is 26%, between Y and T is 18% and between B and Y is 8%. Greater recombination frequencies mean greater distances so you know that B and T are the furthest apart. This corresponds to a gene order of B-Y-T and since frequencies are a direct measure of distance you know exactly how far apart each allele is and can easily calculate the map distances.

15.6.1   Mitochondrial DNA

Mitochondrial DNA (mtDNA or mDNA) has become increasingly popular as a tool to determine how closely populations are related as well as to clarify the evolutionary relationships among species (= phylogenetics). Mitochondrial DNA is circular (BIO 1.2.2, 16.6.3) and can be regarded as the smallest chromosome. In most species, including humans, mtDNA is inherited solely from the mother. The DNA sequence of mtDNA has been determined from a large number of organisms and individuals (including some organisms that are extinct).

15.7   DNA Recombination and Genetic Technology

DNA recombination involves DNA that contains segments or genes from different sources. The foreign DNA can come from another DNA molecule, a chromosome or from a complete organism. Most DNA transferred is done artificially using DNA recombination techniques which use restriction enzymes to cut pieces of DNA. These enzymes originate from bacteria and are extremely specific because they only cut DNA at specific recognition sequences along the strand. These recognition sites correspond to different nucleotide sequences and produce sticky and blunt ends when a double stranded DNA segment is cut.

The sticky end is the unpaired part of the DNA that is ready to bind with a complementary codon (sequence of three adjacent nucleotides; BIO 3.0). These cut pieces or **restriction fragments** are often inserted into plasmids (circular piece of DNA that is able to replicate independently of the chromosomal DNA) which are then able to be introduced into the bacteria via transformation (see BIO 2.2).

Treating the plasmid, or replicon, with the same restriction enzymes used on the original fragment produces the same sticky ends in both pieces allowing base pairing to occur when they are mixed together. This attachment is stabilized by DNA ligase. After the ends are joined and the recombinant plasmid is incorporated into bacteria, the bacteria become capable of producing copious amounts of a

Bacterium and Vector Plasmid

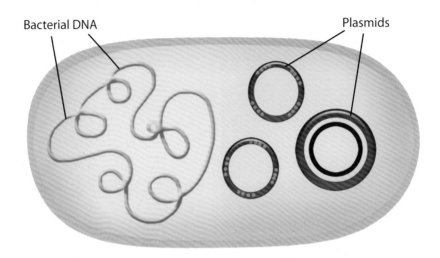

specific protein that was not native to its species (i.e. bacteria with recombinant DNA producing insulin to treat diabetes).

Gel electrophoresis is a method of separating restriction fragments of differing lengths based on their size (as described in the previous section, a restriction fragment is a fragment of DNA cleaved by a restriction enzyme). The DNA fragments are passed through a gel which is under the influence of an electric field. Since DNA is negatively charged it will move towards the cathode (positive electrode). The shorter fragments move faster than the longer ones and can be visualized as a banding pattern using autoradiography techniques.

SDS-PAGE, sodium dodecyl sulfate polyacrylamide gel electrophoresis (ORG 13), also separates proteins according to their electrophoretic mobility. SDS is an anionic detergent (i.e. negatively charged) which has

the following effect: (1) linearize proteins and (2) give an additional negative charge to the linearized proteins. In most proteins, the binding of SDS to the polypeptide chain gives an even distribution of charge per unit mass, thus fractionation will approximate size during electrophoresis (i.e. not dependent on charge).

Restriction fragment length polymorphisms or RFLP is a technique that exploits variations in restriction fragments from one individual to another that differ in length due to polymorphisms, or slight differences in DNA sequences. The process involves digesting DNA sequences with different restriction enzymes, detecting the resulting restriction fragments by gel electrophoresis, and comparing their lengths. In DNA fingerprinting, commonly used to analyze DNA left at crime scenes, RFLP's are produced and compared to RFLP's of known suspects in order to catch the perpetrator.

Sometimes it is necessary to obtain the DNA fragment bearing the required gene directly from the mRNA that codes for the polypeptide in question. This is due to the presence of introns (non-coding regions on a DNA molecule; BIO 3.0) which prevent transcription of foreign genes in the genome of bacteria, a common problem in recombinant technology. To carry this out one can use reverse transcriptase producing complementary DNA (cDNA) which lack the problematic introns.

Rather than using a bacterium to clone DNA fragments, sometimes DNA is copied directly using the polymerase chain reaction (PCR). This method allows us to rapidly amplify the DNA content using synthetic primers that initiate replication at specific nucleotide sequences. This method relies on thermal cycling (repeated heating and cooling) of the DNA primers and can lead to thousands and even millions of copies in relatively short periods of time.

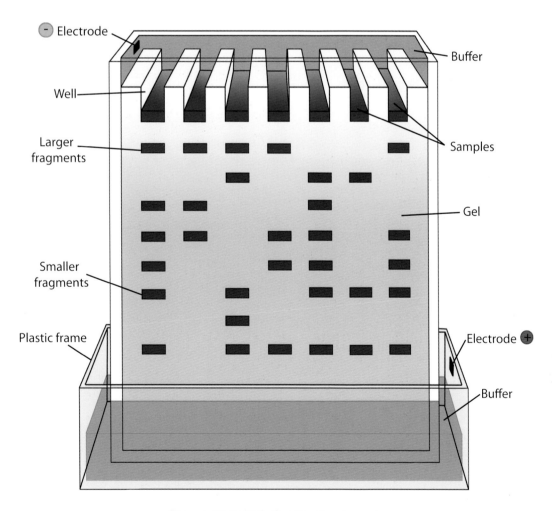

Figure IV.A.15.1: Gel Electrophoresis.

Southern blotting, named after Dr. E. Southern, is the process of transferring DNA fragments from the electrophoresis agarose gel onto filter paper where they are identified with probes. The procedure begins by digesting DNA in a mixture with *restriction endonucleases* to cut out specific pieces of DNA. The DNA fragments are then subjected to gel electrophoresis. The now separated fragments are bathed in an alkaline solution where they immediately begin to denature. These fragments are then placed (or blotted) onto nitrocellulose paper and then incubated with a specific probe whose location can be visualized with autoradiography.

Northern blotting is adapted from the Southern blot to detect specific sequences of RNA by hybridization with cDNA. Similarly, *Western blotting* is used to identify specific amino-acid sequences in proteins. Some students prefer to remember the blotting techniques with the mnemonic SNOW DROP.

SNOW	DROP
Southern	**D**NA
Northern	**R**NA
O	**O**
Western	**P**rotein

DNA microarray technology (= DNA chip or biochip or "laboratory-on-a-chip") helps to determine which genes are active and which are inactive in different cell types. This technology evolved from Southern blotting and can also be used to genotype multiple regions of a genome. DNA microarrays are created by robotic machines that arrange incredibly small amounts of hundreds or thousands of gene sequences on a single microscope slide. These sequences can be a short section of a gene or other DNA element that is used to hybridize a cDNA or cRNA (also called anti-sense RNA) sample. The hybridization is usually observed and quantified by the detection of fluorescent tag.

NB: The molecular biology techniques of FRAP (BIO 1.5) and ELISA (BIO 8.4) were described earlier in this book. Basic lab techniques and equipment are presented in General Chemistry Chapter 12. Electrophoresis and chromatography are discussed in Organic Chemistry Chapter 13.

GOLD STANDARD WARM-UP EXERCISES

CHAPTER 15: Genetics

1) Which of the following is the LEAST likely reason for the phenotype of PKU disease lacking phenylalanine hydroxylase?

   A. An added nucleotide in the genetic code results in an altered sequence of nucleotides which gets translated into an altered sequence of amino acids.

   B. A deletion in the genetic code results in an altered sequence of nucleotides which gets translated into an altered sequence of amino acids.

   C. The stereochemistry of the chromosome becomes altered.

   D. A deletion in the genetic code creates a stop codon in the nucleotide sequence.

2) In general terms, what is the primary genetic difference between a hepatocyte (a liver cell) and a muscle cell?

   A. The amount of DNA
   B. The number of chromosomes
   C. The number of genes
   D. The expression of genes

3) Over 10 million North Americans are treated for thyroid diseases and, overwhelmingly, women are much more likely than men to succumb to these conditions. Is it reasonable to conclude that thyroid disease is sex-linked?

   A. No, because thyroid disease appears to be caused by a defect of the immune system and not a defective DNA sequence.

   B. No, because if the disease was sex-linked, there would be a high incidence in the male, rather than the female, population.

   C. Yes, because the high incidence of the disease in women suggests that a gene found on the X chromosome codes for the disease.

   D. Yes, because the same factor increases the risk of women getting the disease, regardless of familial background.

4) Although the cloned sheep Dolly contains the exact DNA as her genetic mother, there are a few visible and behavioral differences in Dolly. This is most probably due to:

   A. the sheep in which the embryo was implanted.

   B. the induction of specific genes not expressed in the mother.

   C. mutations caused by incubation in the nutrient-deficient solution.

   D. environmental factors.

5) In fruit flies, males have XY sex chromosomes, females have XX, and white eye color is sex linked. If red-eyed (heterozygous) females are crossed with white-eyed males, what would be the expected eye colors and sexes of the progeny?

   A. ¾ white-eyed female and ¼ red-eyed male.

   B. ½ red-eyed female and ½ white-eyed male.

   C. All red eyed, half male and half female.

   D. ¼ red-eyed female, ¼ white-eyed female, ¼ red-eyed male and ¼ white-eyed male.

6) The members of a homologous pair of genes are separated during meiosis of reproductive cells so that each gamete contains one of the alleles. The preceding is an expression of which of the following laws?

A. The law of segregation
B. The law of sorting
C. The law of independent assortment
D. The law of gene isolation

7) Which of the following refers to a cross in which traits are considered simultaneously?

A. Filial cross
B. Double cross
C. Dihybrid cross
D. Punnett cross

8) Which of the following terms refers to the frequency with which a gene is expressed in a detectable way?

A. Penetrance
B. Polygenetics
C. Codominance
D. Allelism

9) Which of the following terms refers to the collection of all alleles of every gene present in the members of a population?

A. Genetic assortment
B. Population
C. Gene diversity
D. Gene pool

10) Although there is some evidence that pronounced differences in DNA content can interfere with chromosome pairing between species, the effect is surprisingly slight; hybrids between related species of grasses that differ by as much as 50 percent in DNA content have virtually normal chromosome pairing, chiasma formation and segregation. Which of the following processes likely occurs to allow the normal chromosome pairing observed in grass species?

A. The interstitial repetitive sequences in one homologous chromosome would loop so that pairing could occur.
B. The unpaired sequences in the homologous chromosome without the interstitial repetitive sequences would duplicate so that pairing could occur.
C. The homologous chromosome with the interstitial repetitive sequence would undergo a translocation so that pairing could occur.
D. The homologous chromosome with the interstitial repetitive sequence would undergo a deletion so that pairing could occur.

11) Von Willebrand's disease is an autosomal dominant bleeding disorder. A man who does not have the disease has two children with a woman who is heterozygous for the condition. If the first child expresses the bleeding disorder, what is the probability that the second child will have the disease?

A. 0.25
B. 0.50
C. 0.75
D. 1.00

12) A transfusion of red blood cells is being considered. Which of the following donors would NOT elicit and immune response in a recipient who is type B and Rh-negative?

A. One who was type A and Rh-negative.
B. One who was type AB and Rh-negative, but had been previously exposed to Rh-positive blood.
C. One who was type B and Rh-negative, but had been previously exposed to Rh-positive blood.
D. One who was type B and Rh-positive.

13) Given that the ABO system elicits a much stronger immune response (i.e. more immunogenic) than the Rh-factor, an Rh-negative type O mother carrying an Rh-positive child will most likely manufacture anti-Rh antibodies if fetal cells enter the maternal circulation if the child is:

A. type A.
B. type B.
C. type O.
D. type AB.

14) The risk of hemolytic disease of the newborn increases with each Rh-positive pregnancy that an Rh-negative woman has. The main reason for this is that:

A. the probability of the fetus being Rh-positive increases with every pregnancy.
B. Rh-negative antibodies in the maternal circulation can cross the placental barrier to attack and hemolyse the erythrocytes of the fetus.
C. anti-Rh antibodies in the maternal circulation can cross the placental barrier to attack and hemolyse the erythrocytes of the fetus.
D. anti-Rh agglutins are not strongly expressed in the fetal circulation.

15) Nonsense mutations and frame shift mutations would most likely originate during which of the following?

A. DNA replication
B. Transcription
C. Translation
D. Splicing

16) Consider the following crossover frequencies:

Crossover	Genes Frequency
B and D	2%
C and A	7%
A and B	15%
C and B	20%
C and D	25%

Which of the following represents the relative positions of the four genes A, B, C and D, on the chromosome?

A. ADCB
B. CABD
C. DBCA
D. ABCD

17) From which grandparent or grandparents did you inherit your mitochondria?

A. Paternal grandfather
B. Maternal grandmother
C. Mother's parents
D. Grandmothers

How can you distinguish the sex chromosomes? Pull down their genes! :)

GS ANSWER KEY

CHAPTER 15

			Cross-Reference
1.	C		BIO 15.1, 15.5
2.	D		BIO 15.1, 14.5.1
3.	B		BIO 15.3
4.	D		BIO 15.1
5.	D		BIO 15.1, 15.3
6.	A		BIO 15.3
7.	C		BIO 15.3
8.	A		BIO 15.6
9.	D		BIO 15.4

			Cross-Reference
10.	A		BIO 15.5, 14.2, deduce
11.	B		BIO 15.3
12.	C		BIO 15.2
13.	C		BIO 15.2
14.	C		BIO 15.2, 15.3.1, 8.2
15.	A		BIO 15.5, 1.2.2, 14.2
16.	C		BIO 1.2.2, ORG 12.5
17.	B		BIO 1.2.2

* Explanations can be found at the back of the book.

Go online to DAT-prep.com for additional chapter review Q&A and forum.

APPENDIX
CHAPTER 15: Genetics

Advanced DAT-30 Passage: Polymerase Chain Reaction

The polymerase chain reaction (PCR) is a powerful biological tool that allows the rapid amplification of any fragment of DNA without purification. In PCR, RNA primers are made to flank the specific DNA sequence to be amplified. These RNA primers are then extended to the end of the DNA molecule with the use of a heat-resistant DNA polymerase. The newly synthesized DNA strand is then used as the template to undergo another round of replication.

The 1st step in PCR is the melting of the target DNA into 2 single strands by heating the reaction mixture to approximately 94 °C, and then rapidly cooling the mixture to allow annealing of the RNA primers to their specific locations (note: annealing is the sticking together of complementary single strands which, of course, involves the formation of hydrogen bonds between the base pairs; BIO 1.2.2). Once the primer has annealed, the temperature is elevated to 72 °C to allow optimal activity of the DNA polymerase. The polymerase will continue to add nucleotides until the entire complimentary strand of the template is completed at which point the cycle is repeated (Figure 1).

One of the uses of PCR is sex determination, which requires amplification of intron 1 of the amelogenin gene. This gene found on the X-Y homologous chromosomes has a 184 base pair deletion on the Y homologue. Therefore, by amplifying intron 1, females can be distinguished from males by the fact that males will have 2 different sizes of the amplified DNA while females will only have 1 unique fragment size.

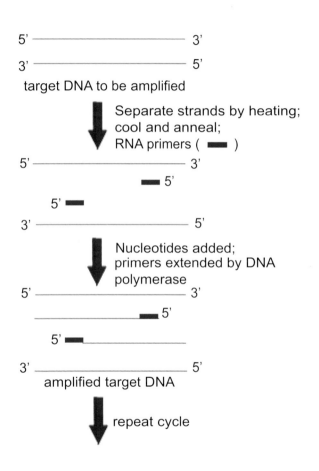

Figure 1

18) The polymerase chain reaction resembles which of the following cellular process?

A. Transcription of DNA
B. Protein synthesis
C. DNA replication
D. Translation

19) Why is a heat resistant DNA polymerase required for successive replication in the polymerase chain reaction, rather than simply a human DNA polymerase?

A. The high temperatures required to melt the DNA double strand may denature a normal human cellular DNA polymerase.

B. The high temperatures required to melt the DNA would cause human DNA polymerase to remain bound to the DNA strand.

C. Heat resistant DNA polymerase increases the rate of the polymerase chain reaction at high temperatures whereas human DNA polymerase lowers the rate.

D. Heat resistant DNA polymerase recognizes RNA primers whereas human DNA polymerase does not.

20) The use of PCR for sex determination relies on the fact that:

A. the amelogenin gene is responsible for an autosomal recessive trait.

B. the X and Y homologous chromosomes have different sizes of intron 1 of the amelogenin gene.

C. females have an X and Y chromosome and males have two X chromosomes.

D. intron 1 has a different nucleotide length than intron 2.

21) What would PCR amplification of an individual's intron 1 of the amelogenin gene reveal if the individual were male?

A. One type of intron 1 since the individual has one X chromosome and one Y chromosome.

B. Two types of intron 1 since the individual has only one X chromosome.

C. One type of intron 1 since the individual has only one X chromosome.

D. Two types of intron 1 since the individual has one X chromosome and one Y chromosome.

22) The technique that utilizes probes to detect specific DNA sequences is known as which of the following?

A. Southern blot

B. RFLP

C. Western blot

D. PCR

Go online to DAT-prep.com for additional chapter review Q&A and forum.

GOLD NOTES

EVOLUTION
Chapter 16

Memorize

...e: species, genetic drift
...ix-Kingdom System: taxonomy,
...res of its members including
...ture and function

Understand

* Natural selection, speciation
* Genetic drift
* Basics: origin of life
* Basics: comparative anatomy
* Basics: eukaryotic, prokaryotic evolution

Importance

2 to 5 out of the 40 Biology
DAT questions are based on content
in this chapter (in our estimation).
* Note that between 25% and 50% of
the questions in DAT Biology are from
5 chapters: 1, 2, 14, 15, and 16.

DAT-Prep.com

Introduction

Evolution is, quite simply, the change in the inherited traits of a population of organisms from one generation to another. This change over time can be traced to 3 main processes: variation, reproduction and selection. The major mechanisms that drive evolution are natural selection and genetic drift. Chemical evolution led to cellular evolution and, ultimately, to the enormous diversity within 3 Domains and 6 Kingdoms.

Additional Resources

Free Online Q&A + Forum

Flashcards

Special Guest

Evolution is the change in frequency of one or more alleles in a population's gene pool from one generation to the next. The evidence for evolution lies in the fossil record, biogeography, embryology, compara-tive anatomy, and experiments from artificial selection. The most important mechanism of evolution is the **selection** of certain pheno-types provided by the **genetic variability** of a population.

16.2 Natural Selection

Natural selection is the non-random dif-ferential survival and reproduction from one generation to the next. Natural selection con-tains the following premises: i) genetic and phenotypic variability exist in populations: offspring show variations compared to par-ents; ii) more individuals are produced than live to grow up and reproduce; iii) the popula-tion competes to survive; iv) individuals with some genes are more likely to survive (greater fitness) than those with other genes; v) indi-viduals that are more likely to survive trans-mit these favorable variations (genes) to their offspring so that these genes become more dominant in the gene pool.

It is not necessarily true that natural selection leads to the the Darwin-era expres-sion "survival of the fittest"; rather it is the genes, and not necessarily the individual, which are likely to survive.

Evolution goes against the foundations of the Hardy-Weinberg Law. For example, natural selection leads to non-random mat-ing due to phenotypic differences. Evolu-tion occurs when those phenotypic changes depend on an underlying genotype; thus non-random mating can lead to changes in allelic frequencies. Consider an example: if female peacocks decide to only mate with a male with long feathers, then there will be a selec-tion pressure against any male with a geno-type which is expressed as short feathers. Because of this differential reproduction, the alleles which are expressed as short feathers will be eliminated from the population. Thus this population evolves.

The three forms of natural selection are: i) **stabilizing selection** in which genetic diver-sity decreases as the population stabilizes on an average phenotype (*phenotypes have a "bell curve" distribution*). This is the most com-mon form of natural selection. It is basically the opposite of disruptive selection, instead of favoring individuals with extreme phenotypes, it favors the intermediate phenotype; ii) **direc-tional selection** when an extreme phenotype has a selective advantage over the aver-age phenotype causing the allele frequency continually shifting in one direction (*thus the curve can become skewed to the left or right*). It occurs most often when populations migrate to new areas with environmental pressures; iii) **disruptive selection** where both extremes

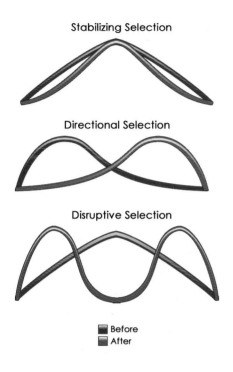

Stabilizing Selection

Directional Selection

Disruptive Selection

■ Before
■ After

are selected over the average phenotype; this would produce a split down the middle of the "bell curve" such that two new and separate "bell curves" would result. For example, if a bird only ate medium sized seeds and left the large and small ones alone, two new populations or groups of seeds would have a reproductive advantage. Thus by selecting against the group of medium sized seeds, two new groups of large and small seeds will result. This is an example of group selection causing *disruptive selection*.

16.3 Species and Speciation

Species can be defined as the members of populations that interbreed or can interbreed under natural conditions. There are great variations within species. A **cline** is a gradient of variation in a species across a geographical area. **Speciation** is the evolution of new species by the isolation of gene pools of related populations. The isolation of gene pools is typically geographic. An ocean, a glacier, a river or any other physical barrier can isolate a population and prevent it from mating with other populations of the same species. The two populations may begin to differ because their mutations may be different, or, there may be different selection pressures from the two different environments, or, *genetic drift* may play a role.

Genetic drift is the random change in frequencies of alleles or genotypes in a population (recall that this is antagonistic to the Hardy-Weinberg Law). Genetic drift normally occurs when a small population is isolated from a large population. Since the allelic frequencies in the small population may be different from the large population (*sampling error*), the two populations may evolve in different directions.

Populations or species can be sympatric, in which speciation occurs after ecological, genetic or behavioral barriers arise within the same geographical boundary of a single population, or allopatric, in which speciation occurs through geographical isolation of groups from the parent population {Sympatric = live together, Allopatric = live apart}. Mechanisms involved in allopatric speciation are represented in the two preceding paragraphs.

The following represents some isolating mechanisms that prevent sympatric populations of different species from breeding together: i) habitat differences; ii) different breeding times or seasons; iii) mechanical differences (i.e. different anatomy of the genitalia); iv) behavioral specificity (i.e. different courtship behavior); v) gametic isolation (= fertilization cannot occur); vi) hybrid inviability (i.e. the hybrid zygote dies before reaching the age of sexual maturity); vii) hybrid sterility; viii) hybrid breakdown: the hybrid offspring is fertile but produces a next generation (F_2) which is infertile or inviable.

16.4 Origin of Life

Evidence suggests that the primitive earth had a reducing atmosphere with gases such as H_2 and the reduced compounds H_2O (vapor), $NH_{3(g)}$ (ammonia) and $CH_{4(g)}$ (methane). Such an atmosphere has been shown (i.e. Miller, Fox) to be conducive to the formation and stabilization of organic compounds. Such compounds can sometimes polymerize (*possibly due to autocatalysis*) and evolve into living systems with metabolism, reproduction, digestion, excretion, etc.

Critical in the early history of the earth was the evolution of: (1) the reducing atmosphere powered with energy (e.g. lightening, UV radiation, outgassing volcanoes) converting reduced compounds (water, ammonia, methane) into simple organic molecules (the 'primordial soup'); (2) self-replicating molecules surrounded by membranes forming protocells (very primitive microspheres, coacervates assembling into the precursor of prokaryotic cells: protobionts); (3) chemosynthetic bacteria which are anaerobes that used chemicals in the environment to produce energy; (4) photosynthesis which releases O_2 and thus converted the atmosphere into an oxidizing one; (5) respiration, which could use the O_2 to efficiently produce ATP; and (6) the development of membrane bound organelles (*a subset of prokaryotes which evolved into eukaryotes*, BIO 16.6.3) which allowed eukaryotes to develop meiosis, sexual reproduction, and fertilization.

It is important to recognize that throughout the evolution of the earth, organisms and the environment have and will continue to shape each other.

16.5 Comparative Anatomy

Anatomical features of organisms can be compared in order to derive information about their evolutionary histories. Structures which originate from the same part of the embryo are called homologous. **Homologous** structures may have similar anatomical features shared by two different species as a result of a common ancestor but with a late divergent evolutionary pattern in response to different evolutionary forces. Such structures may or may not serve different functions. **Analogous** structures have similar functions in two different species but arise from different evolutionary origins and entirely different developmental patterns (see Figure IV.A.16.1).

Vestigial structures represent further evidence for evolution since they are organs which are useless in their present owners, but are homologous with organs which are important in other species. For example, the appendix in humans is a vestige of an organ that had digestive functions in ancestral species. However, it continues to assist in the digestion of cellulose in herbivores.

Taxonomy is the branch of biology which deals with the classification of organisms. Humans are classified as follows:

Kingdom	Animalia
Phylum (= Division)	Chordata
Subdivision	Vertebrata
Class	Mammalia
Order	Primates
Family	Hominidae
Genus	*Homo*
Species	*Homo sapiens*

{Mnemonic for remembering the taxonomic categories: <u>K</u>ing <u>P</u>hilip <u>c</u>ame <u>o</u>ver for <u>g</u>reat <u>s</u>oup}

The subphyla Vertebrata and Invertebrata are subdivisions of the phylum Chordata. Acorn worms, tunicates, sea squirts and amphioxus are invertebrates. Humans, birds, frogs, fish, and crocodiles are vertebrates. We will examine features of both the chordates and the vertebrates.

Chordates have the following characteristics at some stage of their development: i) a <u>notochord</u>; ii) <u>pharyngeal gill slits</u> which lead from the pharynx to the exterior; iii) a <u>hollow dorsal nerve cord</u>. Other features which are less defining but are nonetheless present in chordates are: i) a more or less segmented anatomy; ii) an internal skeleton (= *endoskeleton*); iii) a tail at some point in their development.

Vertebrates have all the characteristics of chordates. In addition, vertebrates have: i) a vertebral column; ii) well developed sensory and nervous systems; iii) a ventral heart with a closed vascular system; iv) some sort of a liver, endocrine organs, and kidneys; and v) cephalization which is the concentration of sense organs and nerves to the front end of the body producing an obvious head.

16.6 Patterns of Evolution

The evolution of a species can be divided into four main patterns:

1. Divergent evolution – Two or more species originate from a common ancestor.

2. Convergent evolution – Two unrelated species become more alike as they evolve due to similar ecological conditions. The traits that resemble one another are called analogous traits. Similarity in species of different ancestry as a result of convergent evolution is homoplasty. For example, flying insects, birds and bats have evolved wings independently.

3. Parallel evolution – This describes two related species that have evolved similarly after their divergence from a common ancestor. For example, the appearance of similarly shaped leaves in many genera of plant species.

4. Coevolution – This is the evolution of one species in response to adaptations gained by another species. This most often occurs in predator/prey relationships where an adaptation in the prey species that makes them less vulnerable leads to new adaptations in the predator species to help them catch their prey (BIO 19.2, 19.4).

16.6.1 Macroevolution

Macroevolution describes patterns of evolution for groups of species rather than individual species. There are two main theories:

1. **Phyletic gradualism** – This theory argues that evolution occurs through gradual accumulation of small changes. They point to fossil evidence as proof that major changes in speciation occur over long periods of geological time and state that the incompleteness of the fossil record is the reason why some intermediate changes are not evidenced.

2. **Punctuated equilibrium** – This theory states that evolutionary history is marked

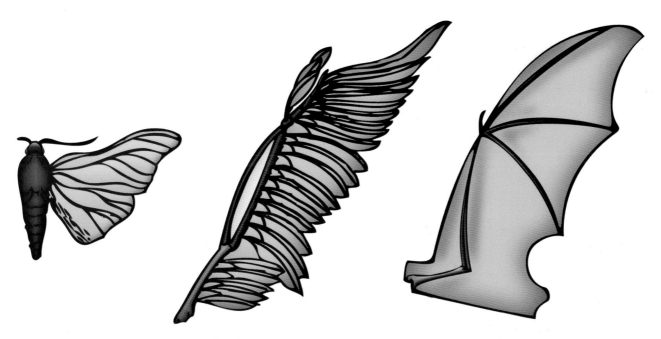

Figure IV.A.16.1: Analogous and homologous structures. The light blue wings represent analogous structures between different species: a flying insect, a bird and a bat, respectively. The bones are homologous structures. For example, green represents the humerus, purple represents the radius and ulna, red represents metacarpals and phalanges. Of course, insects have no bones. See the skeleton in BIO 11.3 to remind yourself of the meaning of some of these bony structures homologous in humans.

by sudden bursts of rapid evolution with long periods of inactivity in between. Punctuated equilibrium theorists point to the absence of fossils showing intermediate change as proof that evolution occurred in short time periods.

16.6.2 Basic Patterns for Changes in Macroevolution

1. Phyletic change (anagenesis): gradual change in an entire population that results in an eventual replacement of ancestral species by novel species and ancestral populations can be considered extinct.

2. Cladogenesis: one lineage gives rise to two or more lineages each forming a "clad". It leads to the development of a variety of sister species and often occurs when it is introduced to a new, distant environment.

3. Adaptive radiation: a formation of a number of lineages from a single ancestral species. A single species can diverge into a number of different species, which are able to exploit new environments.

4. Extinction: more than 99.9% of all species are no longer present.

16.6.3 Eukaryotic Evolution

Eukaryotes evolved from primitive heterotrophic prokaryotes in the following manner:

1. Heterotrophs first formed in the primordial soup (mixture of organic material) present in the early Earth (BIO 16.4). As the cells reproduced, competition increased and natural selection favored those heterotrophs who were best suited to obtain food.

2. Heterotrophs evolved into autotrophs (capable of making own food) via mutation. The first autotrophs were highly successful because they were able to manufacture their own food supply using light energy or energy from inorganic substrates (i.e. cyanobacteria).

3. As a by-product of the photosynthetic activity of autotrophs, oxygen was released into the atmosphere. This lead to formation of the ozone layer which prevented UV light from reaching the earth's surface. The interference of this major autotrophic resource was caused by the increased blockage of light rays.

4. Mitochondria, chloroplasts, and possibly other organelles of eukaryotic cells, originate through the symbiosis between multiple microorganisms. According to this theory, certain organelles originated as free-living bacteria that were taken inside another cell as endosymbionts. Thus mitochondria developed from proteobacteria and chloroplasts from cyanobacteria. This is the belief of the endosymbiotic theory which counts the following as evidence that it bodes true:

   A. Mitochondria and chloroplasts possess their own unique DNA which is very similar to the DNA of prokaryotes (circular). Their ribosomes also resemble one another with respect to size and sequence.

   B. Mitochondria and chloroplasts reproduce independently of their eukaryotic host cell.

   C. The thylakoid membranes of chloroplasts resemble the photosynthetic membranes of cyanobacteria.

16.6.4 The Six-Kingdom, Three-Domain System

Organisms are classified into categories called *taxa* whereas species receive a name followed by a *genus*. Closely related animals are grouped in the same genus. Genera that share related features are grouped in a family which is then grouped into orders. Orders become grouped into classes, phyla and finally kingdoms (BIO 16.5).

The following is an example of how a dog is classified:

Kingdom > Animalia

　Phylum > Chordata

　　Class > Mammalia

　　　Order > Carnivora

　　　　Family > Canidae

　　　　　Genus > Canis

　　　　　　Species > Canis familiaris

Five vs. Six Kingdoms

Over generations, taxonomists have developed several systems for the classification of organisms. From the model based on Linnaeus' hierarchical system grouping organisms based on common physical char-

acteristics (1735), the 'classic' Five-Kingdom system evolved (1969): Monera, Protista, Fungi, Plantae, and Animalia.

Genetic sequencing has given researchers tools to group organisms based on molecular differences (primarily ribosomal RNA structure). By 1990, Woese's Three-Domain System was established. The domains are Archaea, Bacteria, and Eukarya.

Under this system, there are six kingdoms: Archaebacteria (ancient bacteria), Eubacteria (true bacteria), Protista, Fungi, Plantae, and Animalia. The Archaea and Bacteria domains contain prokaryotic organisms. Eubacteria are classified under the Bacteria domain and archaebacteria are classified as Archaeans.

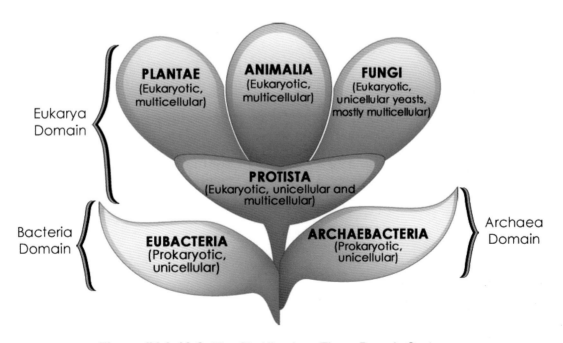

Figure IV.A.16.2: The Six-Kingdom, Three-Domain System.

The Eukarya domain includes eukaryotes and is subdivided into the kingdoms Protista, Fungi, Plantae, and Animalia.

Three-Domain System

- Archaea Domain
  Kingdom Archaebacteria

- Bacteria Domain
  Kingdom Eubacteria

- Eukarya Domain
  Kingdom Protista
  Kingdom Fungi
  Kingdom Plantae
  Kingdom Animalia

Kingdom Archaebacteria and Kingdom Eubacteria

The old designation of these 2 kingdoms was "Kingdom Monera". Every organism in this kingdom is a prokaryote which lack nuclei and various cellular organelles. Cell walls of most prokaryotes contain peptidoglycans. Many prokaryotes are categorized by their mode of nutrition. Autotrophs manufacture their own food and consist of photoautotrophs (use light energy) and chemoautotrophs (use inorganic sources). Various examples of inorganic substances used are H_2S, NH_3 and NO. Heterotrophs on the other hand must obtain their energy by consuming organic substances produced by autotrophs. Parasites prey on living tissues from a host while saprobes feed on decaying organic matter.

Prokaryotes are further divided based on their ability to survive with or without oxygen. Obligate aerobes require oxygen while obligate anaerobes can only survive in the absence of oxygen (see BIO 2.2).

Archaebacteria – The archaebacteria are classified by cell walls which lack peptidoglycan, ribosomes that resemble eukaryotic ribosomes and plasma membranes that differ in their lipid content. Examples of archaebacteria are methanogens, halophiles (salt lovers) and thermoacidophiles that can only live in hot, acidic environments such as springs or volcanic vents.

Eubacteria – Eubacteria (BIO 2.2) are mainly categorized by their mode of nutrition and by their means of motility (flagella or gliding). They are classified into three main shapes; cocci (spherical), bacilli (rod shaped) and spirilla (spiral). Finally, they are divided into either gram negative or gram positive. Bacteria that stain positive with the gram stain technique have a thick peptidoglycan wall while gram negative bacteria have a thin wall with very little peptidoglycan. Examples of eubacteria are cyanobacteria, chemosynthetic bacteria, nitrogen-fixing bacteria and spirochetes.

Kingdom Protista

Organisms in this kingdom can be algae-like, animal-like, fungus-like, unicellular or multicellular and do not generally possess strong evolutionary ties. The algae-like protists, such as phytoplankton which are important sources of food for marine organisms, all obtain their

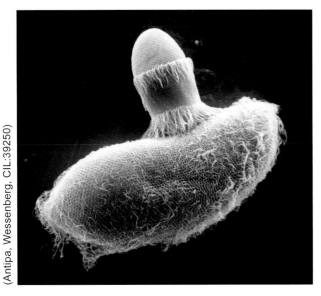

(Antipa, Wessenberg, CIL:39250)

Figure IV.A.16.3: David and Golliath: Two animal-like unicellular, ciliated protists in an epic struggle. The larger of the two carnivores, Paramecium, is attacked from above by the smaller Didinium. In this case, the organisms were preserved for this SEM micrograph before the outcome could be determined. Like other ciliates (ciliaphora), they can reproduce asexually (binary fission) or sexually (conjugation); osmoregulation is via contractile vacuoles; and, they are also visible using a light microscope.

energy via photosynthesis and possess chlorophyll pigments. They are further characterized by the form of carbohydrate in which they use to store energy, the number of flagella present and the composition of their cells walls. Various examples of algae-like protists are euglenophyta, dinoflagellata, chlorophyta (green algae with both chlorophyll a and b and cellulose in their cell walls) and rhodophyta. The animal-like protists are all heterotrophic and include rhizopoda (amoebas), sporozoa, ciliophora and zoomastigophora. Fungus-like protists resemble fungi by forming spore-bearing bodies and include acrasiomycota (cellular

slime molds), myxomycota (plasmodial slime molds) and oomycota (water molds). They exist in alternative forms between an aggregate form and an individual cell. The aggregate form consists of a large mass of cytoplasm (protoplasm) with many nuclei. It is not truly multicellular and such an arrangement is called coenocytic (many nuclei).

Kingdom Fungi

Fungi grow as a mass of hyphae called a *mycelium*. With the exception of yeast, fungi are multicellular (yeast are unicellular). Some fungi have septa which divide the hyphae into separate compartments containing individual nuclei. The fungi cell walls consist of chitin and they are either parasites or saprobes. Fungi are predominantly haploid and can reproduce sexually or asexually. The sexual reproduction involves temporary diploid structures while the asexual method of reproduction occurs through budding, fragmentation or asexual spores (sporangiospores and conidia). All fungi are heterotrophs. They may be parasitic or saprophytic (= saprobe; see detritivores, BIO 19.6). In either case, they absorb rather than ingest their food from the environment by secreting digestive enzymes outside their bodies.

Examples of fungi include *zygomycota* (lack septa and reproduce sexually by fusion of their hyphae with different strains of other neighboring hyphae), *ascomycota* (have septa and reproduce sexually by producing haploid ascospores), *basidiomycota* (have septa and reproduce sexually through haploid basidiospores), *deuteromycota* (no sexual reproduction observed, i.e. penicillin) and *lichens* (mutualistic associations between fungi and algae). See BIO 2.3 for an introduction to fungi.

Kingdom Plantae

The major adaptation for plants in order to survive the transition from water to land was evolving increasingly efficient methods of water conservation. Besides being vital for growth, water also played a major role in reproduction by providing a medium for the delivery of flagellated sperm to eggs. Plants also became much more susceptible to ultraviolet radiation. In order to combat these new problems plants have evolved several methods for survival on land:

1. Except for bryophytes (mosses) all plants have a diploid sporophyte as the dominant generation in their sexual reproduction. Diploid (2N) is more likely to survive radiation damage because of the presence of two alleles which allows recessive mutations to be masked. Plants undergo an alteration of generations with a sexual haploid stage (gametophyte) followed by an asexual diploid stage (sporophyte).

2. A waxy cuticle that limits desiccation (being dried out).

3. The development of a vascular system which eliminated the need for close proximity to water. Two groups of vascular tissues evolved, xylem and phloem, specializing in water transport and food transport, respectively.

4. Sperm became packaged as pollen allowing distribution via wind or animals; in advanced divisions of plants such as the anthophyta, the gametophytes are enclosed within an ovary.

The following is a list of the major plant divisions. All plants are multicellular, non-motile, photosynthetic autotrophs. Notice how each division shows an increasingly greater adaptation to survival on land:

1. **Bryophyta** – The Bryophyta consist of the mosses, liverworts and hornworts. They are characterized by still being dependent on water for sexual reproduction and a lack of organized vascular tissue. Therefore, most bryophytes must live in moist places. Bryophytes undergo alteration of generations. The dominant life cycle stage is the haploid gametophyte, which is large and nutritionally independent. The sporophyte is small, short-lived and nutritionally dependent on the gametophyte for survival.

2. **Tracheophyta** – These divisions all contain vascular tissue xylem (water conducting) and phloem (food conducting) and are informally classified as tracheophytes. In contrast to Bryophytes, the sporophyte generation is dominant in Tracheophytes. The gametophyte is short-lived and nutritionally dependent.

3. **Coniferophyta** – The conifers include pines, firs, cedars and redwoods and are part of the gymnosperm group. Conifers produce seeds that contain a

partially developed sporophyte that has been arrested in its development. The gametophyte stage is short-lived. The male microsporangia meiotically produce many haploid microspores, which mature into the pollen grains (male gametophyte). As pollen grains can be carried by wind, the requirement of a water environment is eliminated for conifers. The pollen grain grows into a tube and provides a path for the sperm to reach the egg through an opening called the micropyle. The female macrosporangia produce haploid cells. Three of the four degenerate and the fourth one survives to become the megaspore (female gametophyte). The ovule is the final result.

4. **Angiosperms** – These are the flowering plants and consist of some major parts, including the pistil which is the female reproductive structure and consists of the ovary, style and stigma. The ovary develops into the fruit. The stamen is the male counterpart and consists of a pollen-bearing anther and a filament stalk. The petals attract the pollinators (= biotic vectors that move pollen from the male anthers to the female stigma for fertilization like bees or other insects). The anther of the male stamen produces microspores and the ovary of the female pistil produces megaspores. Fertilization occurs when pollen lands on the sticky stigma and a pollen tube grows down the style towards the ovule. One sperm cell fertilizes the egg forming a diploid zygote while the other sperm cell fuses with polar nuclei forming the triploid endosperm (3N) which is the food source for the growing embryo. This is collectively referred to as double fertilization. {Note: Plants will be further explored in Chapter 17; see BIO 1.5 to see an endosperm cell in mitosis.}

Kingdom Animalia

All members of Kingdom Animalia are multicellular, heterotrophic, display motility, have a dominant diploid generation in their life cycle and undergo a period of embryonic development with two or three germ layers (BIO 14.5). The coelomate can also be divided into two branches: deuterostomes and protostomes. There is however tremendous diversity which is evidenced in the following characteristics:

1. **Tissue complexity** – Most animals are part of the eumetazoa (true tissues) group and are diploblastic (possessing two germ layers) or triploblastic (three layers). However, the parazoan cells are not organized into true tissues and no organs develop.

2. **Body symmetry** – Animals are either radial or bilateral. Radial symmetry features a top and bottom but no front nor back; bilateral symmetry features top, bottom, front and back. Radial symmetry animals consist of two phyla: cnidaria and ctenophore, which are diploblastic. All the rest belong to bilateral symmetry, which are triploblastic (possessing a third germ layer, the mesoderm) and can be further divided into acoelomate (lack

of coelom), pseudocoelomate (incomplete lining of coelom) and true coelom.

3. **Cephalization** – A progressively greater increase in nerve tissue towards the head.

4. **Coelom** – A fluid filled *coelom* (= body cavity) cushions the internal organs and its presence correlates with body size. An acoelomate lacks a coelom (platyhelminthes and rhynchocoela) while a pseudocoelomate possesses a cavity that is not completely lined by mesoderm (rotifera and nematoda). A true coelom consists of a fluid filled cavity within the mesoderm, which is completely lined by epithelium (annelida, mollusca, arthropoda, echinoderm and chordates).

5. **Protostomes and deuterostomes** – The coelomates can also be divided into two branches: deuterostomes and protostomes. This has to do with the type of cleavage, or cell division that takes place during the development of the zygote. Protostomes features spiral cleavage and the archenteron (infolding of the gut during embryogenesis) develops into the mouth followed by anus formation. Deuterostomes display radial cleavage and the archenteron forms the anus followed by mouth formation. Major protostome phyla include platyhelminthes, nematoda, mollusca, annelida and arthropoda. Major deuterostome phyla include echinodermata and chordates.

6. **Differentiation of tissue and organs** – Animals exhibit variant degrees of differentiation. Simple animals develop few systems (i.e. reproductive system, digestive system) to support life. Advanced animals present with higher degrees of differentiation (i.e. digestive system, reproductive system, nervous system, circulatory system, etc.). For example, regarding the circulatory system: (1) Porifera, Cnidaria, Platyhelminthes and Nematoda have none; (2) the open circulatory system is common to molluscs and arthropods and other invertebrates. "Blood" (= *hemolymph*) is pumped by a heart into a body cavity (= *hemocoel*) where tissues are bathed so they can access oxygen and nutrients by diffusion. The blood moves slowly and the animal must move its muscles to move the blood within the cavities (compare with the human lymphatic system: BIO 7.6); (3) the closed circulatory system is present in all vertebrates (i.e. humans; see BIO 7.1-7.5) and a few invertebrates (i.e. annelids, cephalopods). Closed circulatory systems have the blood within vessels at higher pressure and moving at greater speeds. In this type of system, blood is pumped by a heart through vessels, and does not normally fill body cavities. Birds and mammals (also crocodilians) have a four-chambered heart which acts as two separate pumps (BIO 7.2, 7.3).

7. **Locomotion** – All animals exhibit some form of locomotion, in contrast to plants, which are considered non-motile. Animals can have a support structure for muscle that is external (exoskeleton, i.e. Mollusca, Arthropoda) or internal (endoskeleton, i.e. Porifera, Echinodermata,

Chordata). A hydrostatic skeleton, composed of fluid under pressure in closed compartments, is used by soft bodied animals like Cnidaria, Nematoda, Annelida, Echinodermata, etc.

There are ten major phyla:

1. **Porifera** – Sponges are classified with the parazoa because they do not display true tissues. They feed via a filtering mechanism ("suspension feeders") where food is drawn in by flagellated cells called choanocytes (also called "collar cell" because there is a collar of cytoplasm surrounding the flagellum), through a cavity (= *spongocoel*) and out through an opening (= *osculum*). The body is two layered: an outer epidermis layer and an inner sheet consisting of choanocytes. Their spongy wall contains spicules made from $CaCO_3$. Most sponges are *hermaphrodites* which means that each individual functions as both male and female.

2. **Cnidaria** – Hydrozoans, jellyfish and corals. Cnidarians are also composed of two layers: the ectoderm and the endoderm and contain a digestive sac that is sealed at one end. A single opening functions as both mouth and anus. They display radial symmetry and feature two body types: the medusa (floating umbrella shaped structure) and the sessile (= *attached*) polyp (cylindrical in shape and elongated at the axis of the body). Cnidarians are *carnivores* (BIO 19.3) and their specialized features include: a nerve net and tentacles armed with *cnidocytes* which are cells with organelles (= *nematocysts*) that eject a stinging thread. This is responsible for the stings delivered by jellyfish.

3. **Platyhelminthes** – Flatworms (planarians, flukes and tapeworms) that are bilaterally symmetrical and develop from three germ layers and are thus known as triploblastic. They do not have digestive tracts (acoelomates) or circulatory systems. Many flatworms have evolved adaptations to suit their parasitic nature; for example, tapeworms feature hooks and suckers near the "head" (= *scolex*) which help them attach to the digestive tracts of humans. The bodies of platyhelminthes are divided into segments (*proglottids*) which contain the male and female reproductive structures, so each segment can reproduce independently.

4. **Nematoda** –Roundworms with locomotion by peristalsis and possess pseudocoelomate bodies with complete digestive tracts. However, they lack circulatory systems. Some species of nematodes are important parasites of plants and animals.

5. **Rotifera** – Rotifers with complete digestive tracts and that are mostly filter feeders (through action of their cilia).

6. **Mollusca** – Snails, oysters, clams, squids and octopuses. Most possess shells and are coelomates with complete digestive tracts. They secrete a calcium carbonate substance which is later incorporated into their exoskeleton

(= external skeleton; i.e. shell). They breathe by gills and contain an open circulatory system, except for the cephalopods, and a highly developed nervous system. The class Cephalopoda (squids, octopuses, cuttlefish) are carnivores with beak-like jaws surrounded by tentacles.

7. **Annelida** – Earthworms and leeches that all display segmentation. Annelida have true coeloms (true body cavity completely lined with epithelium). They have well defined systems including nervous, digestive and closed circulatory systems. Earthworms have *setae* (tiny bristles) on their bodies which help them move around in the soil while leeches possess suckers at opposite ends of their bodies that are used for attachment and movement. Leeches suck blood and can secrete a chemical (= *hirudin*) to prevent blood from clotting.

8. **Arthropoda** – Spiders, insects and crustaceans (= crabs, lobsters, shrimp, etc.). All have jointed appendages, well developed nervous systems, specialization of body segments and an exoskeleton (= shell or *cuticle*) made of layers of protein and the polysaccharide chitin (BIO 20.3.3). When an arthropod grows, it sheds its exoskeleton (= *molting*) through a process called *ecdysis*. Arthropods have an open circulatory system and are true coelomates. They are the most successful of the invertebrates with respect to the numbers of species.

9. **Echinodermata** – Sea stars ("starfish"), urchins and sand dollars. Unlike the previous phyla, the echinodermata are deuterostomes that most closely resemble the next and final phyla, the chordates. Evolutionary evidence suggests a link between echinoderms and chordates. Echinoderms are radially symmetrical as adults (with multiples of 5, like traditional starfish) and bilaterally symmetrical as larvae or embryos. They possess true coeloms. Most echinoderms, including starfish, are slow-moving or sessile marine animals. They have a thin epidermis covering an endoskeleton of hard calcareous plates. They have a unique water vascular system which is a network of hydraulic canals branching into tube feet that aid in locomotion and feeding. Males and females are usually separate. Starfish can regrow lost arms.

10. **Chordata** – These are deuterostomes and include invertebrates (tunicates and lancelets) or vertebrates (sharks, fish, amphibians, birds and humans). All possess four principle features:

   A A notochord during development
   B A dorsal hollow nerve cord that forms the basis of the nervous system
   C Pharyngeal gill slits in adulthood or at some early stage of embryonic development
   D A muscular tail at some stage

Humans are, of course, vertebrates. Details of the various body systems of humans have already been reviewed in Chapters 6 to 14.

Taxonomy is not being truly respected when the word "invertebrates" is being used.

You might have already noticed that the term "invertebrate" covers several phyla: Porifera, Cnidaria, Echinodermata, Platyhelminthes, etc., and, of course, the subphylum Invertebrata! In fact, it would be easier to state the reverse: all Animalia are invertebrates and thus do not develop a vertebral column, except for 3% of all animals which are in the subphylum Vertebrata. Although the preceding states a fact, it is an imperfect and, almost random, way to divide the immense Kingdom Animalia.

GOLD STANDARD WARM-UP EXERCISES

CHAPTER 16: Evolution

1) All of the following can provide evidence for evolution EXCEPT one. Which is the EXCEPTION?

   A. Fossil record
   B. Embryology
   C. Spontaneous generation
   D. Comparative anatomy

2) Which one of the following would cause the Hardy-Weinberg principle to be inaccurate?

   A. Individuals mate with each other at random.
   B. There is no source of new copies of alleles from outside the population.
   C. The size of the population is very large.
   D. Natural selection is present.

3) Which statement most accurately reflects what geneticists refer to as "fitness"?

   A. Fitness reflects the number of mates each individual of the population reproduces with.
   B. Fitness is a measure of the contribution of a genotype to the gene pool of the next generation.
   C. Fitness refers to the relative health of a population as a whole.
   D. Fitness is the measure of the relative health of individuals within a population.

4) The increasing occurrence over time of very colorful male birds with a reduction in moderately colorful male birds is an example of:

   A. directional selection.
   B. stabilizing selection.
   C. disruptive selection.
   D. the bell curve.

5) Which one of the following populations would most quickly lead to two groups with few shared traits?

   A. A population with stabilizing selection
   B. A population with disruptive selection
   C. A population with no selection
   D. A population with directional selection

6) The random loss of alleles in a population is called:

   A. natural selection.
   B. mutation.
   C. genetic drift.
   D. nondisjunction.

7) Which of the following molecules is thought to have been absent from the primitive reducing atmosphere?

   A. Ammonia (NH_3)
   B. Water vapor (H_2O)
   C. Oxygen (O_2)
   D. Hydrogen (H_2)

8) All of the following is true about a protocell EXCEPT one. Which is the EXCEPTION?

   A. It would have contained a biochemical pathway for energy metabolism and self-replicating molecules.
   B. It would have been present before the development of a true cell.
   C. It might have been like a coacervate droplet in which a semipermeable boundary allows some materials to be absorbed from the surrounding environment.
   D. It did not contain a nucleus but had a cell wall and circular DNA.

9) The appearance of photosynthetic cyanobacteria and aerobic bacteria in the early history of the Earth:

   A. eliminated the conditions that originally led to the first life on Earth.
   B. resulted in the development of an oxidizing atmosphere on Earth.
   C. led to the production of the ozone layer and thus reduced the amount of UV light reaching the Earth.
   D. All of the above.

10) A taxon consisting of the most closely related species is called a(n):

   A. genus.
   B. family.
   C. order.
   D. class.

11) The structural similarities between the flippers of whales and the arms of humans are used to show that:

   A. humans and whales have a common ancestry.
   B. humans began life in water.
   C. whales evolved from humans.
   D. whales can swim but humans are not meant to swim.

12) All chordates possess a:

   A. hollow dorsal nerve cord.
   B. vertebral column.
   C. closed vascular system.
   D. tail in the adult form.

13) The theory that evolutionary change is slow and continuous is known as:

   A. punctuated equilibrium.
   B. geographic isolation.
   C. gradualism.
   D. speciation.

14) Unicellular eukaryotes could be found in:

   A. Fungi and Eubacteria.
   B. Fungi and Protista.
   C. Fungi, Protista and Eubacteria.
   D. only Protista.

15) Sponges are included in which of the following phyla?

   A. Annelida
   B. Cnidaria
   C. Porifera
   D. Rotifera

16) The most successful of the invertebrate groups with respect to the numbers of species is:

A. Mollusca.

B. Echinodermata.

C. Arthropoda.

D. Annelida.

17) Which of the following groups is characterized by radially symmetrical members?

A. Annelids

B. Cnidaria

C. Mollusks

D. Arthropods

18) A flatworm lacks:

A. a true coelom.

B. bilateral symmetry.

C. bilateral symmetry and a true coelom.

D. bilateral symmetry, a true coelom, and mesodermal tissue.

19) Which of the following has a gut with two openings, a mouth and an anus?

A. Annelids

B. Cnidarians

C. Tapeworms

D. Flatworms

20) Exoskeletons are characteristic of which of the following?

A. Echinoderms

B. Mollusks

C. Arthropods

D. B and C

GS ANSWER KEY

CHAPTER 16

		Cross-Reference				Cross-Reference
1.	C	BIO 16.1	11.	A	BIO 16.5
2.	D	BIO 15.4, 16.2	12.	A	BIO 16.5, 16.6.4
3.	B	BIO 16.2	13.	C	BIO 16.6.1
4.	A	BIO 16.2	14.	B	BIO 16.6.4
5.	B	BIO 16.2	15.	C	BIO 16.6.4
6.	C	BIO 16.3	16.	C	BIO 16.6.4
7.	C	BIO 16.4, 16.6.3	17.	B	BIO 16.6.4
8.	D	BIO 16.4	18.	A	BIO 16.6.4
9.	D	BIO 16.4, 16.6.3, 16.6.4	19.	A	BIO 16.6.4
10.	A	BIO 16.5	20.	D	BIO 16.6.4

* Explanations can be found at the back of the book.

Go online to DAT-prep.com for additional chapter review Q&A and forum.

Go online to DAT-prep.com for additional chapter review Q&A and forum.

GOLD NOTES

Memorize	Understand	Importance
...gdom Plantae: basic taxonomy, ...hemistry, structures and function	* Monocots vs. dicots * Seeds, tissues, roots, leaves * Sap transportation * Plant hormones, responses to stimuli * Photosynthesis: light/dark, C3/C4/CAM	**0 to 2 out of the 40 Biology** DAT questions are based on content in this chapter (in our estimation). * Note that between 25% and 50% of the questions in DAT Biology are from 5 chapters: 1, 2, 14, 15, and 16.

DAT-Prep.com

Introduction

Plants are eukaryotes with cell walls with cellulose and obtain most of their energy from sunlight via photosynthesis using chlorophyll contained in chloroplasts, which gives them their green color. Plants provide most of the world's free oxygen and basic foods. We have already explored the basic features of Kingdom Plantae in BIO 16.6.4.

Additional Resources

Free Online Q&A + Forum

Flashcards

Special Guest

A major distinction in plants lies within the angiosperms (see BIO 16.6.4 for an overview of Kingdom Plantae). The angiosperms, along with the gymnosperms comprise the seed plants. Angiosperms, however, can be divided into *monocots* and *dicots*. The differences are as follows:

1. Monocots have only one cotyledon (nutritive tissue for developing seedling) where as dicots have two.

2. Monocots have a parallel pattern of veins in their leaves while dicots display a netted pattern.

3. Monocot petals come in multiples of three while dicots are multiples of four or five.

4. The vascular bundle (xylem and phloem tissue) is scattered in monocots and ring-patterned in dicots.

5. Monocots have fibrous roots and dicots have taproots (large single root).

17.2 Plant Tissues

There are three major groups of plant tissue:

1. **Ground tissue** – This includes the parenchyma cells (most common type, can be specialized in gas exchange, storage and photosynthesis or can remain totipotent and be able to divide to produce new populations of undifferentiated cells), the collenchyma (thick walls, function in mechanical support and meanwhile offer flexibility, therefore also known as "plastic support" cells) and schlerenchyma (similar to collenchyma but with thicker walls, provide load-bearing support). The hypodermis can be found below (= *hypo*) the epidermis and includes some ground tissue. Two groups of sclerenchyma cells exist: fibers and sclereids. Their walls consist of cellulose, hemicellulose and lignin.

2. **Dermal tissue** – Epidermal portion of the plants, covered by a waxy cuticle in the aerial parts and consists of guard cells that surround the stomata, glandular cells and epidermal hair cells.

3. **Vascular tissue** – Consists of the xylem and phloem which together form vascular bundles. The xylem cells are often located toward the center of the vascular bundle. Their thick cell walls provide mechanical support and are made up of dead cells. Its primary function is to conduct water and minerals up the plant. There are two types of xylem cells: trancheids and vessel elements.

The water passes through tracheids, specialized types of xylem cells, which are long and tapered. They also travel through vessel members which have small perforations in them to make the movement of water more efficient. Phloem are located toward the outside of the vascular bundle and are made up of sieve-tube members that form tubes. Unlike xylem, the phloem is comprised of living tissue even though they lack nuclei. Cambium cells are a type of actively dividing, undifferentiated cell known as meristem lying between the phloem and xylem. They provide for lateral growth of plants by adding to phloem or xylem. The vascular cambium is the source of both the secondary xylem (cambium located near the xylem) and the secondary phloem (cambium located near the phloem). Their primary function is to transport nutrients (i.e. carbohydrates) down the stem.

17.2.1   Seeds

The formation of a seed after fertilization completes the process of reproduction in seed plants. The seed itself consists of an embryo, a seed coat and endosperm which surrounds the embryo and provides nutrition in the form of starch, though it can also contain oils and protein. The zygote divides mitotically to form a mass of cells (= embryo), which is an immature plant that will develop into a new plant under proper conditions.

An embryo is composed of different parts, the epicotyl which forms the shoot (stems, flowering stems and leaves), the hypocotyl which connects the epicotyl, the radicle which develops into the primary root, the cotyledons which form the seed leaves, the endosperm which stores nutrition, and the seed coat which develops from integument of the ovule and forms the outer covering of the seed.

In monocotyledonous plants, a protective sheath (= coleoptile) is present to protect emerging shoots. Germination is a process in which metabolic pathways in a seed embryo are reactivated leading to growth and the emergence of a seedling above the soil surface. It occurs when the seed receives an environmental cue (most likely water). In order for the seed coat to split, the embryo soaks up water during the water imbibition phase. The seed coat cracks and the hypocotyl begins to elongate forming the early shoot. Primary growth now begins at the tips called the *apical meristems* which contain actively dividing meristematic (undifferentiated) cells, much like stem cells in humans. The root grows via a zone of cell

Dicot Seed

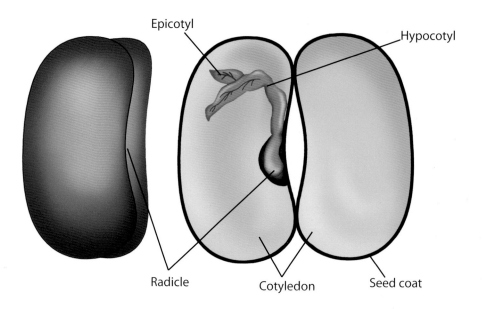

division located in the apical meristem. The cells now elongate in the zone of elongation and are followed by the zone of maturation where cells differentiate into xylem, phloem or epidermal tissues.

17.2.2 Roots

Roots consist of the following specialized tissues:

1. **Epidermis** – Lines the outside of the root and feature root hairs which increase the surface area for better absorption.

2. **Cortex** – The cortex, composed mostly of undifferentiated cells, makes up the bulk of the root and functions in storage and transportation of materials into the center of the root through diffusion.

3. **Endodermis** – Found at the innermost portion of the cortex. Contains suberin that creates a water-impenetrable barrier called the Casparian strip. All water is forced to pass through the endodermal cells and not between them. Therefore, water moving into or out of the xylem through the diffusional space outside the plasma membranes can be regulated by endodermal cells to control the degree of movement of water and the uptake of ions or molecules.

Monocot Root

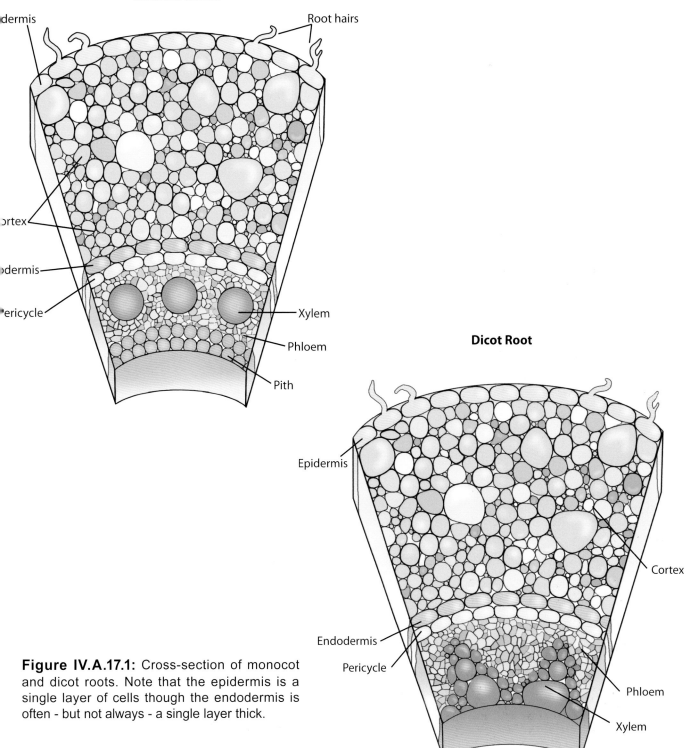

dermis

Root hairs

ortex

odermis

ericycle

Xylem

Phloem

Pith

Dicot Root

Epidermis

Cortex

Endodermis

Pericycle

Phloem

Xylem

Figure IV.A.17.1: Cross-section of monocot and dicot roots. Note that the epidermis is a single layer of cells though the endodermis is often - but not always - a single layer thick.

4. **Stele** – The stele makes up the tissues inside the endodermis and consists of the pericycle from which the lateral roots arise, xylem found in the center and phloem cells which occupy the regions between the xylem lobes. In monocot roots, there is a pith, or medulla, which is surrounded by the xylem and phloem. The pith is composed of soft, spongy parenchyma cells, which store and transport nutrients throughout the plant. Observe the illustrations and BIO 17.2.4 for the differences between monocots and dicots.

17.2.3 Leaves

Leaves display the following structures:

1. **Epidermis** – Covered by a waxy, acellular cuticle which reduces transpiration (loss of water through evaporation). The epidermis serves several functions: protection against water loss through transpiration, regulation of gas exchange and absorption of water.

2. **Palisade mesophyll** – tightly packed cells directly under the epidermis. This layer contains many more chloroplasts than the spongy layer below. The regular arrangement of these cells allows maximal absorption of sunlight for photosynthesis to occur.

3. **Spongy mesophyll** – Consists of loosely arranged parenchyma cells with the intercellular air spaces acting as chambers that provide CO_2 to photosynthesizing cells.

4. **Guard cells** – Flank the stomata and function as specialized cells that control opening and closing allowing gas exchange.

5. **Vascular bundles** – Consist of xylem, phloem and bundle sheath cells that surround the vascular bundles.

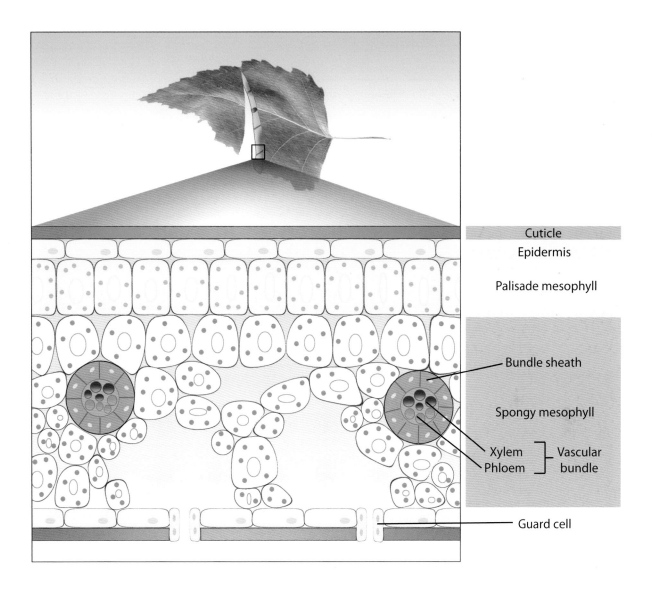

Figure IV.A.17.2: Cross-section of a leaf.

Now that we have reviewed many features of plants, we can summarize previous and additional characteristics that help to distinguish monocots and dicots.

	Monocots	**Dicots**
Embryo	Single cotyledon	Two cotyledons
Seeds	One-piece (i.e. corn)	Two-piece (i.e. beans)
Petals of flower	Multiples of 3	Multiples of 4 or 5
Leaf veins	Mostly parallel each other	Branch out from a central vein (= net pattern = reticulated)
Root systems	mostly branch out equally from base (fibrous roots)	mostly have one major root from which smaller ones grow (taproot)
Stems	• Do not grow in ring pattern • Herbaceous, never woody • Hypodermis: sclerenchyma	• Sometimes grow in ring pattern • Herbaceous, sometimes woody • Hypodermis: collenchyma
Vascular bundles	• Form ring pattern in roots • Scattered in stems • Conjoint, collateral and closed in stems	• In middle of root • Can form ring in stems • Conjoint, collateral and open in stems
Pollen	Single furrow or pore	Three furrows or pores
Secondary growth	Rare (i.e. palm tree)	Often present (i.e. secondary xylem is commercially important as wood)
Examples	Grains (wheat, corn, millet, rice), grasses, lilies, daffodils, sugar cane, ginger, onions, bamboo, palm tree, banana tree	Legumes (pea, beans, lentils, peanuts), daisies, mint, grass, lettuce, tomato, oak tree, cacti

Table IV.A.17.1: Summary of monocots vs. dicots. When xylem and phloem elements are found in the same line, the arrangement is called conjoint; if phloem is only external to xylem it is called collateral (i.e. in many stems); if xylem and phloem alternate with each other as in roots, it is called radial. Cambium is the cellular plant tissue from which phloem, xylem, or cork grow by division, resulting in secondary thickening (= woody plants). Open vascular bundles have cambium and the possibility of further xylem and phloem. There is no cambium in closed vascular bundles. {Note: "closed" does NOT mean that the vascular bundles are blocked at the ends.}

17.3 Transport of Water and Sugar

Sap is a fluid transported in xylem cells (tracheids or vessel elements) or phloem sieve tube elements.

Xylem sap is mostly water, with some hormones, mineral elements and other nutrients in aqueous form. It flows from the roots towards the leaves - best explained by the cohesion-tension theory.

Phloem sap is mostly water, with some sugars, hormones, and mineral elements in aqueous form. It flows from where carbohydrates are produced or stored to where they are used - best explained by the pressure flow hypothesis.

Note: Glucose is known as the principle carbohydrate. Glucose is one of the main products of photosynthesis (BIO 17.6) and the primary fuel for cellular respiration (BIO 4.4-4.10).

Sucrose (a disaccharide of fructose and glucose) is the *translocatable* carbohydrate (i.e. *moves* within the phloem of the plant). Starch is called the storage carbohydrate and cellulose is the structural carbohydrate (for more about carbohydrates: BIO 20.3).

17.3.1 Transportation in Xylem

As mentioned before, water is transported through the plant via dead, hardened tracheids found in xylem tissue (BIO 17.2). The water initially enters by osmosis and can move in either the *symplast* or the *apoplast* pathway. Apoplast is a diffusional space outside the plasma membrane formed by the continuum of cell walls of adjacent cells. In the apoplast pathway, water moves through this space without ever entering the cells.

In the symplast pathway, the plasmodesmata (small tubes that connect the cytoplasm of adjacent cells; see BIO 1.4) allow direct cytoplasm-to-cytoplasm flow of water and other nutrients between cells along concentration gradients. In particular, it is used in root systems to bring in nutrients. The apoplast pathway is eventually blocked by the Casparian strip (BIO 17.2.2) and the water can only enter the stele via the symplast pathway. There are three main mechanisms in the movement of water in plants:

1. **Osmosis** – A concentration gradient is maintained between the soil and the root via the higher mineral concentration inside the stele. As a result, water moves from the soil and into the root where it can reach the xylem.

2. **Capillary action** – Results from the forces of adhesion and causes the water to move up the xylem towards the apical region.

3. **Cohesion-tension theory** – Accounts for most movement of water in the xylem and is based on transpiration (a negative pressure within the leaves that builds up due to evaporative loss of water), cohesion (a result of hydrogen bonding in water which allows it to behave as a single column) and bulk flow (occurs when water molecules evaporate from the leaf surface causing the drawing up of another column).

17.3.2 Transportation in Phloem

The Pressure Flow Hypothesis (= Mass Flow Hypothesis) is the best-supported theory to explain the movement of food through the phloem (mnemonic: PFFP – **P**ressure **F**low **F**ood **P**hloem). Movement occurs by bulk flow (mass flow) by means of turgor pressure, also described as hydrostatic pressure.

Sucrose is the primary translocatable carbohydrate (= *sugar that moves within the plant*) in the great majority of plants. Translocation of sugars is accomplished through phloem cells and begins at a source and ends at a sink. The sink refers to the site where the carbohydrates are utilized by the plant. The sugar enters sieve-tube members through active transport and causes the concentration of solutes to be much higher in the source than in the sink. Water now enters by osmosis and the pressure builds due to the inability of the rigid cell wall to expand. The sugars now move upwards via bulk flow towards the sink where the carbohydrates are used. Some sugars are stored as starch which is insoluble in water allowing any cell to act as a sink when the soluble sugars are converted to starch.

17.4 Plant Hormones

Much like in human physiology, plant hormones also function in affecting the division, growth or differentiation of their target cells. They are signal chemicals only required in very small quantities and their effects depend on the particular hormone, its concentration and the presence or absence of other hormones.

There are five main classes of plant hormones:

1. **Auxin or IAA (indolacetic acid)** – Auxins promote plant growth by loosening cellulose fibers inside the cells which raises turgor pressure causing the cell

wall to expand. It is most often found at the tips of shoots and roots where it plays a role in influencing a plant's response to light and gravity (discussed later). They stimulate the production of new xylem cells by the cambium. Auxins inhibit development of lateral buds. They also promote lateral root development while inhibit root elongation.

2. **Gibberellins** – Also promote cell growth and are synthesized in young leaves and seeds. In contrast to auxins which stimulate production of new xylem cells, gibberellins stimulate the production of new phloem cells by the cambium. They also reverse the dormancy of seeds. In addition, they reverse the inhibition of shoot growth induced by inhibitors such as abscisic acid.

3. **Cytokinins** – Stimulate cell division and are produced in roots. They also stimulate the growth of lateral buds, weakening apical dominance (dominant growth of the apical meristem) and delay senescence (aging). Cytokinins (= kinins) work synergistically with auxins, and the ratio of these two groups of plant hormones is important in affecting major growth periods and the timing of differentiation of a plant.

4. **Ethylene** – This hormone is a gas that promotes fruit ripening and the production of flowers. They also, in concert with auxins, inhibit the elongation of roots and stems, counteracting the effect of gibberellins.

5. **Abscisic acid** – A chief growth inhibitor, it serves to maintain dormancy in seeds which is eventually broken by the presence of gibberellins or by environmental cues such as water or light. At the beginning of a plants' life, there is high abscisic acid (ABA) levels. Just before the seed germinates, ABA levels decrease and growth commences. As plants become more mature with fully functional shoots and leaves, ABA levels increase again, slowing down the cellular growth.

17.5 Plant Responses to Stimuli

Rather than change their location, plants alter their growth patterns in response to an environmental stimulus. This is referred to as a tropism and there are three main forms:

1. **Phototropism** – This is a plant's response to light and is governed by auxin. When there is an equal amount of light hitting all sides of the plant, the growth of the stem is uniform and proceeds straight upward. In the event that one side does not receive as much light as the other the auxin concentrates on the shady side of the stem and causes differential growth with the shady side growing more than the sunny side, causing the stem to bend towards the light.

2. **Gravitropism** – A plant responds to gravity in the following manner: If the stem is horizontal the auxins will concentrate on the lower side stimulating the lower side to elongate faster than the upper and thus causing the stem to bend upwards as it grows. This is known as negative geotropism. If a root is horizontal the auxins will again concentrate on the lower side, however the effect on the root cells is the opposite. In roots auxins inhibit growth due to a large presence of auxins already found in the roots, allowing the upper side to elongate faster than the lower and thus causing the root to bend downwards as it grows. And this is known as positive geotropism.

3. **Thigmotropism** – This is a plant's response to touch. Its mechanism is not well understood.

Photoperiodism is a plant's response to changes in the length of day and night. They are able to detect shorter days or shorter nights due to the presence of an endogenous clock (keeps track of time even in the absence of external cues) which allows them to maintain a circadian rhythm (= an intrinsic oscillation of about 24 hours). External cues in this case would be dawn or dusk.

A protein called phytocrome plays a role in maintaining this rhythm and comes in two forms: red (P_r) or far-red (P_{fr}). The far-red form resets the clock while the red form is what is synthesized in plant cells. Flashes of red or far-red light during the night resets the clock; however, flashes of darkness during the day do nothing. This leads to the conclusion that night length is responsible for resetting the circadian rhythm.

Flowering plants can either be long-day (only flower when daylight is increasing such as in the early summer), short-day (flower when daylight is less than a critical length or when night exceeds a critical length) or day-neutral (do not flower in response to daylight changes). A hormone called *florigen* is believed to play a major role in the initiation of flowering when the photoperiod allows for it.

17.6 Photosynthesis

17.6.1 Overview

Photosynthesis is the process of converting light energy into energy stored within chemical bonds that plants can access to meet their metabolic demands. A typical plant can convert sunlight into chemical energy (i.e. carbohydrates such as glucose and other sugars, cellulose, lignin) with an efficiency of approximately 1%. In plants, photosynthesis takes place in a specialized organelle - the chloroplast (BIO 17.6.4). Some bacteria lack chloroplasts but may have membranes that function in a similar manner. The equation breaks down as follows:

$$Light + 6H_2O + 6CO_2 \rightarrow C_6H_{12}O_6 + 6O_2$$

The process begins when light is captured by one of the three main photosynthetic pigments: *chlorophyll a*, *chlorophyll b* and the *carotenoids*. Each is capable of absorbing light at a specific wavelength allowing them to optimize energy absorption. The chlorophylls are both green while the carotenoids show a red/orange or yellow color. When light hits one of these pigments the electrons associated with the atoms of the molecule become excited and immediately re-emit the absorbed energy due to their instability. This process continues until the energy is ultimately absorbed by either *chlorophyll a* or *chlorophyll b*. Chlorophyll a and b are part of the two photosystems, photosystem I and II. A photosystem is composed of chlorophyll molecules coupled to other proteins and is the functional and structural unit of protein complexes that carry out the absorption of light and the transfer of energy and electrons. Each photosystem can be identified by the wavelength of light to which it is most reactive. Photosystem I (PS I) contains the chlorophyll a molecule that absorbs best at 700 nm and uses ferredoxin iron sulfur protein as the terminal electron acceptor. Photosystem II (PS II) contains the chlorophyll dimer molecule that absorbs best at 680 nm and uses quinine as the terminal electron acceptor.

Photosynthesis involves the conversion of CO_2 to carbohydrate accompanied by the release of oxygen using the energy from sunlight. The net reaction is as follows:

$$6CO_2 + 12H_2O + light\ energy \rightarrow$$
$$C_6H_{12}O_6 + 6O_2 + 6H_2O$$

Photosynthesis occurs in two distinct stages and both take place in the chloroplast. In the first stage, the light-dependent stage, energy of the sunlight is captured and converted into chemical energy in the form of ATP and NADPH. In the second stage, the light-independent stage, the former ATP and NADPH drive the conversion of CO_2 into sugars in a process called carbon fixation. Therefore, this process is also called reduction synthesis. Although the light-independent stage is also called the dark reaction, it is not completely independent of light as it is coupled to the light-dependent reaction for an energy source.

Photophosphorylation begins with PS II and is the process of making ATP from ADP and inorganic phosphate P_i using light energy. Electrons trapped by P_{680} are energized by light and are passed to the primary electron acceptor. Next, the electrons pass through the electron transport chain (ETC), which consists of proteins whose job it is to pass electrons from one carrier protein to the next (i.e. ferredoxin and cytochrome). The electrons lose energy as they move down the ETC and terminate at P_{700} (PS I). The energy lost is used to phosphorylate 1.5 ATP molecules. Once they reach PS I, the electrons are re-energized by sunlight and passed to a different primary electron acceptor. Two elec-

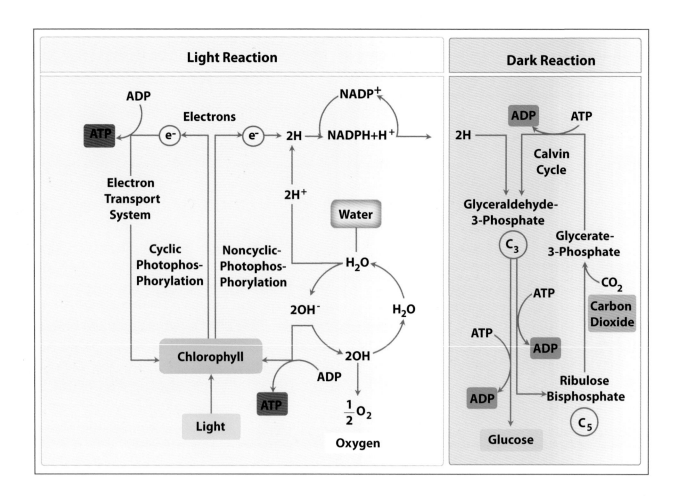

trons pass through another shorter ETC and combine with NADP$^+$ and H$^+$ to form NADPH which is an important energy-rich coenzyme. The two electrons that have now been incorporated into NADPH and were originally lost from PS II, are replaced when H$_2$O is split into 2H$^+$ and ½O$_2$. The remaining H$^+$ provides the H in NADPH. This process is called photolysis and is catalyzed by a manganese containing protein complex.

Cyclic photophosphorylation is very similar to noncyclic except that here the electrons energized in PS I are recycled and eventually return to PS I instead of being incorporated into NADPH. It is considered a primitive form of photosynthesis.

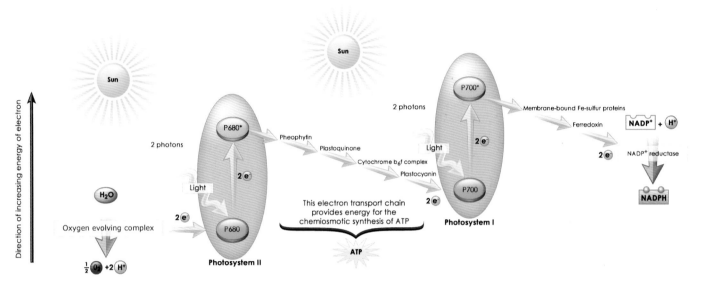

Figure IV.A.17.3: The first stage of photosynthesis: Light-dependent reactions (photoreduction) in which light energy is converted to chemical energy ATP and NADPH on the thylakoid membranes of chloroplasts.

17.6.2 The Light-Dependent Reactions: A Closer Look

The light-dependent reactions, or *photoreduction*, is the first stage of photosynthesis, and has two forms: cyclic electron flow and non-cyclic electron flow. In the non-cyclic form, the chlorophyll molecule within photosystem II (P_{680}) absorbs photons and the light energy excites electrons to a higher energy level. These high energy electrons are then shuttled through an electron transport chain (ETC), whose job is to pass electrons from one carrier protein to the next (i.e. ferredoxin and cytochrome) and to generate an electrochemical proton gradient across the membrane. The proton gradient across the thylakoid membrane creates a proton-motive force, which is used by ATP synthase to form ATP (= *chemiosmosis* which is the same process used in mitochondria).

The electrons lose energy as they move down the ETC and terminate at photosystem I (P_{700}). Once they reach P_{700}, the electrons are re-energized by photons and passed to a different electron acceptor, which again is passed down lowering energies of electron acceptors. Instead of returning to P_{700} along the carrier chain, the electrons are transferred to NADP to form NADPH. The electron hole that P_{700} is left with will be filled by electrons coming from P_{680} and the electron hole that P_{680} is left with will be filled by electrons coming from photolysis of water. Therefore, the net result of the non-cyclic reaction is the production of NADPH and ATP and the photolysis of water.

The cyclic form is similar to that of the non-cyclic form, but differs in that it generates only ATP but no NADPH. The cyclic reaction takes place only at photosystem I (P_{700}). The electron energized in photosystem I is displaced and passed down the electron acceptor molecules and returns to photosystem I, from where it is emitted, hence the name cyclic reaction.

17.6.3 The Light-Independent Reactions: A Closer Look

The next step of photosynthesis involves the Calvin-Benson cycle which fixes CO_2 in the sense that it takes the inert, inorganic CO_2 and incorporates it into a usable form capable of integration into biological systems. The end result is the formation of a single molecule of glucose which takes six complete turns of the Calvin cycle and consumes six CO_2 molecules.

It begins with the enzyme *rubisco* (= ribulose-1,5-bisphosphate carboxylase oxygenase = RuBisCO) which catalyzes the merging of CO_2 and ribulose biphosphate. The CO_2 that is incorporated into ribulose-1,5-bisphosphate (RuBP) produces a six-carbon intermediate that immediately splits in half forming two molecules of 3-phosphoglycerate (PGA), and is the reason why the Calvin cycle is referred to as C3 photosynthesis (12 PGA are made from 6 CO_2 and 6 RuBP).

What follows is that in the presence of ATP and NADPH, 3-phosphoglycerate is reduced to phosphoglyceraldehyde (PGAL). For every six cycles, 12 ATP and 12 NADPH are used to convert 12 PGA into 12 PGAL. Five out of every 6 molecules of the PGAL produced is used to regenerate RuBP to keep the process continuing. However, the 1 out of every 6 molecules of the PGAL that is not recycled will be combined with another PGAL to form hexose phosphates, which ultimately yield sugar compounds. Next, the 6 RuBP originally used to combine with 6 CO_2 are regenerated (6 ATP are used to convert 10 PGAL or G3P to 6 RuBP). Lastly, the remaining 2 PGAL are used to form glucose.

Since no light is directly involved with this reaction, the Calvin cycle can also be referred to as the *dark reaction* even though it cannot proceed in the dark. This is because

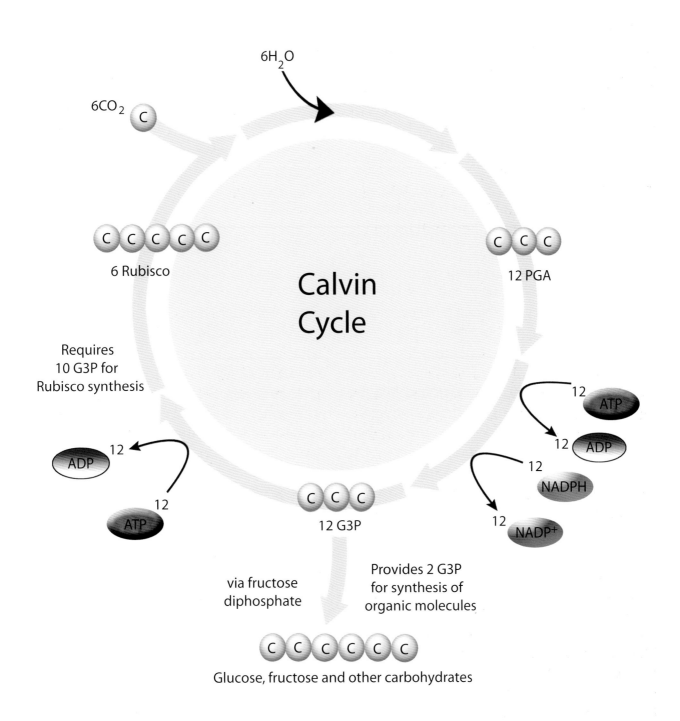

Figure IV.A.17.4: The Calvin Cycle (C3).

it is dependent on energy from NADPH and ATP, formed during the light reactions of photosynthesis. Keep in mind that none of these reactions occur spontaneously. Each one is dependent on a coenzyme or metal cofactor.

The sum of reactions in the Calvin cycle is the following (P_i = inorganic phosphate):

$$3\ CO_2 + 6\ NADPH + 5\ H_2O + 9\ ATP \rightarrow$$
$$glyceraldehyde\text{-}3\text{-}phosphate\ (G3P) + 2\ H^+$$
$$+ 6\ NADP^+ + 9\ ADP + 8\ P_i$$

17.6.4 Characteristic Features of Plant Cells

In Chapter 1, we explored many features of the generalized eukaryotic cell. We will now take a closer look at 3 characteristic - though *not* necessarily unique - features of plant cells: the cell wall, vacuoles and plastids.

The cell wall: Imagine that a cell is like a floppy water balloon. Well, the cell wall is like putting the balloon in a box. The cell wall is a fairly rigid layer that lies outside of the cell's plasma membrane. The cell wall provides structural support and acts as a pressure vessel, preventing overexpansion when water enters the cell.

There are specialized pores through the wall called plasmodesmata that provide a cytoplasmic connection between adjacent plant cells (BIO 17.3.1; compare with gap junctions, BIO 1.5). The cytoplasm of a plant is, therefore, more or less contiguous throughout the entire plant.

Cell walls are made of carbohydrates (BIO 20.3) and are found in plants (cellulose, hemicellulose and the 'glue' that binds cell walls together - pectin); bacteria (peptidoglycan; BIO 2.2); fungi (chitin; BIO 2.3, 16.6.4); algae (glycoproteins and polysaccharides); and some archaea (glycoproteins and polysaccharides). Animals and protozoa do not have cell walls.

Vacuoles: Membrane-bound organelles present in all plant and fungal cells, and some protist, animal and bacterial cells. Vacuoles are filled with water and some inorganic and organic molecules including enzymes in solution, and rarely engulfed solids.

Plant cells can have one large central vacuole instrumental in maintaining internal hydrostatic pressure and pushing the plasma membrane against the cell wall (= *turgor pressure*). Incredibly, the vacuole may occupy from 20% to up to 80-90% of the cell's volume.

Plastids: All arise from a common precursor: *proplastid*. Plastids are all surrounded by a double plasma membrane and contain their own double stranded DNA molecule (see endosymbiotic theory; BIO 16.6.3). However, similar to mitochondria, most plastid proteins are coded by nuclear DNA. Plastids can be found in plants and other eukaryotes (protists; BIO 16.6.4).

Here are some common plastids:

- Amyloplasts – store starch
- Chromoplasts – contain colorful pigments
- Chloroplasts – photosynthesis which we will continue to examine.

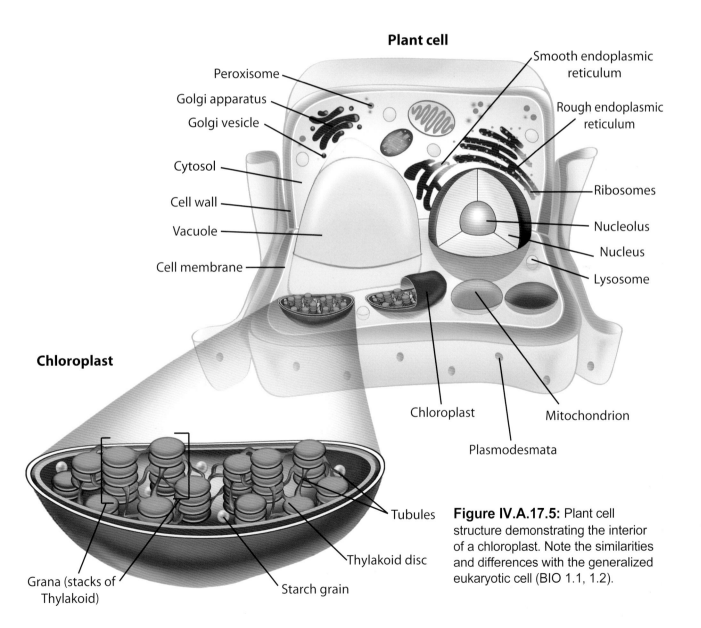

Plant cell

Peroxisome
Golgi apparatus
Golgi vesicle
Cytosol
Cell wall
Vacuole
Cell membrane

Smooth endoplasmic reticulum
Rough endoplasmic reticulum
Ribosomes
Nucleolus
Nucleus
Lysosome

Chloroplast

Chloroplast
Mitochondrion
Plasmodesmata

Grana (stacks of Thylakoid)
Starch grain
Thylakoid disc
Tubules

Figure IV.A.17.5: Plant cell structure demonstrating the interior of a chloroplast. Note the similarities and differences with the generalized eukaryotic cell (BIO 1.1, 1.2).

Both the light and dark reactions occur in chloroplasts. Within the inner membrane, in the region called the *stroma*, there is a system of interconnecting flattened membrane compartments, called the *thylakoids*, which stacked collectively form a granum (plural: *grana*). Chlorophyll resides within the thylakoid membranes. It is within the thylakoids where the machinery and pigments for the light-dependent reactions are found. The light independent reaction, or the dark reactions, occur in the stroma.

17.6.5 Photorespiration

Photorespiration is the biosynthetic pathway that leads to the fixation of oxygen. This occurs because rubisco is capable of fixing both CO_2 and O_2. This is undesirable as the products formed when rubisco fixes O_2 are not of any use to the plant. Peroxisomes, a specialized organelle, are found near chloroplasts and break down the wasteful products of photorespiration (BIO 1.2.1).

17.6.6 Other Photosynthetic Pathways

Some plants have managed to evolve more efficient ways of photosynthesis. The C4 pathway and CAM method are the two main modifications to the original C3 photosynthesis and they overcome the tendency of the enzyme rubisco to fix oxygen rather than carbon dioxide thus avoiding the production of undesirable products of photorespiration. In C4 photosynthesis the CO_2 combines with PEP (phosphoenolpyruvate) rather than rubisco and forms OAA (oxaloacetate). OAA has 4 carbons and is immediately converted to malate which is then shuttled to the bundle sheath cells (see BIO 17.2.3). There the malate is converted to pyruvate and CO_2. The pyruvate is converted back to PEP, which is transported back to the mesophyll cell and CO_2 now enters the Calvin cycle.

The process repeats with the ultimate goal being the movement of CO_2 from mesophyll cells to the bundle sheath cells. This is key as the bundle sheath cells are more or less isolated from O_2 and the C3 pathway can now proceed as normal, minimizing photorespiration. The C4 pathway is usually found in arid, hot climates. Stomata must be open in order to allow CO_2 to enter. However, when these stomata are open the plant loses water. C4 plants are extremely efficient at photosynthesis and this allows them to minimize the time in which they have their stomata open, reducing H_2O loss.

CAM photosynthesis is very similar to C4 except that in CAM the OAA is converted to malic acid instead of malate and is shuttled to the vacuole of the cell rather than the bundle

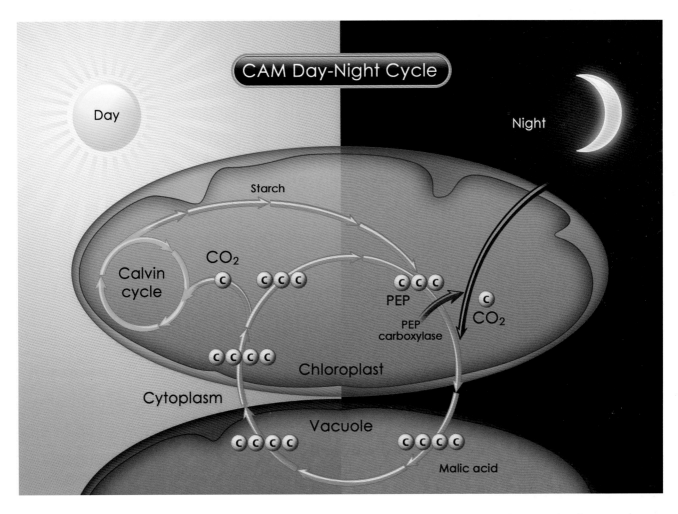

Figure IV.A.17.6: The CAM Day-Night Cycle. In CAM plants the photosynthesis and initial carbon fixation occur at night and a 4-carbon acid is stored in the cell's vacuole. During the day, the Calvin cycle operates in the same chloroplasts.

sheath cells. Stomata remain open at night where PEP carboxylase is active and the malic acid accumulates in the vacuoles. However, instead of being immediately passed on to the Calvin cycle, the malic acid is stored for later use. During the day the stomata are closed which is the reverse of most other plants. During this time the CO_2 is fixed by rubisco and the Calvin cycle proceeds. Being able to keep stomata closed during the day minimizes the loss of water through evaporation, allowing plants that utilize the CAM method to grow in environments that would otherwise be too dry for C3 plants. Therefore, CAM plants are also found in hot, dry climates with cool nights.

GOLD STANDARD WARM-UP EXERCISES

CHAPTER 17: Plants

NOTE: these Warm-up Questions refer to this chapter on Plants as well as content covering Kingdom Plantae from Chapter 16.

1) The ovary of a flowering plant can develop into a:

A. cone.
B. seed.
C. fruit.
D. spore.

2) The part of the flower that is adapted to catch pollen is the:

A. stigma.
B. anther.
C. ovule.
D. style.

3) The part of a stamen containing the pollen sacs in flowers is known as the:

A. style.
B. filament.
C. pistil.
D. anther.

4) The ancestors of land plants were aquatic algae. All of the following are evolutionary adaptations to life on land EXCEPT one. Which is the EXCEPTION?

A. Xylem and phloem
B. A waxy cuticle
C. Sperm packaged as pollen
D. The Calvin cycle

5) Which of the following nourishes a developing seed?

A. Endosperm
B. Nectar
C. Zygote
D. Pollen tube

6) Match the following:

I. Epidermal tissue
II. Parenchyma
III. Collenchyma
IV. Sclerenchyma
V. Meristem

i. Storage and photo-synthesis
ii. Mechanical support
iii. Stomata
iv. Actively dividing
v. Sclereid cells

A. I-iv, II-v, III-iii, IV-ii, V-i
B. I-iii, II-i, III-ii, IV-v, V-iv
C. I-ii, II-iv, III-v, IV-i, V-iii
D. I-i, II-iii, III-v, IV-ii, V-iv

7) In a plant, the layer of persistently meriste-matic tissue, giving rise to secondary tissues, resulting in growth in diameter is which of the following?

A. Pores
B. Bark
C. Cambium
D. Capsule

8) Which of the following describes the loss of water vapor by plants?

A. Transpiration
B. Perspiration
C. Respiration
D. Absorption

9) An important function of root hairs is that they:

A. anchor a plant in the soil.
B. increase the surface area for absorption.
C. store and transport starches.
D. provide a niche for bacteria.

10) Which of the following is correct regarding the Casparian strip in plant roots?

A. It ensures that all water must pass through a cell membrane before entering the stele.
B. It provides increased surface area for the absorption of water.
C. It is located between the epidermis and the cortex.
D. It supplies ATP for the active transport of minerals into the stele from the cortex.

11) All of the following form part of a plant's apoplast EXCEPT one. Which one is the EXCEPTION?

A. The lumen of a sieve tube
B. The lumen of a xylem vessel
C. The cell wall of a root hair
D. The cell wall of a mesophyll cell

12) What regulates the flow of water through xylem?

A. Active transport by tracheids and vessel elements
B. Passive transport by the endodermis
C. Active transport by sieve tube members
D. The evaporation of water from the leaves

13) What is theorized to be the driving force for the transport of sap in phloem?

A. Water transpiration
B. Root pressure
C. Gravity
D. Hydrostatic pressure

14) Which of the following plant hormones are produced in roots and stimulate cell division?

A. Cytokinins
B. Ethylene
C. Abscisic acid
D. Gibberellins

15) The tendency of a plant to grow toward light is called:

A. phototropism.
B. photosynthesis.
C. photorespiration.
D. photoinduction.

16) In the first stage of photosynthesis, light energy is used to:

A. produce carbohydrates.
B. move water molecules.
C. denature chlorophyll.
D. split water.

17) What percent of the total radiant energy received by a plant is converted to chemical energy?

A. Less than 2%
B. 10%
C. 30%
D. 50%

18) Molecular oxygen formed during plant photosynthesis is derived exclusively from:

A. carbohydrates.
B. proteins.
C. water.
D. CO_2.

19) During the light phase of photosynthesis, choose the molecule that is oxidized and the molecule that is reduced, respectively.

A. Water and NADP
B. Water and CO_2
C. NADPH and CO_2
D. CO_2 and Water

20) The oxygen molecule in glucose formed during photosynthesis comes from:

A. fructose.
B. water.
C. NADP.
D. CO_2.

21) The light-dependent reactions of photosynthesis result in the formation of which of the following?

A. ATP
B. O_2
C. NADPH + H^+
D. All of the above

22) All of the following are true EXCEPT one. Which one is the EXCEPTION?

A. In C3 plants, the light and dark reactions can take place at the same time.
B. In C4 plants, the light and dark reactions can take place at the same time.
C. CAM and C3 plants are adapted to arid environments but C4 plants are not.
D. CAM plants keep their stomata closed during the day to reduce the loss of water.

23) What directly powers the light-independent reactions?

A. Carbon dioxide
B. Sunlight
C. ADP and $NADP^+$ produced by the light-dependent reactions
D. ATP and NADPH produced by the light-dependent reactions

GS ANSWER KEY

CHAPTER 17

Cross-Reference

1.	C	BIO 16.6.4 (Kingdom Plantae)
2.	A	BIO 16.6.4 (Kingdom Plantae)
3.	D	BIO 16.6.4 (Kingdom Plantae)
4.	D	BIO 16.6.4 (Kingdom Plantae);
		BIO 17.6.3
5.	A	BIO 17.1, 17.2.1
6.	B	BIO 17.2, 17.2.2
7.	C	BIO 17.2, 17.2.4
8.	A	BIO 17.2.3, 17.3
9.	B	BIO 17.2.2
10.	A	BIO 17.2.2
11.	A	BIO 17.2.3, 17.3, 17.3.1
12.	D	BIO 17.3, 17.3.1

Cross-Reference

13.	D	BIO 17.3, 17.3.2
14.	A	BIO 17.4
15.	A	BIO 17.5
16.	D	BIO 17.6.1, 17.6.2
17.	A	BIO 17.6.1
18.	C	BIO 17.6.1
19.	A	BIO 4.7–4.9, 17.6.1, 17.6.2;
		CHM 1.5.1, 1.6, 10.1, 10.2
20.	D	BIO 17.6.1
21.	D	BIO 17.6.1
22.	C	BIO 17.6
23.	D	BIO 17.6.3

* Explanations can be found at the back of the book.

Go online to DAT-prep.com for additional chapter review Q&A and forum.

GOLD NOTES

Memorize	Understand	Importance
nal movement	* Different forms of behavior * Chemical communication * Social behavior	**0 to 1 out of the 40 Biology** DAT questions are based on content in this chapter (in our estimation). * Note that between 25% and 50% of the questions in DAT Biology are from 5 chapters: 1, 2, 14, 15, and 16.

DAT-Prep.com

Introduction

Behavior is what an animal does. Nature and nurture shape the behavior of animals. Nature is innate, described as "instinct" where genes determine the behavior. Nurture is learned, described as "experience" where learning influences behavior. The two extremes are not mutually exclusive and both nature and nurture are deeply influenced by evolution.

Additional Resources

Free Online Q&A + Forum

Flashcards

Most behavior exhibited by animals is molded by natural selection and evolutionary forces. It can also be inherited through genes (innate). There are six main forms of behavior:

1. **Instinct** – This type of behavior is inherited (= innate, i.e. a mother caring for her offspring).

2. **Fixed action pattern** – This pattern is also innate and is initiated by a specific stimulus. It is always carried out to completion (i.e. mating dance with the female acting as the stimulus or cows herding). Because this pattern is innate, it is less likely to be modified by learning. In addition, an animal has a limited ability to develop any new fixed-action patterns.

3. **Imprinting** – An irreversible behavior that is acquired during a critical period via an appropriate stimulus (i.e. Konrad Lenz's famous gosling experiment where he discovered that during the first two days of life the goslings will recognize any moving object as their mother. Lenz himself swam with the goslings during this critical period and was accepted as their mother). If the proper environmental pattern or object is not presented during this critical period, the behavior pattern will not develop properly.

4. **Associative learning** – Occurs when an animal learns that two or more events are connected. Classical conditioning is an example of this behavior as is seen in Ivan Pavlov's legendary experiment where he discovered that dogs would salivate in response to a ringing bell even when food did not immediately follow as was normally the case. The dogs associated the bell (substitute stimulus) with the food (normal stimulus) and the bell itself was able to elicit the salivary response. This type of conditioning involves the association of an autonomic response with an environmental stimulus. In Pavlov's experiment the normal stimulus, known as unconditioned stimulus as it elicits response naturally, is replaced by a neutral stimulus (substitute stimulus) chosen by the experimenter that will not elicit a response by itself. During conditioning, the neutral stimulus (substitute stimulus) and the unconditioned stimulus are linked together and eventually, the neutral stimulus is able to elicit a response without the presence of the unconditioned stimulus and it becomes the conditioned stimulus.

5. **Trial and error learning** – A second form of associative learning where an animal connects its own behavior with a particular environmental response. The response can be positive or negative, thereby encouraging or discouraging the animal's likeliness in repeating the behavior (i.e. B.F. Skinner's rat experiment where he trained them to push levers to obtain food pellets or avoid mild electrical shocks). This type of behavior is also known as operant or instrumental conditioning. Under certain conditions, random activities are directed into a behavior pattern with the use of reward or reinforcement. Conversely, lack of certain activities is directed into a

behavior pattern with the use of punishment. The loss of an acquired behavior is called extinction as would be the case if the rats stopped receiving food after pushing on the lever.

6. **Habituation** – A learned behavior that allows an animal to decrease their response to a certain stimulus after they have seen it many times before. This is seen in virtually every organism on the planet. However, if a stimulus is removed, the response tends to recover and this is called spontaneous recovery.

18.2 Animal Movement

Three kinds of movement are commonly found in animals:

1. **Kinesis** – An undirected, random change in speed in an animal's movement in response to a certain stimulus. It will slow down in a favorable situation and speed up in unfavorable ones (i.e. woodlice becoming sluggish as humidity increases).

2. **Taxis** – A directed movement in response to a stimulus. Can be either toward or away from the stimulus (i.e. moths move towards the light at night).

3. **Migration** – The long distance, seasonal movement of animals (i.e. many species of birds migrate south for the winter).

18.3 Chemical Communication

Animals use pheromones in order to communicate on the chemical level. Pheromones are secreted or excreted chemical factors, usually in minute quantities, that trigger a social response in members of the same species. Releaser pheromones cause immediate and reversible behavioral changes in the recipient. For example, releaser pheromones can be secreted as an alarm substance. Primer pheromones cause long term, physiological changes in the recipient. For example, primer pheromones can play a role in the regulation of reproductive capacities of animals. Bombykol was the first known pheromone and is released by the female silkworm in order to attract mates.

Most social behaviors have evolved in order to optimize individual fitness. All animals must at some point communicate with others in order to reproduce. There are four main types:

1. **Agonistic behavior** – Aggressive displays of behavior that usually originate from competition for a particular resource, most often food or mates.

2. **Dominance hierarchies** – Established in order to maintain power and status relationships between individuals within a group. This is referred to as a pecking order in chickens.

3. **Territoriality** – Involves the defense of one's territory and ensures adequate food supplies and ample room to rear young. Territoriality functions in distributing members of species to minimize intraspecific aggressions. Therefore, the larger the population the smaller the territories can be. Overt fighting is usually avoided by some form of clear display, which can be visual (i.e. the red breast of the robin), auditory (i.e. bird song) or olfactory, through scent marking (i.e. urination, defecation or through the smearing of excretions from scent glands).

4. **Altruistic behavior** – An unselfish, sacrificing behavior that reduces the overall fitness of the individual. This type of behavior is seen when animals risk their safety by defending a friend or family member or when they sacrifice their reproduction to help another individual (always of the same species). Altruism is, in part, correlated with the "coefficient of relatedness" which is the ratio of identical genes in two individuals. The interaction between related individuals can affect gene frequencies (*kin selection*).

GOLD STANDARD WARM-UP EXERCISES

CHAPTER 18: Animal Behavior

1) Which of the following is consistent with associative learning?

   A. Operant conditioning
   B. Classical conditioning
   C. Pavlovian conditioning
   D. All of the above

2) Fish in aquariums tend to swim to the water's surface when a person approaches. Their behavior has likely formed through:

   A. insight.
   B. instinct.
   C. classical conditioning.
   D. imprinting.

3) After a young duck imprints on a plastic mechanical toy, the young duck will:

   A. follow only that plastic mechanical toy.
   B. follow all plastic mechanical toys .
   C. then imprint on any real adult duck.
   D. then imprint on its mother.

4) You want to train a puppy to "sit". You give the dog a treat every time he does as you ask. You are applying:

   A. habituation.
   B. imprinting.
   C. classical conditioning.
   D. operant conditioning.

5) Animals that help other animals are expected to be:

   A. carrying the most "fit" genes.
   B. carrying the least "fit" genes.
   C. related to the animals they help.
   D. stronger than other animals.

GS ANSWER KEY

CHAPTER 18

Cross-Reference

1.	D	BIO 18.1
2.	C	BIO 18.1
3.	A	BIO 18.1
4.	D	BIO 18.1
5.	C	BIO 18.1

* Explanations can be found at the back of the book.

Go online to DAT-prep.com for additional chapter review Q&A and forum.

Go online to DAT-prep.com for additional chapter review Q&A and forum.

GOLD NOTES

ECOLOGY
Chapter 19

Memorize	Understand	Importance
ic ecology nomenclature, graphs interactions ulation growth equation mids, percentage transfer nes	* Population, community ecology * Coevolution, ecosystems * Biomes	**0 to 2 out of the 40 Biology** DAT questions are based on content in this chapter (in our estimation). * Note that between 25% and 50% of the questions in DAT Biology are from 5 chapters: 1, 2, 14, 15, and 16.

DAT-Prep.com

Introduction

Ecology is the study of the relationships that living organisms have with each other and with their natural environment. Areas of interest include the distribution, number, total amount (biomass), composition, and changing states of organisms within and among ecosystems. Biodiversity is the variety of species in ecosystems and the genetic variations they contain.

Additional Resources

Free Online Q&A + Forum

Flashcards

Special Guest

The studying of ecology encompasses both the biotic (living) and abiotic (non living) environment as it involves the interaction of species with other organisms as well as with their physical surroundings. There are six key terms that must be defined before we go any further:

1. **Population** – A group of individuals of the same species living in the same area.

2. **Community** – A group of populations of different species interacting with each other in the same area.

3. **Ecosystem** – The interaction between organisms in a community and their physical environment.

4. **Biosphere** – Comprises all regions of the earth that contain living things.

5. **Habitat** – The specific place where an organism dwells.

6. **Niche** – The unique role an organism plays in the biotic and abiotic environment, focusing on all the resources used by that particular animal. Organisms occupying the same niche compete for the same resources; therefore, no two species can occupy the same niche: the competition will drive either extinction of one of the species or divergent evolution leading to two species with greater differences. A niche is such a specific segment of ecospace that a species can be identified by the niche it occupies.

19.2 Population Ecology

The first major subtopic of ecology is population ecology, specifically the study of the growth and distribution of populations. It is described by its size, density, dispersion (they can be either random, clumped or uniformly distributed), age structure and the type of survivorship curve. There are three types of survivorship curves:

(a) **Type I** – Species who generally are able to survive until middle age, at which point mortality rates are high when you pass this midpoint (i.e. humans).

(b) **Type II** – Species who display a random pattern of survivorship (i.e. rodents).

(c) **Type III** – Species where most individuals die young. Typical of many insects, oysters and any other species that produces free swimming larvae.

Population growth is characterized by the biotic potential, the carrying capacity and any limiting factors that prevent said population from reaching its full potential. *Biotic potential* is the maximum growth rate of a population under ideal circumstances. Such a scenario is rarely achieved as any number of resource or growth restriction problems can negatively affect the rate and limit growth. The *carrying capacity* refers to the maximum

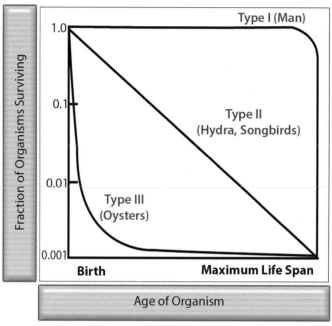

Scaled to maximum life span for each species.

number of individuals of a certain population that can be sustained in a particular habitat. Limiting factors can be density-dependent (become important when population size increases and resources become scarce) or density-independent (factors that occur independently of population density such as natural disasters or climate changes).

The growth of a population can be described by the following equation:

$$r = (births - deaths)/N$$

r = growth rate
N = population size
numerator = the net increase in individuals

When births exceed deaths, r will be positive and the population will increase. If births and deaths are equal, then the population size remains constant. When deaths exceed births, r will be negative and the population will decrease.

There are two general patterns of population growth:

1. **Exponential growth** – Occurs whenever the reproductive rate is greater than zero. Forms a J shaped curve.

2. **Logistic growth** – Occurs when limiting factors keep the population in check. Produces an S shaped curve. The point at which the growth rate levels off is the carrying capacity. Once growth is reduced below the carrying capacity,

resources become more readily available and the population is often able to recover. This is not always the case. Sometimes the population may crash into extinction or in milder cases it will establish a new lower carrying capacity.

Exponential and logistic growth drives evolution in one of two types of life-history strategies: r- or K-selection.

1. **r-selected species (unstable environment)** – In unstable environments, r selection predominates and exhibits the ability to reproduce many offspring, each of which has a relatively low probability to survive to adulthood. Other characteristics of r-selection include small body size of individuals, early maturity, little parent care requirement, high fertility, and short generation time.

2. **K-selected species (stable environment)** – In stable environments, K-selection predominates and exhib-

its the ability to compete successfully for limited resources. In contrast to r-selected populations, which can vary significantly, K-selected population size remains constant and is close to the maximum that the environment can allow (close to the carrying capacity). A small number of offspring is produced that require extensive parental care until they mature. Other characteristics of K-selection include large body size of individuals and longer life expectancy.

One key example of a population cycle seen in nature is the relationship between a predator and its prey. This type of association tends to fluctuate (when the predator population decreases the prey population increases and vice versa). However; it is not always a given that changes in one predator population directly lead to changes in the prey population. Food or seasonal factors may also affect the relationship.

19.3 Community Ecology

Community ecology deals with the interaction of populations. Interspecific competition refers to competition between different species while intraspecific competition is between members of the same species. There are three ways that organisms can go about reducing competiton:

1. **Competitive exclusion (Gause's principle)** – Gause's principle states that no two species can occupy the same niche and coexist. Species occupying the same niche compete for at least one resource in common. What inevitably occurs is that one species outcom-

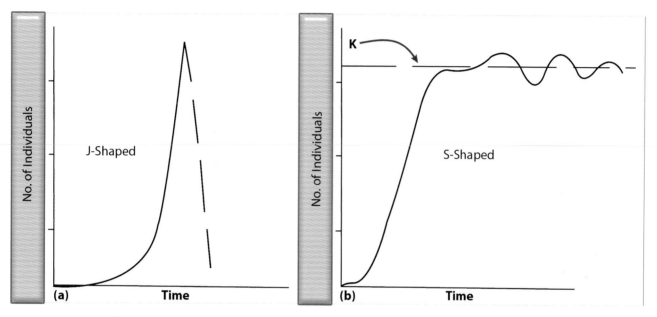

Population Growth Forms: (a) J-shaped; (b) S-shaped - K represents the carrying capacity.

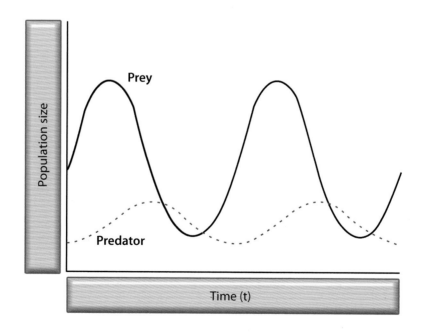

petes the other leading to the extinction of the weaker, less adaptable species.

2. **Resource partitioning** – When species adapt to occupy slightly different niches in order to coexist.

3. **Niche shift** – Selection of characteristics that enable one species to better obtain resources leads to an eventual niche shift and leads to divergence of features or character displacement.

A community is an integrated system of species living within the same area. The major types of interspecific interactions include symbiosis, predation, saprophytism and scavengers.

1. **Symbiosis** is a term that applies to two species living in close proximity with each other, which may or may not benefit both sides. There are four main types of symbiotic relationships: mutualism, commensalism, parasitism and amensalism.

   a) **Mutualism** – Any relationship between individuals of different species where both individuals derive some benefit. An example of mutual symbiosis can be seen in lichens, a very close association between fungus and algae. The algae supply sugars obtained via photosynthesis for itself and the fungus, while the fungus provides carbon dioxide and nitrogenous wastes for the algae to use for photosynthesis and protein synthesis. Another example is between legumes and symbiotic nitrogen-fixing bacteria that live together. The bacteria grow on the roots of legumes to form root nodules. In the nodule, the legume provides nutrients for itself and the bacteria while the bacteria fixes nitrogen, making it useable for the legume.

   b) **Commensalism** – Any relationship between two living organisms where one benefits and the other is not significantly affected. An example is between a remora (a 'suckerfish') and a shark, where the remora attaches itself to the shark and uses it for transportation (wide geographic dispersal) and for protection. The shark is completely unaffected.

   c) **Parasitism** – Any relationship where one member of the association, the parasite, benefits at the expense of the other, the host. Parasitic symbioses take many forms, from endoparasites that live within the host to ectoparasites that live on the exterior surface of the host. In addition, parasites may even have parasites of their own. For example, an animal may have a parasitic worm, which in turn is parasitized by bacteria. A classic example of parasitism is between a virus and the host cell. All viruses are parasites (BIO 2.1). Once they enter into the host, the viruses take over the host cell function and use it for their own.

   d) **Amensalism** – Any relationship between two living organisms where one is completely obliterated (harmed) and the other is unaffected (not benefited). A common example is between the bread mold penicillium and bacteria. Penicillium secretes penicillin which kills bacteria. Throughout the process the penicillium is unaffected.

2. **Predation** is a term that describes an interspecific interaction where a predator feeds on other living organisms. This definition includes carnivores (diet: mainly or exclusively animal tissue), herbivores (diet: plant based) and omnivores (diet can include plants, animals, algae and fungi). A key characteristic of the predator-prey relationship is the predator's direct impact in controlling the prey's population but not so as to threaten its existence.

3. **Saprophytism** is a term that describes the process of chemical decomposition of dead or decayed organic matter extracellularly through which nutrients are later absorbed. They play a vital role in the ecosystem by completing the cycling of organic matter within the system.

4. **Scavenger** is a term that can be applied to both carnivorous and herbivorous in which the scavengers consume dead animal or plants or decaying matter. They play a vital role in the ecosystem by contributing to the decomposition of dead or decaying matter.

19.4 Coevolution

Coevolution is the evolution of one species in response to new adaptations found in another species. Organisms need to be able to coexist. This is paramount to the continued viability of the ecosystem and the planet as a whole. Important examples of coevolution include camouflage (an animal blending in with its surroundings to avoid predation), secondary compounds (toxic chemicals produced in plants to discourage herbivores), aposematic coloration (conspicuous colorations or patterns found on the body of an organism that warn predators of their defense mechanisms) and mimicry (two or more species resemble one another in appearance). There are two specific types:

1. **Mullerian mimicry** – Occurs when several harmful species, may or may not be closely related, share the same warning signals. This helps protect all species involved by making their coloration/patterns better known to their shared predators (i.e. bees, wasps and hornets).

2. **Batesian mimicry** – In contrast to Mullerian mimicry where both parties are harmful, this type of mimicry occurs when a harmless species, known as the mimic, mimics the warning signals of a harmful species, known as the model (i.e. a harmless fly adopting a yellow/black pattern to resemble bees).

The concept of ecological succession is seen when one community with a certain species inhabiting it is gradually replaced by another community consisting of a different species until a climax community is established. As succession progresses species diversity and biomass (total mass of all living organisms) increases. The final stage, or *sere*, is called the climax community where the combination of species and their habitat remains the same until it is destroyed by some sort of catastrophic event such as a forest fire or earthquake. Some of the factors that change over time before the climax stage is reached include substrate texture, soil pH, light availability and crowding.

The plants and animals that are the first to colonize a new habitat are called the pioneer species (most often r-selected species that grow quickly and produce many offspring). The pioneer species are eventually replaced by K-selected species which are more stable and live longer.

There are two types of succession:

1. **Primary succession** – Occurs on substrates that never previously supported living things such as volcanic islands. In this scenario succession often begins with the establishment of lichens followed by many species of bacteria, mosses, insects and other arthropods. Grasses, herbs and plants appear next when the soil becomes arable. More r-selected species follow and are eventually replaced by K-selected ones.

2. **Secondary succession** – Begins in habitats where there has been prior colonization by various communities of organisms. Areas damaged by fires, floods or insect devastation are prime candidates. This occurs faster than primary succession because conditions are already in place to support life.

19.6 Ecosystems

The study of ecosystems focuses on the production and utilization of energy and organizes different plant and animal groups into trophic (= feeding/nutrition) levels that are each associated with a particular energy source. There are five types:

1. **Primary producers** – Autotrophs such as plants and chemotrophs such as oxi-dizing bacteria that utilize light energy or simple raw materials, respectively, to synthesize all the necessary organic compounds.

2. **Primary consumers** – Herbivores that eat the primary producers.

3. **Secondary consumers** – Primary carnivores that eat the primary consumers.

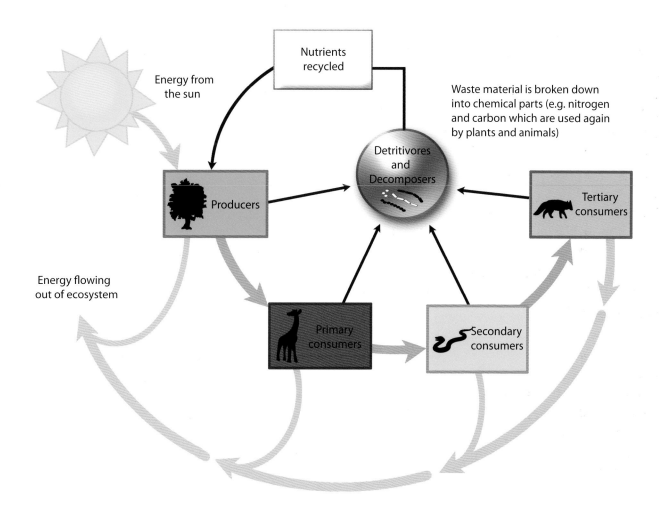

4. **Tertiary consumers** – Secondary carnivores that eat the secondary consumers.

5. **Detritivores** – Consumers that obtain their energy from dead plants and animals.

   Ecological pyramids are used to show the relationship between the different trophic levels. The horizontal bars represent the sizes and the order of the levels represents how energy is transferred. There are three main types of pyramids:

1. **Pyramid of energy:** The producer at the base of the pyramid contains the most amount of energy. Less energy becomes available for primary consumers and even less for secondary or tertiary consumers. The least amount of energy is present at the top of the pyramid.

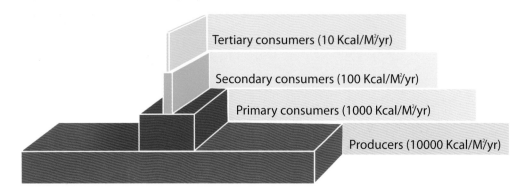

Tertiary consumers (10 Kcal/M²/yr)

Secondary consumers (100 Kcal/M²/yr)

Primary consumers (1000 Kcal/M²/yr)

Producers (10000 Kcal/M²/yr)

2. **Pyramid of numbers:** The producer at the base of the pyramid contains the greatest number of organisms. As the pyramid is ascended, there is a smaller number of organisms. The least number of organisms is present at the top of the pyramid.

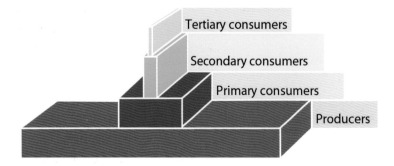

Tertiary consumers

Secondary consumers

Primary consumers

Producers

3. **Pyramid of biomass:** The producer at the base of the pyramid contains the most amount of mass since organisms from upper levels of the pyramid derive their food from lower levels. The least amount of biomass is present at the top of the pyramid.

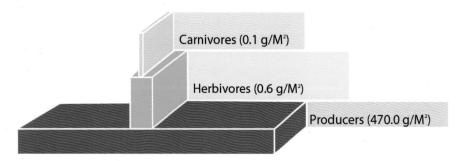

Carnivores (0.1 g/M²)

Herbivores (0.6 g/M²)

Producers (470.0 g/M²)

The concept of ecological efficiency relates to the pyramids by describing the proportion of energy in one trophic level that is transferred to the next level. Large horizontal bars represent energy that is transferred with high efficiency while the narrower bars are indicative of decreased efficacy. On average, only about 10% of the energy produced at one trophic level is transferred to the next. The remaining 90% is consumed by metabolic demand of the plant or animal found in that level. Food chains (linear flow charts of who eats whom) and food webs (more complete version of the food chain) diagram the flow of energy between organisms.

19.7 Biomes

Biomes are occupied by unique communities of plants and animals that possess adaptations tailored to the conditions of their collective habitat. Each biome is a component of the biosphere (BIO 19.1):

1. **Tropical rain forest** – Characterized by high temperatures, heavy rainfall, lush vegetation and many different types of species (monkeys, lizards and snakes). Little plant growth occurs on the floor due to lack of sunlight, a direct result of the tall trees that form a canopy and shade the surface. Epiphytes are commonly found in rain forests and are small plants that grow on the branches of the larger trees, further shading the ground surface.

2. **Savannas** – Grasslands with scattered plant life that receive less water than the rain forests. As suggested by its name, "grasslands" are areas where the vegetation is dominated by grasses and other non-woody (= herbaceous) plants.

3. **Temperate grasslands** – Receive even less water than the savannas and are subject to lower temperatures (i.e. North American prairie).

4. **Temperate deciduous forests** - Occupy regions which have warm summers, cold winters and moderate precipitation.

5. **Alpine** - Upper altitudes of mountains, where cooler climates give rise to communities which resemble (but do not duplicate) the taiga, tundra and frozen biomes.

6. **Deserts** – Arid and hot with little precipitation. Feature cacti and species of animal that have tremendous water conservation adaptations (i.e. camels and kangaroo rats).

7. **Taigas** – Coniferous forests with cold winters and snow. Pines and firs occupy this region. Taiga is also knows as boreal forest. {"Coniferous" refers to trees or shrubs that bear cones and

evergreen leaves (see Kingdom Plantae, BIO 16.6.4).}

8. **Tundra** – Extremely harsh winters with little if any vegetation. Animals living in the tundra have adaptations to the cold and cannot survive in moderate biomes (i.e. polar bears and penguins). Tundra has short growing seasons, a large variation in annual temperatures and usually has permafrost (= a thick layer of soil that remains frozen). The ecological boundary (= ecotone) between the forest and tundra is called the tree line (= timberline). Depending on the classification system, Tundra is sometimes referred to as Arctic, Antarctic or Frozen. The latter two cannot support vegetation because it is too cold and dry.

GOLD STANDARD WARM-UP EXERCISES

CHAPTER 19: Ecology

1) A certain plant requires light, moisture, oxygen, carbon dioxide and minerals in order to survive. The preceding information is consistent with the idea that the plant depends on:

A. symbiotic relationships.
B. amensalism.
C. biotic factors.
D. abiotic factors.

2) Which of the following graphs best describes logistic growth?

A. J shaped curve
B. S shaped curve
C. K-selected species
D. r-selected curve

3) The idea that two different species cannot occupy the same niche for long is consistent with the:

A. Competitive Exclusion Principle.
B. Principle of Ecology.
C. Hardy-Weinberg Law.
D. Theory of Natural Selection.

4) Certain bacteria living in the human colon help to produce vitamin K is an example of:

A. mutualism.
B. commensalism.
C. amensalism.
D. parasitism.

5) The trophic structure of an ecosystem can be represented as a pyramid of:

A. biomass.
B. numbers.
C. energy.
D. all of the above.

6) Which of the following is a producer?

A. A silkworm
B. A mushroom
C. A pregnant lioness
D. An oak tree

7) Organisms that use inorganic nutrients and an outside energy source to produce sugars and other organic nutrients for themselves and other members of the community are:

A. autotrophs.
B. producers.
C. heterotrophs.
D. both A and B.

8) An example of a detritus feeder is a(n):

A. cow.
B. dog.
C. earthworm.
D. photosynthetic bacterium.

9) Tertiary consumers feed on:

A. producers.
B. chemoautotrophs.
C. primary consumers.
D. secondary consumers.

10) Solar energy is first transformed by which of the following when it enters an ecosystem?

    A. Chemoautotrophs

    B. Detritivores

    C. Producers

    D. Primary consumers

11) As nutrients cycle through an ecosystem, the inorganic nutrients are returned to autotrophs by:

    A. detritivores.

    B. producers.

    C. chemoautotrophs.

    D. primary consumers.

12) The main difference between a tropical rainforest and a savanna is the difference in:

    A. precipitation.

    B. temperature.

    C. animals.

    D. hemisphere.

13) On the Arctic tundra, only the topmost layer of earth thaws but the layer beneath is referred to as:

    A. subsoil.

    B. permafrost.

    C. temperate earth.

    D. arctic vegetation.

14) Which of the following is (are) treeless?

    A. Desert

    B. Tundra

    C. Grasslands

    D. All of the above

15) Which of the following is consistent with a coniferous forest?

    A. Deciduous forest

    B. Temperate Forest

    C. Boreal Forest

    D. Tropical Rainforest

GS ANSWER KEY

CHAPTER 19

		Cross-Reference				Cross-Reference
1.	D	BIO 19.1	9.	D		BIO 19.6
2.	B	BIO 19.2, 19.3	10.	C		BIO 19.6
3.	A	BIO 16.2, 19.3	11.	A		BIO 19.6
4.	A	BIO 2.2, 9.5, 19.3	12.	A		BIO 19.7
5.	D	BIO 19.6	13.	B		BIO 19.7
6.	D	BIO 16.6.4, 19.6	14.	D		BIO 19.7
7.	D	BIO 2.2, 19.6	15.	C		BIO 19.7
8.	C	BIO 16.6.4, 19.6				

* Explanations can be found at the back of the book.

Go online to DAT-prep.com for additional chapter review Q&A and forum.

APPENDIX
CHAPTER 19: Ecology

Advanced DAT-30 Passage: Coevolution: A Closer Look

Much of the study of evolution of interspecific interactions had focused on the results rather than the process of coevolution. In only a few cases has the genetic bases of interspecific interactions been explored. One of the most intriguing results has been the description of "gene-for-gene" systems governing the interaction between certain parasites and their hosts. In several crop plants, dominant alleles at a number of loci have been described that confer resistance to a pathogenic fungus; for each such gene, the fungus appears to have a recessive allele for "virulence" that enables the fungus to attack the otherwise resistant host. Cases of <u>character displacement</u> - the evolutionary divergence of similar traits among competing sympatric species - are among the best evidence that interspecific interactions can result in genetic change.

Assuming that parasites and their hosts coevolve in an "arms race," we might deduce that the parasite is "ahead" if local populations are more capable of attacking the host population with which they are associated than other populations. Whereas the host may be "ahead" if local populations are more resistant to the local parasite than to other populations of the parasite.

Several studies have been done to evaluate coevolutionary interactions between parasites and hosts, or predators and prey. In one, the fluctuations in populations of houseflies and of a wasp that parasitized them were recorded. The results of the experiment are shown in Fig. 1.

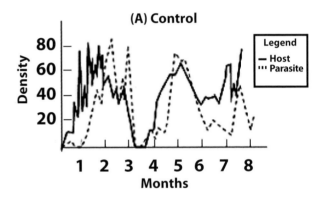

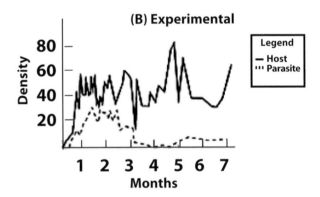

Figure 1

16) A pathogenic fungus is more capable of growth and reproduction on its native population of its sole host, the wild hog peanut, than on plants from other populations of the same species. It is reasonable to conclude that:

A. the fungus, in this instance, was capable of more rapid adaptation to its host than vice versa.

B. the fungus, in this instance, was capable of more rapid adaptation to all populations of the host species than vice versa.

C. the host, in this instance, was capable of more rapid adaptation to the fungus than vice versa.

D. all populations of the host species were capable of more rapid adaptation to the fungus than vice versa.

17) According to Fig. 1, the experiment showed that over time:

A. coevolution caused a decrease in both the host and parasite populations.

B. coevolution caused both a decrease in fluctuation of the host and parasite populations, and a lowered density of the parasite population.

C. coevolution caused a marked increase in the fluctuation of only the host population, and lowered the density of the parasite population.

D. coevolution caused a decrease in the population density of the parasite population but caused a marked increase in the density of the host population.

18) The control in the experiment likely consisted of:

A. members from different populations of the host and parasite species used in the experimental group, that had a short history of exposure to one another.

B. members of the host and parasite species used in the experimental group, that had a long history of exposure to one another.

C. members of the host and parasite species used in the experimental group that had no history of exposure to one another.

D. members from different populations of the host and parasite species used in the experimental group, that had a long history of exposure to one another.

19) Which of the following is the least likely explanation of the results obtained for the control group in Fig. 1?

A. A low parasite population results in a lowered host population by the sheer virulence of the parasite.

B. A very low host population can increase a parasite population by forcing the parasite to seek an alternate source for food.

C. A high parasite population destroys the host population resulting in a lowered host population.

D. A high host population creates a breeding ground for parasites thus increasing the parasite population.

20) Penicillin is an antibiotic which destroys bacteria by interfering with cell wall production. Could the development of bacterial resistance to Penicillin be considered similar to coevolution?

A. Yes, a spontaneous mutation is likely to confer resistance to Penicillin.

B. No, an organism can only evolve in response to another organism.

C. Yes, as antibiotics continue to change there will be a selective pressure for bacterial genes which confer resistance.

D. No, bacteria have plasma membranes and can survive without cell walls.

ANSWER KEY

ADVANCED TOPICS - CHAPTER 19

Cross-Reference

16.	A	BIO 2.1, 2.3, 16.2, 16.6, 19.2, 19.3, 19.4
17.	B	BIO 16.2, 16.3, 16.6, 19.2, 19.3, 19.4
18.	C	BIO 2.5, 2.5.1, 16.6, 19.2, 19.3, 19.4
19.	A	BIO 2.5, 2.5.1, 16.3, 16.6, 19.2, 19.3, 19.4
20.	C	BIO 16.3, 16.6, 19.2, 19.3, 19.4

P = paragraph; S = sentence; E = equation; T = table; F = figure

Go online to DAT-prep.com for additional chapter review Q&A and forum.

GOLD NOTES

BIOCHEMISTRY
Chapter 20

Memorize	Understand	Importance
enclature and structures of non molecules ectric point equation ae: amphoteric, zwitterions	* Effect of H, S, hydrophobic bonds * Basic mechanisms of reactions * Effect of pH, isoelectric point * Protein structure * Basics: carbohydrates, lipids, steroids, phosphorus * Biological buffers	**0 to 2 out of the 40 Biology** DAT questions are based on content in this chapter (in our estimation). * Note that between 25% and 50% of the questions in DAT Biology are from 5 chapters: 1, 2, 14, 15, and 16.

DAT-Prep.com

Introduction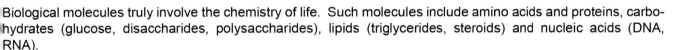

Biological molecules truly involve the chemistry of life. Such molecules include amino acids and proteins, carbo-hydrates (glucose, disaccharides, polysaccharides), lipids (triglycerides, steroids) and nucleic acids (DNA, RNA).

Additional Resources

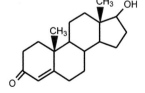

Free Online Q&A + Forum

Video: Online or DVD

Flashcards

Special Guest

If Biochemistry is not your favorite subject, here is the good news: most biochemistry has been covered in previous chapters including our review of DNA, RNA and protein (chapters 1 and 3), enzymes and cellular metabolism (chapters 4 and 17), etc. Thermodynamics, enthalpy, thermochemistry, and rate processes in chemical reactions are reviewed in GS DAT General Chemistry (chapters 7, 8 and 9).

In this chapter, we will only review those aspects of biochemistry that could be asked in DAT Biology but not reviewed elsewhere in the GS series of DAT books. This chapter overlaps GS DAT Organic Chemistry Chapter 12 (Biological Molecules) which has more details regarding stereochemistry, reactions and mechanisms.

20.1 Amino Acids

Amino acids are molecules that contain a side chain (R), a carboxylic acid, and an amino group at the α carbon. Thus the general structure of α-amino acids is:

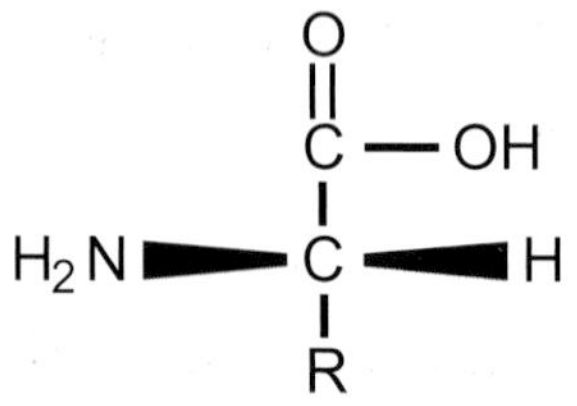

L - amino acid 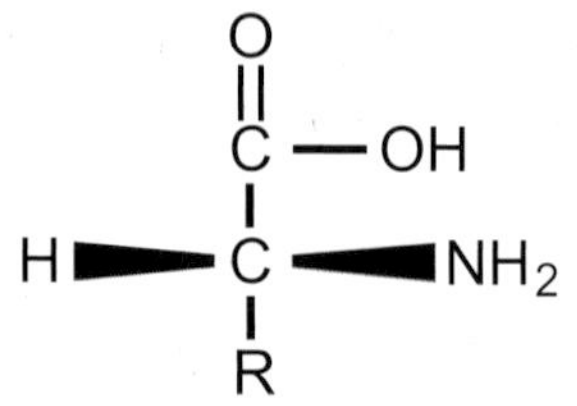   D - amino acid

Amino acids may be named systematically as substituted carboxylic acids, however, there are 20 important α-amino acids that are known by common names. These are naturally occurring and they form the building blocks of most proteins found in humans. The following are a few examples of α-amino acids:

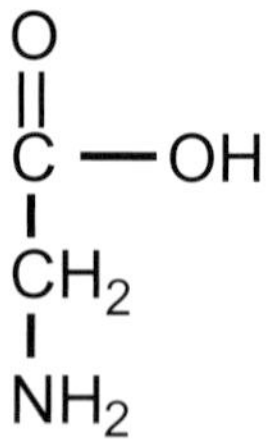

Glycine 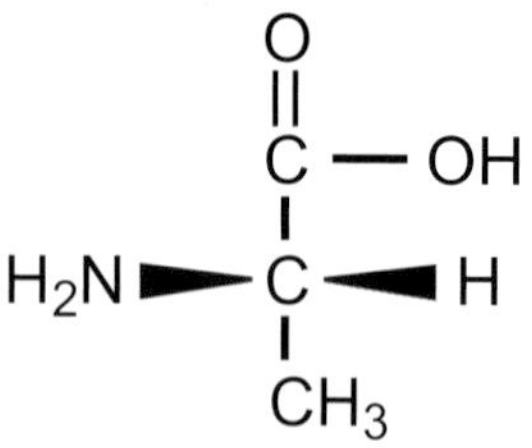   Alanine

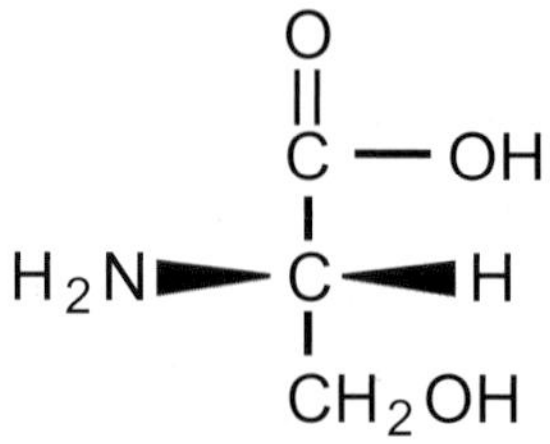

Serine 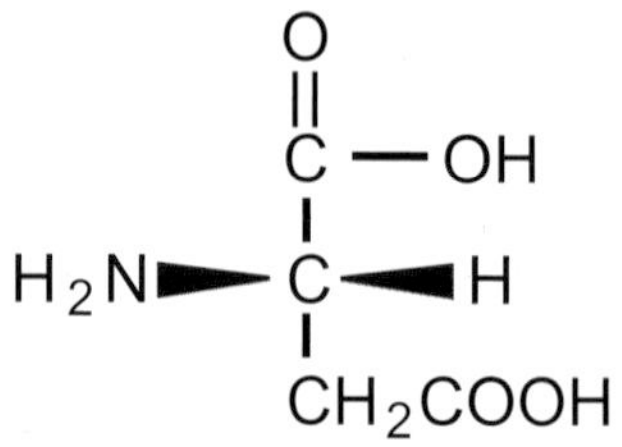   Aspartic acid

Note that all amino acids have the same relative configuration, the L-configuration. However, the absolute configuration depends on the priority assigned to the side group (*see* ORG 2.3.1 *for rules*). In the preceding amino acids, the S-configuration prevails.

20.1.1 Hydrophilic vs. Hydrophobic

Different types of amino acids tend to be found in different areas of the proteins that they make up. Amino acids which are ionic and/or polar are hydrophilic, and tend to be found on the exterior of proteins (i.e. *exposed to water*). These include aspartic acid and its amide, glutamic acid and its amide, lysine, arginine and histidine. Certain other polar amino acids are found on either the interior or exterior of proteins. These include serine, threonine, and tyrosine. Hydrophobic amino acids which may be found on the interior of proteins include methionine, leucine, trypto-phan, valine and phenylalanine. Hydrophobic molecules tend to cluster in aqueous solutions (= *hydrophobic bonding*). Alanine is a nonpolar amino acid which is unusual because it is less hydrophobic than most nonpolar amino acids. This is because its nonpolar side chain is very short.

Glycine is the smallest amino acid, and the only one that is not optically active. It is often found at the 'corners' of proteins. Alanine is small and, although hydrophobic, is found on the surface of proteins.

20.1.2 Acidic vs. Basic

Amino acids have both an acid and basic components (= *amphoteric*). The amino acids with the R group containing an amino ($-NH_2$) group, are basic. The two basic amino acids are lysine and arginine. Amino acids with an R group containing a carboxyl ($-COOH$) group are acidic. The two acidic amino acids are aspartic acid and glutamic acid. One amino acid, histidine, may act as either an acid or a base, depending upon the pH of the resident solution. This makes histidine a very good physiologic buffer. The rest of the amino acids are considered to be neutral.

The basic $-NH_2$ group in the amino acid is present as an ammonium ion, $-NH_3^+$. The acidic carboxyl $-COOH$ group is present as a carboxylate ion, $-COO^-$. As a result, amino acids are dipolar ions, or *zwitterions*. In an aqueous solution, there is an equilibrium present between the dipolar, the anionic, and the cationic forms of the amino acid:

$$H_3\overset{+}{N} - CH - CO_2H \underset{H_3O^+}{\rightleftharpoons} H_3\overset{+}{N} - CH - CO_2^- \underset{H_3O^+}{\rightleftharpoons} H_2N - CH - CO_2^-$$

$$\underset{\text{Acidic}}{\overset{|}{CH_3}} \qquad \underset{\text{Neutral}}{\overset{|}{CH_3}} \qquad \underset{\text{Basic}}{\overset{|}{CH_3}}$$

Therefore the charge on the amino acid will vary with the pH of the solution, and with the isoelectric point. This point is the pH where a given amino acid will be neutral (i.e. have no net charge). This isoelectric point is the average of the two pK_a values of an amino acid (*depending on the dissociated group*):

$$\text{isoelectric point} = pI = (pK_{a1} + pK_{a2})/2$$

As this is a common exam question, let's further summarize for the average amino acid: When in a relatively acidic solution, the amino acid is fully protonated and exists as a cation, that is, it has two protons available for dissociation, one from the carboxyl group and one from the amino group. When in a relatively basic solution, the amino acid is fully deprotonated and exists as an anion, that is, it has two proton accepting groups, the carboxyl group and the amino group. At the isoelectric point, the amino acid exists as a neutral, dipolar zwitterion, which means that the carboxyl group is deprotonated while the amino group is protonated.

20.1.3 The 20 Alpha-Amino Acids

Approximately 500 amino acids are known - of these, only 22 are proteinogenic ("protein building") amino acids. Of these, 20 amino acids are known as "standard" and are found in human beings and other eukaryotes, and are encoded directly by the universal genetic code (BIO 3). The 2 exceptions are the "non-standard" pyrrolysine — found only in some methanogenic organisms but not humans — and selenocysteine which is present in humans and a wide range of other organisms.

Of the 20 standard amino acids, 9 are called "essential" for humans because they cannot be created from other compounds by the human body, and so must be taken in as food.

The following summarizes the categories of amino acids based on side chains, pK_a and charges at physiological pH:

1. Nonpolar amino acids: R groups are hydrophobic and thus decrease solubility. These amino acids are usually found within the interior of the protein molecule.

2. Polar amino acids: R groups are hydrophilic and thus increase the solubility. These amino acids are usually found on the protein's surface.

3. Acidic amino acids: R groups contain an additional carboxyl group. These amino acids have a negative charge at physiological pH.

4. Basic amino acids: R groups contain an additional amine group. These amino acids have a positive charge at physiological pH. Note that asparagine and glutamine have amide side chains and are thus not considered basic (see ORG 9.3).

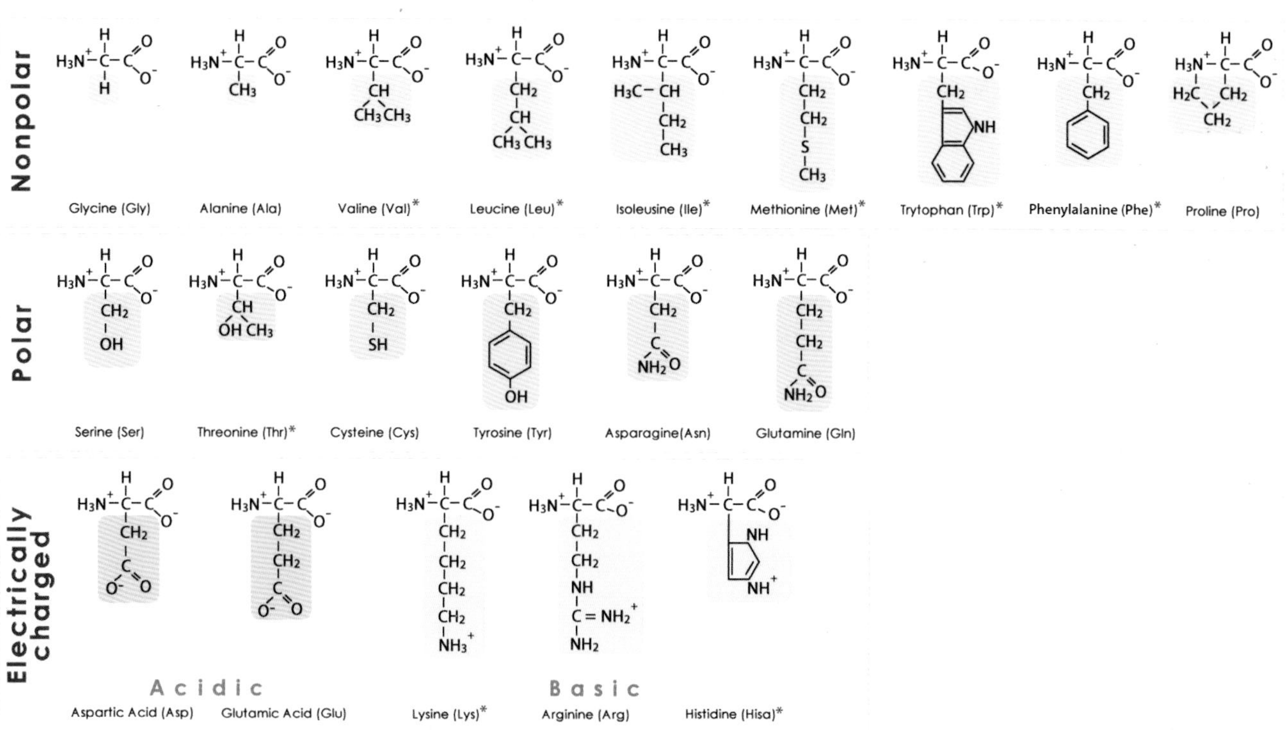

Figure IV.A.20.1: The 20 Standard Amino Acids. A red asterix * is used to indicate the 9 essential amino acids.

20.2 Proteins

20.2.1 General Principles

An oligopeptide consists of between 2 and 20 amino acids joined together by amide *(peptide)* bonds. Oligopeptides include dipeptides (2 amino acids), tripeptides (3), tetrapeptides (4), pentapeptides (5), etc. Poly-peptides - generally regarded to be between the size of oligopeptides and proteins - are polymers of up to 100 or even 1000 α-amino acids (depending on the molecule and the reference). Proteins are long chain polypeptides which often form higher order structures. These peptide bonds are derived from the amino group of one amino acid, and the acid group of another. When a peptide bond is formed, a molecule of water is released (*condensation = dehydration*). The bond can be broken by adding water (*hydrolysis*).

Since proteins are polymers of amino acids, they also have isoelectric points. Classification as to the acidity or basicity of a protein depends on the numbers of acidic and basic amino acids it contains. If there is an excess of acidic amino acids, the isoelectric point will be at a pH of less than 7. At $pH = 7$, these proteins will have a net negative charge.

Similarly, those with an excess of basic amino acids will have an isoelectric point at a pH of greater than 7. Therefore, at $pH = 7$, these proteins will have a net positive charge. Proteins can be separated according to their isoelectric point on a polyacrylamide gel (*electrophoresis*; BIO 15.7; ORG 13).

20.2.2 Protein Structure

Protein structure may be divided into primary, secondary, tertiary and quaternary structures. The <u>primary structure</u> is the sequence of amino acids as determined by the DNA and the location of covalent bonds (*including disulfide bonds*). This structure determines the higher order structures.

The <u>secondary structure</u> is the orderly inter- or intramolecular *hydrogen bonding* of the protein chain. The resultant structure may be the more stable α-helix (e.g. keratin), or a β-pleated sheet (e.g. silk). Proline is an amino acid which cannot participate in the regular array of H-bonding in an α-helix. Proline disrupts the α-helix, thus it is usually found at the beginning or end of a molecule (i.e. hemoglobin).

The <u>tertiary structure</u> is the further folding of the protein molecule onto itself. This structure is maintained by *noncovalent bonds* like hydrogen bonding, Van der Waals forces,

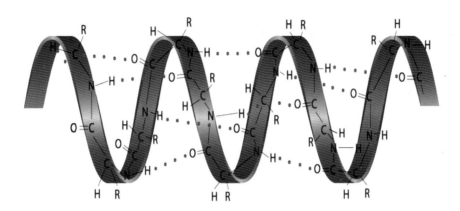

Hydrogen bonds between amino acids
at different locations in polypeptide chain

α helix

R = Amino acid side chain

Figure IV.A.20.2: Secondary Structure: α-helix. This is a structure in which the peptide chain is coiled into a helical structure around a central axis. This helix is stabilized by hydrogen bonding between the N-H group and C=O group four residues away. A typical example with this secondary structure is keratin.

Pleated sheet

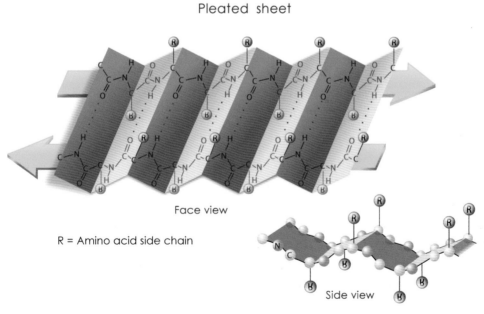

Face view

R = Amino acid side chain

Side view

Figure IV.A.20.3: Secondary Structure: β-pleated sheet. Peptide chains lie alongside each other in a parallel manner. This structure is stabilized by hydrogen bonding between the N-H group on one peptide chain and C=O group on another. A typical example with this secondary structure is produced by some insect larvae: the protein fiber "silk" which is mostly composed of fibroin.

hydrophobic bonding and electrostatic bonding (CHM 4.2). The resultant structure is a globular protein with a hydrophobic interior and hydrophilic exterior. Enzymes are classical examples of such a structure. In fact, enzyme activity often depends on tertiary structure.

The covalent bonding of cysteine (*disulfide bonds or bridge*) helps to stabilize the tertiary structure of proteins. Cysteine will form sulfur-sulfur covalent bonds with itself, producing *cystine*.

$$2H_2N\!-\!CH\!-\!CO_2H \xrightarrow{-H_2}$$

cysteine

cystine

The quaternary structure is when there are two or more protein chains bonded together by noncovalent bonds. For example, hemoglobin consists of four polypeptide sub-units (*globin*) held together by hydrophobic bonds forming a globular almost tetrahedryl arrangement.

20.3 Carbohydrates

20.3.1 Description and Nomenclature

Carbohydrates are sugars and their derivatives. Formally they are 'carbon hydrates,' that is, they have the general formula $C_m(H_2O)_n$. Usually they are defined as polyhydroxy aldehydes and ketones, or substances that hydrolyze to yield polyhydroxy aldehydes and ketones. The basic units of carbohydrates are monosaccharides (sugars).

There are two ways to classify sugars. One way is to classify the molecule based on the type of carbonyl group it contains: one with an aldehyde carbonyl group is an *aldose*; one with a ketone carbonyl group is a *ketose*. The second method of classification depends on the number of carbons in the molecule: those with 6 carbons are *hexoses*, with 5 carbons are *pentoses*, with 4 carbons are *tetroses*, and with 3 carbons are *trioses*. Sugars may exist in either the ring form, as hemiacetals, or in the straight chain form, as polyhydroxy aldehydes. *Pyranoses* are 6 carbon sugars in the ring form; *furanoses* are 5 carbon sugars in the ring form.

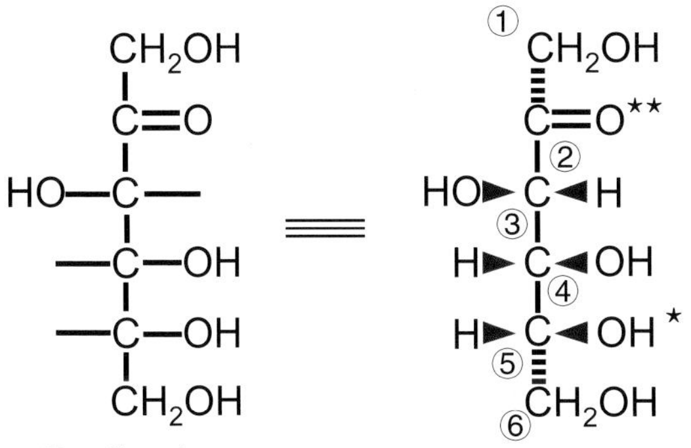

D - fructose

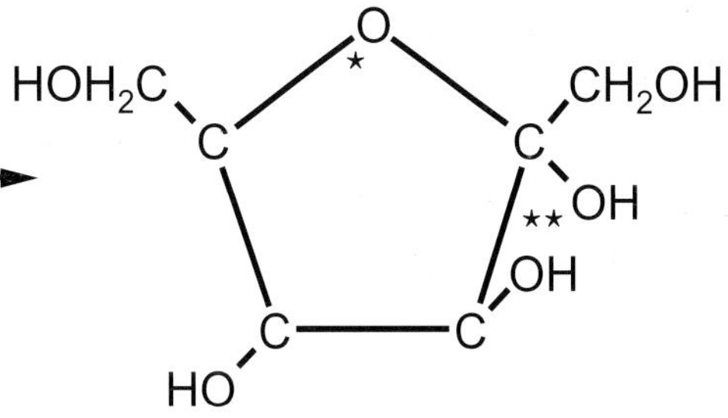

α - D - fructose
(a furanose)

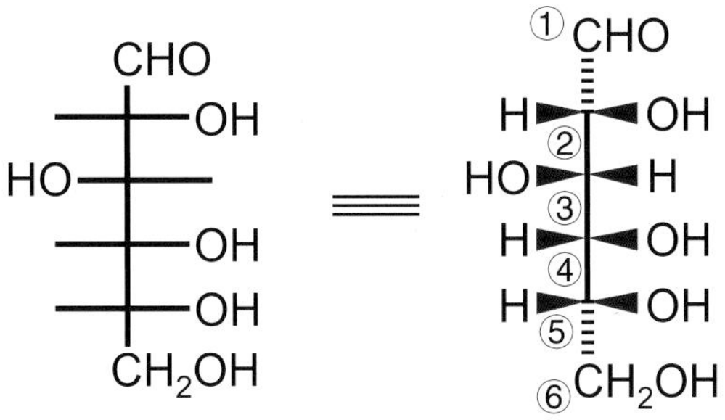

D - Glucose
(an aldose hexose)

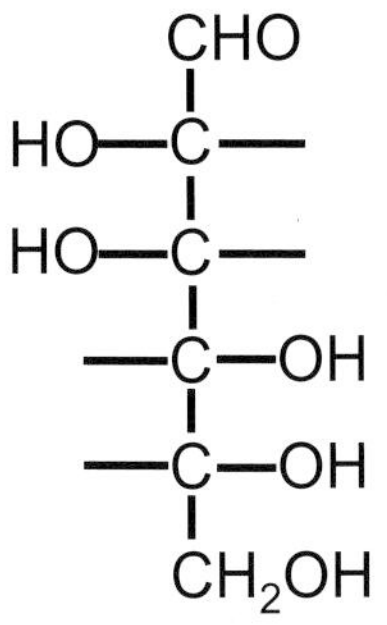

D - Mannose
(C_2 epimer
of glucose)

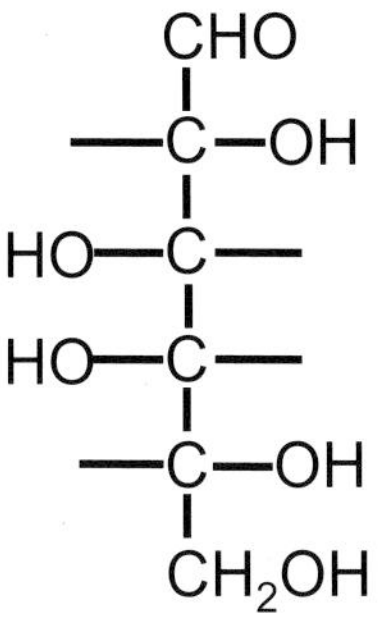

D - Galactose
(C_4 epimer
of glucose)

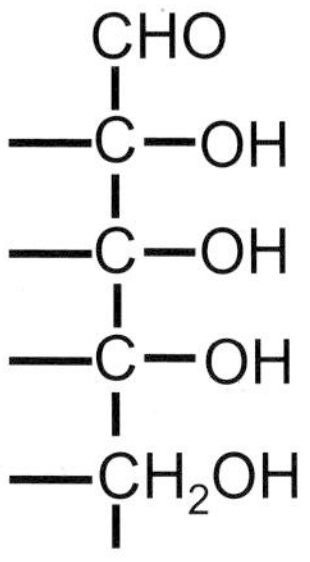

D - Ribose
(in RNA)

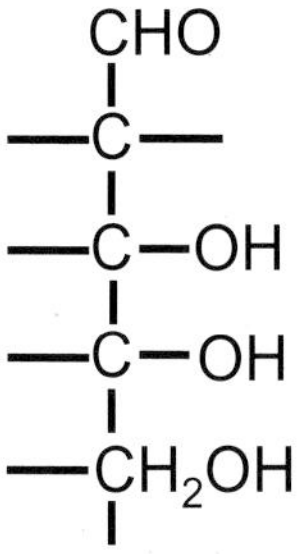

2 - Deoxy - D - ribose
(in DNA)

Figure IV.A.20.4: Names, structures and configurations of common sugars.

In the ring form, there is the possibility of α or β *anomers*. Anomers occur when 2 cyclic forms of the molecule differ in conformation only at the hemiacetal carbon (carbon 1). Generally, pyranoses take the 'chair' conformation, as it is very stable, with all (usually) hydroxyl groups at the equatorial position. *Epimers* are diastereomers that differ in the configuration of only one stereogenic center. For carbohydrates, epimers are 2 monosaccharides which differ in the conformation of one hydroxyl group.

Most but not all of the naturally occurring aldoses have the D-configuration. Thus they have the same *relative* configuration as D-glyceraldehyde.

The names and structures of some common sugars are shown in Figure IV.A.20.4.

20.3.2 Important Reactions of Carbohydrates

A disaccharide is a molecule made up of two monosaccharides, joined by a *glycosidic bond* between the hemiacetal carbon of one molecule, and the hydroxyl group of another. The glycosidic bond forms an α-1,4-glycosidic linkage if the reactant is an α anomer. A β-1,4- glycosidic linkage is formed if the reactant is a β anomer. When the bond is formed, one molecule of water is released (condensation). In order to break the bond, water must be added (hydrolysis):

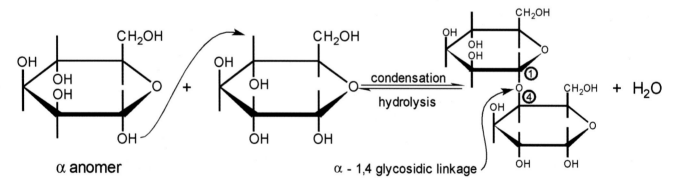

α anomer   α - 1,4 glycosidic linkage

- Sucrose (common sugar) = glucose + fructose
- Lactose (milk sugar) = glucose + galactose

- Maltose (α-1,4 bond) = glucose + glucose
- Cellobiose (β-1,4 bond) = glucose + glucose

20.3.3 Polysaccharides

Polymers of many monosaccharides are called polysaccharides. As in disaccharides, they are joined by glycosidic linkages. They may be straight chains, or branched chains. Some common polysaccharides are:

- Starch (plant energy storage; BIO 17.3)
- Cellulose (plant structural component; BIO 17.3)
- Glycocalyx (associated with the plasma membrane; BIO 1.1)
- Glycogen (animal energy storage in the form of glucose; BIO 4.1, 4.4, 9.4.1)

- Chitin (structural component found in shells or arthropods; BIO 16.6.4: Fungi and Arthropoda)

Carbohydrates are the most abundant organic constituents of plants. They are the source of chemical energy in living organisms, and, in plants, they are used in making the support structures. Cellulose consists of $\beta(1\rightarrow4)$ linked D-glucose. Starch and glycogen are mostly $\alpha(1\rightarrow4)$ glycosidic linkages of D-glucose.

20.4 Lipids

Lipids are a class of organic molecules containing many different types of substances, such as fatty acids, fats, waxes, triacyl glycerols, terpenes and steroids.

Triacyl glycerols are oils and fats of either animal or plant origin. In general, fats are solid at room temperature, and oils are liquid at room temperature.

Triacyl glycerols are also commonly referred to as triglycerides (= triacylglycerides) and are, by definition, fatty acid triesters of the trihydroxy alcohol glycerol.

> Glycerol + 3 Fatty acids = Triglyceride

The general structure of a triacyl glycerol is:

$$
\begin{array}{l}
\quad\quad\quad\quad\;\; O \\
\quad\quad\quad\quad\;\; || \\
CH_2O-C-R \\
\\
\quad\quad\quad\quad\;\; O \\
\quad\quad\quad\quad\;\; || \\
CH_2O-C-R' \\
\\
\quad\quad\quad\quad\;\; O \\
\quad\quad\quad\quad\;\; || \\
CH_2O-C-R''
\end{array}
$$

The R groups may be the same or different, and are usually long chain alkyl groups.

Upon hydrolysis of a triacyl glycerol, the products are three fatty acids and glycerol (*see* ORG 9.4.1). The fatty acids may be saturated (= no multiple bonds, i.e. *palmitic acid*) or unsaturated (= containing double or triple bonds, i.e. *oleic acid*). Unsaturated fatty acids are usually in the cis configuration. Saturated fatty acids have a higher melting point than unsaturated fatty acids. Some common fatty acids are:

$$CH_3(CH_2)_{14}COOH$$

palmitic acid

$$CH_3(CH_2)_{16}COOH$$

stearic acid

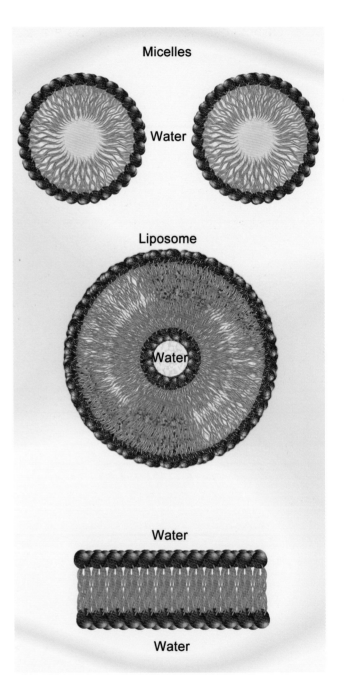

$$CH_3(CH_2)_7 \overset{\displaystyle}{\underset{H}{C}} = \overset{\displaystyle (CH_2)_7CO_2H}{\underset{H}{C}}$$

oleic acid

"Essential" fatty acids are fatty acids that humans - and other animals - must ingest because the body requires them but cannot synthesize them. Only two are known in humans: alpha-linolenic acid and linoleic acid. Because they have multiple double bonds that begin near the methyl end, they are both known as polyunsaturated omega fatty acids.

Soap is a mixture of salts of long chain fatty acids formed by the hydrolysis of fat. This process is called saponification. Soap possesses both a nonpolar hydrocarbon tail and a

Figure IV.A.20.5. Amphipathic molecules arranged in micelles, a liposome and a bilipid layer.

polar carboxylate head. When soaps are dispersed in aqueous solution, the long nonpolar tails are inside the sphere while the polar heads face outward. Recall that a sphere is the shape that minimizes surface tension (i.e. the smallest surface area relative to volume; CHM 4.2).

Soaps are surfactants (BIO 12.3). They are compounds that lower the surface tension of a liquid because of their amphipathic nature (i.e. they contain both hydrophobic tails and hydrophilic heads; see BIO 1.1).

Of course, the cellular membrane is a lipid bilayer (Biology Chapter 1). The polar heads of the lipids align towards the aqueous environment, while the hydrophobic tails minimize their contact with water and tend to cluster together. Depending on the concentration of the lipid, this interaction may result in micelles (spherical), liposomes (spherical) or other lipid bilayers.

Micelles are closed lipid monolayers with a fatty acid core and polar surface. The main function of bile (BIO 9.4.1) is to facilitate the formation of micelles, which promotes the processing or emulsification of dietary fat and fat-soluble vitamins.

Liposomes are composed of a lipid bilayer separating an aqueous internal compartment from the bulk aqueous environment. Liposomes can be used as a vehicle for the administration of nutrients or pharmaceutical drugs.

20.4.1 Steroids

Steroids are derivatives of the basic ring structure:

The IUPAC-recommended ring-lettering and the carbon atoms are numbered as shown. Many important substances are steroids, some examples include: cholesterol, D vitamins, bile acids, adrenocortical hormones, and male and female sex hormones.

Testosterone
(an androgen)

Estradiol
(an estrogen)

The rate limiting step in the production of steroids (= *steroidogenesis*) in humans is the conversion of cholesterol to pregnenolone, which is in the same family as progesterone. This occurs inside of mitochondria and serves as the precursor for all human steroids.

Since such a significant portion of a steroid contains hydrocarbons, which are hydrophobic, steroids can dissolve through the hydrophobic interior of a cell's plasma membrane (BIO 1.1, 6.3). Furthermore, steroid hormones contain polar side groups which allow the hormone to easily dissolve in water. Thus steroid hormones are well designed to be transported through the vascular space, to cross the plasma membranes of cells, and to have an effect either in the cell's cytosol or, as is usually the case, in the nucleus.

20.5 Phosphorous in Biological Molecules

Phosphorous is an essential component of various biological molecules including
adenosine triphosphate (ATP), phospholipids
in cell membranes (BIO 1.1), and the nucleic
acids which form DNA (BIO 1.2.2). Phosphorus can also form phosphoric acid and several phosphate esters:

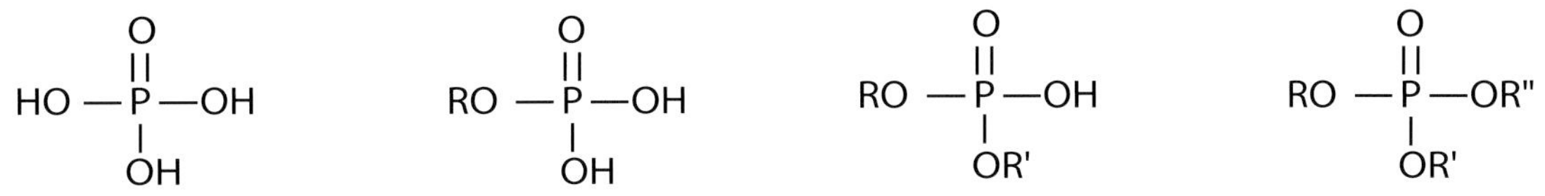

$$HO-\overset{\overset{\textstyle O}{\|}}{\underset{\underset{\textstyle OH}{|}}{P}}-OH \qquad RO-\overset{\overset{\textstyle O}{\|}}{\underset{\underset{\textstyle OH}{|}}{P}}-OH$$

phosphoric acid

$$RO-\overset{\overset{\textstyle O}{\|}}{\underset{\underset{\textstyle OR'}{|}}{P}}-OH \qquad RO-\overset{\overset{\textstyle O}{\|}}{\underset{\underset{\textstyle OR'}{|}}{P}}-OR''$$

phosphate esters

A phospholipid is produced from three
ester linkages to glycerol. Phosphoric acid
is ester linked to the terminal hydroxyl group
and two fatty acids are ester linked to the two
remaining hydroxyl groups of glycerol (*see
Biology Section 1.1 for a schematic view of a
phospholipid*).

In DNA, the phosphate groups engage
in two ester linkages creating phosphodiester
bonds. It is the 5' phosphorylated position of
one pentose ring which is linked to the 3' position of the next pentose ring (*see* BIO 1.2.2):

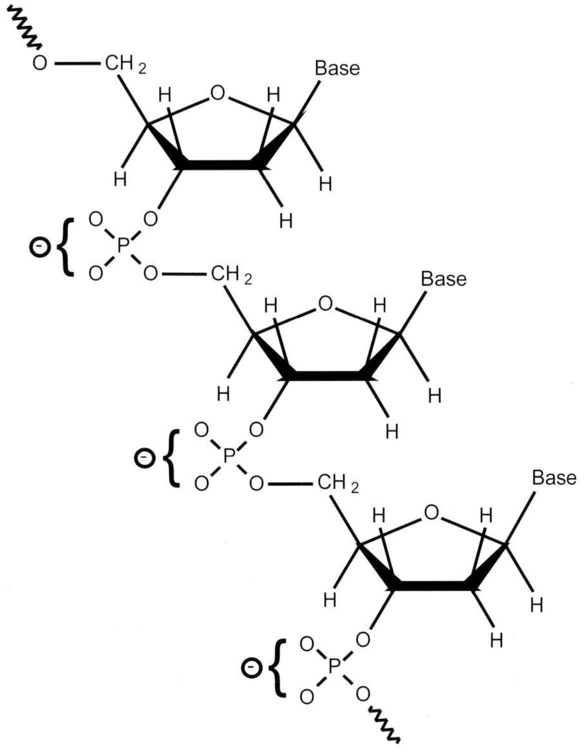

In Biology Chapter 4, the production of ATP was discussed. In each case, the components ADP and P_i (= *inorganic phosphate*) combined using the energy generated from a coupled reaction to produce ATP. The linkage between the phosphate groups are via *anhydride bonds*:

$$\text{adenine}\!-\!\text{ribose}\!-\!\text{O}\!-\!\overset{\displaystyle \overset{O}{\|}}{\underset{\underset{O^-}{|}}{P}}\!-\!\text{O}\!-\!\overset{\displaystyle \overset{O}{\|}}{\underset{\underset{O^-}{|}}{P}}\!-\!\text{OH}$$

adenosine   diphosphate

$$+\ \ \text{HO}\!-\!\overset{\displaystyle \overset{O}{\|}}{\underset{\underset{O^-}{|}}{P}}\!-\!\text{O}^- \xrightarrow{\text{energy}}$$

inorganic
phosphate

$$\text{A}\!-\!\text{O}\!-\!\overset{\displaystyle \overset{O}{\|}}{\underset{\underset{O^-}{|}}{P}}\!-\!\text{O}\!-\!\overset{\displaystyle \overset{O}{\|}}{\underset{\underset{O^-}{|}}{P}}\!-\!\text{O}\!-\!\overset{\displaystyle \overset{O}{\|}}{\underset{\underset{O^-}{|}}{P}}\!-\!\text{O}^- +\ \text{H}_2\text{O}$$

adenosine triphosphate

20.6 Biological pH Buffers

A pH buffer is like a molecular sponge for protons. They are molecules which have the ability to minimize changes in pH when an acid - or base - is added to it.

Plasma pH is normally maintained at 7.4. A pH less than 7.35 is acidosis, whereas a pH of greater than 7.45 is alkalosis. Either condition can be a result of either respiratory or metabolic changes.

It is expected for the DAT that you have an understanding of the chemistry of buffers including equilibrium constants, pH, pK_a, titration and the Henderson-Hasselbalch Equation (GS DAT General Chemistry Chapter

6). These fundamental concepts will not be reviewed here.

It should be noted that the major buffer system in extracellular fluids is the CO_2-bicarbonate buffer system mediated by the enzyme carbonic anhydrase (BIO 12.4.1). This is responsible for about 75% of extracellular buffering. Protein and phosphate buffers dominate the intracellular space. Other buffer systems, though important, have a lesser impact and include ammonia (urine), calcium carbonate (bone), hemoglobin (red blood cells), and many others.

The amino acid histidine is a very good physiologic buffer (mentioned in BIO 20.1.2). Among the reasons is that its pK_a of 6.5 is not far from plasma pH and when protonated, it is resonance stabilized. Histidine is one of the building blocks of carbonic anhydrase, hemoglobin and many other proteins.

Major Buffer Systems of the Human Body		
Bicarbonate buffer	$CO_2 + H_2O \rightleftharpoons H_2CO_3 \rightleftharpoons$ $H^+ + HCO_3^-$	In blood plasma, interstitial fluids
Hemoglobin	$Hb\text{-}H \rightleftharpoons Hb^- + H^+$	Interior of red blood cells
Phosphate buffer	$H_2PO_4^- \rightleftharpoons H^+ + HPO_4^{2-}$	Most important in urine but also intracellular fluid
Protein	$Pr\text{--}H \rightleftharpoons Pr^- + H^+$	Most important in intracellular fluid with a relatively minor effect in blood

GOLD STANDARD WARM-UP EXERCISES

CHAPTER 20: Biochemistry

1) The functional groups of the amino acids located in the interior of the enzyme phenylalanine hydroxylase are mostly likely:

   A. basic.
   B. acidic.
   C. hydrophilic.
   D. hydrophobic.

2) A student is synthesizing tripeptides using three different amino acids. How many distinct molecules can she create?

   A. 3
   B. 4
   C. 6
   D. 9

3) Which of the following best describes the primary structure of proteins?

   A. The arrangement of different protein subunits in a multiprotein complex.
   B. The order in which amino acids are linked together in a protein.
   C. Regions of ordered structure within a protein.
   D. The overall three dimensional shape of a protein.

4) It has been found that proinsulin, the precursor molecule to insulin, contains a portion that is held together by disulfide bonds. This information provides data most characteristic to what level of protein structure?

   A. Primary structure
   B. Secondary structure
   C. Tertiary structure
   D. Quaternary structure

5) Which of the following best identifies the following organic compound?

$$HOCH_2 \overset{\overset{\displaystyle O}{\overset{\displaystyle \|}{}}}{C} CH–CH–CHCH_2OH$$
$$\hspace{3.5cm} | \hspace{0.3cm} | \hspace{0.3cm} |$$
$$\hspace{3.5cm} OH \hspace{0.1cm} OH \hspace{0.1cm} OH$$

   A. Aldehyde
   B. Triacyl glyceride
   C. Protein
   D. Carbohydrate

6) Streptococcus mutans produces glucan, a sticky polymer of glucose that acts like a cement and binds the bacterial cells together and to the tooth surface. Glucan is formed only in the presence of the disaccharide sucrose (the type of sugar found in sweets), through a process catalyzed by an enzyme of the cocci. The enzyme links glucose molecules together to form glucan, while fructose molecules are fermented by the streptococci into lactic acid. Lactic acid can etch the surface of the teeth, enhancing microbial adherence.

   Given the preceding, the enzyme produced by Streptococcus mutans likely initially acts by:

   A. catalyzing the formation of glycosidic bonds between glucose molecules.
   B. splitting sucrose into fructose and glucose.
   C. catalyzing the formation of glycosidic bonds between fructose molecules.
   D. catalyzing the fermentation of fructose.

7) Fructose and glucose are:

A. isotopes.

B. monosaccharides.

C. six-carbon sugars.

D. both B and C.

8) Cholesterol, cortisone and cortisol are best identified as:

A. cholesterols.

B. corticosteroids.

C. bile acids.

D. steroids.

9) ATP is considered an "energy rich" compound because of what kind of bonds?

A. Phosphoanhydride

B. Phosphodiester

C. Phosphoglycosidic

D. Adenosine

10) The three most important buffer systems in body fluids include the bicarbonate buffer system, the phosphate buffer system, and which of the following?

A. Hemoglobin

B. Protein

C. Sodium benzoate

D. Calcium carbonate

11) What is the most effective intracellular inorganic buffer?

A. Phosphate

B. Protein

C. Hemoglobin

D. Bicarbonate

12) What is the normal pH of blood?

A. 7.3-7.4

B. 7.25-7.35

C. 7-8

D. 7.35-7.45

GS ANSWER KEY

Chapter 20

		Cross-Reference				Cross-Reference
1.	D	BIO 20.1.1	7.	D	BIO 20.3.1, 20.3.2
2.	C	BIO 20.2.1; QR 7	8.	D	BIO 6.3, 6.3.2, 20.4.1
3.	B	BIO 20.2.2	9.	A	BIO 4.4–4.10, 20.5
4.	C	BIO 20.2.2	10.	B	BIO 20.6
5.	D	BIO BIO 20.3.1	11.	A	BIO 20.6
6.	B	BIO BIO 20.3.2	12.	D	BIO 20.6.1

* Explanations can be found at the back of the book.

Go online to DAT-prep.com for additional chapter review Q&A and forum.

APPENDIX

CHAPTER 20: Biochemistry

Advanced DAT-30 Passage: Acidosis and Alkalosis

Although buffers in the body fluids help resist changes in pH, the respiratory system and the kidneys regulate the pH of the body fluids. Malfunctions of either the respiratory system or renal system can result in acidosis or alkalosis which may be beyond the capacity of the buffers to repair without the intervention of one of these organ systems.

Respiratory acidosis occurs with an increase in concentration (= *partial pressure*) of carbon dioxide (i.e. impaired breathing or ventilation as seen in COPD, chronic obstructive pulmonary disease which includes chronic bronchitis and emphysema). The result is a lowered ratio of bicarbonate to pCO_2 resulting in a decrease in pH (acidosis; see BIO 12.4.1). The acidosis is reversed gradually when kidneys increase the rate at which they secrete hydrogen ions into the filtrate and increase the absorption of bicarbonate.

Metabolic acidosis can result from the loss of bicarbonate ions (i.e. severe diarrhea) or the accumulation of metabolic acids (i.e. lactic acid, keto acids). This can lead to severe metabolic complications warranting intravenous bicarbonate therapy. The reduced pH stimulates the respiratory center which causes hyperventilation. During hyperventilation, carbon dioxide is eliminated at a greater rate.

Respiratory alkalosis occurs during hyperventilation, when excessive carbon dioxide is eliminated from the system (which lowers pCO_2), the pH of the blood increases, resulting in alkalosis. This can be seen in conditions such as hysteria, stroke and hepatic failure. The kidneys help to compensate for respiratory alkalosis by decreasing the rate of hydrogen ions secretion into the urine and the rate of bicarbonate ion reabsorption.

Metabolic alkalosis generally results when bicarbonate levels are higher in the blood. This can be observed, for example, after sustained vomiting of acidic gastric juices. Kidneys compensate for alkalosis by increasing the excretion of bicarbonate ions. The increased pH inhibits respiration. Reduced respiration allows carbon dioxide to accumulate in the body fluids.

13) Diabetic ketoacidosis is an example of which of the following imbalances?

   A. Respiratory acidosis
   B. Respiratory alkalosis
   C. Metabolic acidosis
   D. Metabolic alkalosis

14) All of the following can be seen as a consequence of vomiting EXCEPT one. Which one is the EXCEPTION?

   A. Metabolic alkalosis
   B. Dehydration
   C. Metabolic acidosis
   D. Respiratory alkalosis

15) Normal pCO_2 is 40 mmHg with the normal range being 35-45 mmHg. If a patient's pH is 7.3 and pCO_2 is 50 mmHg, the patient must have:

A. respiratory acidosis.

B. respiratory alkalosis.

C. metabolic acidosis.

D. metabolic alkalosis.

GOLD STANDARD
MULTIMEDIA EDUCATION

Don't forget to create your own Gold Notes and review them frequently. Please visit our Forum at dat-prep.com/forum and let us know how we can improve. Good luck with your studies!

- The Gold Standard Team

ANSWER KEY

ADVANCED TOPICS - CHAPTER 20

Cross-Reference

13.	C	BIO 20 App.
14.	D	BIO 9.4.2, BIO 20 App.
15.	A	BIO 12.4.1, BIO 20 App.

P = paragraph; S = sentence; E = equation; T = table; F = figure

GOLD NOTES